AF760002

The Application of Neural Networks in the Forecasting of Share Prices

Robert J. Van Eyden

FINANCE & TECHNOLOGY ™

FINANCE &
TECHNOLOGY
™

For further information on Finance & Technology Publishing and the NEUROVE$T JOURNAL, contact us at:

Finance & Technology Publishing
P.O. Box 764, Haymarket, VA 22069 USA
voice: 703-754-0696 fax: 703-753-2634

Cover: a 3D surface graph of daily closing data for the Dow Jones Industrial Average and New York Stock Exchange volume over the first 20 trading days in 1995, using cubic spline interpolation, and sampled as input to a multilayer feedforward neural network.

ISBN 0-9651332-0-6

About the Author

Robert J. Van Eyden has a Ph.D. in Financial Management from the University of Pretoria, South Africa, where he worked as an Associate Professor in Finance. He is currently a fixed-income analyst at Nick Fredericksz, Britz & Co. Dr. Van Eyden's current research interest is in the area of applying neural networks and genetic algorithms to the capital markets. His hobbies include flying light-powered aircraft.

PREFACE

This book represents the end product of a comprehensive study on applying neural networks to the financial markets. As it is built upon the work of numerous practitioners and researchers referenced within its pages, it provides a foundation for future work -- work which can extend to other markets, other neural network architectures, even other emerging technologies. It reflects not only a research perspective but its author's practical sense. As a young Ph.D. graduate, Robert quickly transitioned into industry where he is now actively involved with real-world financial applications.

Perhaps the book's most important contribution exists in its comprehensive consideration of so many issues relevant to the task -- issues in fundamental and technical market analysis and indicators, traditional forecasting methods, neural networks and other new technologies. Much of the research that culminated in this work was completed prior to the introduction of the *NEUROVE$T JOURNAL*. Therefore, it serves a dual purpose. It presents a foundation of research as a prelude to ongoing work regularly published in the Journal, and it describes practical methods immediately accessible to both practitioners and applied researchers in finance.

My first recollection of the author's work occurred through his submission of a manuscript for publication in the Journal. Reviewers of the manuscript were quick to recognize the practical quality of the material. That same quality is apparent throughout this book. Though it is not intended to be a definitive work, its author provides an admirable job of covering many of the topics important to a growing audience of investors, traders, money managers, economists, market technicians, financial analysts, developers, students, and applied researchers, all in pursuit of leveraging new and emerging technologies and tools relevant to their needs.

What first struck me most positively about the material when I first reviewed it was not that its author always pursued the same path that others might have followed, given similar objectives to those of the study. Rather, it was its straightforward discussion and analysis, free of the biases and assumptions that sometimes result from years in the trenches, that I found refreshing. In short, it provides a clear illustration of the path that many newcomers to finance and technology traverse, within a world awash with "advice" from the masters and "information" from everywhere. And it does so using a healthy dose of discipline and skepticism. Newcomers and experienced practitioners and applied researchers should pursue the subject of finance as well.

As the publisher of the *journal of record* for many of the subjects described in the book, Finance & Technology Publishing is delighted to bring this work to the general public. As a colleague in research and practice, I am certain that you will be reading more from Robert.

Randall B. Caldwell
Finance & Technology Publishing
February 1996

TABLE OF CONTENTS

CHAPTER 1

THE SCOPE AND METHODS OF THE STUDY

Theory helps us bear our ignorance of fact.
-- George Santayna

1.1 INTRODUCTION

In the past, forecasting the evolution of share prices has been achieved by both qualitative and quantitative methods. However, after a decade of research, financial economists remain unsatisfied with simple accounts of share price fluctuations. The traditional concept of the efficient market hypothesis requires that the predictability of share prices be unpredictable. Any excess returns that are predictable should quickly be reflected in equilibrium of the share price. Over the last decade, there has been research on the subject of share price predicability. The studies by Boshoff (1983), Du Toit (1986) and Terespolsky (1991) provide strong evidence of share price predictability.

Previous research has been based on linear or simple nonlinear models employing traditional and econometric analysis. In recent years, models for stochastically nonlinear processes have gained increasing importance in economic time series forecasting. The reason for this is that linear models fail to estimate the underlying parameters successfully when the parameters are highly non-Gaussian. While linear models take information only from first and second order moments of a time series, nonlinear models require higher moments to be characterized. In adddition, linear models are inadequate when the underlying economic time series exhibits highly non-Gaussian characteristics. According to Liang (1991:12) there has been an increase in the use of nonlinear models but they are still not extensively used. This is because there is no particular theoretical reason to choose any particular nonlinear model since it is not possible to examine all nonlinear specifications for improved forecastability. For this reason, an alternative forecasting method should be sought that is rich in the class of nonlinear optimization models.

1.2 PROBLEM DEFINITION

The problem regarding present share evaluation models is that they assume that linearity exists in their respective underlying variables. It is certainly difficult to imagine that the behavior of the stock market could be captured completely in a system of linear equations, usually having a finite number of parameters, yet this is the postulation on which existing share evaluation models are based. Consequently, these models are unable to determine the magnitude and direction of share prices with an acceptable degree of accuracy, which supports the suspicion that the true dynamics of the share market are those of nonlinear deterministic processes.

Knowledge of the existence of nonlinear dependency in share price data on the Johannesburg Stock Exchange is not sufficient to capitalize on the construction of a share market fluctuation model. The research and development of a nonlinear prediction and classification model is required, which, when applied to share price data, will provide a potential framework for the characterizing of the time series that has been traditionally referred to as pure random error, chaotic, and having low correlation estimates (Scheinkman and LeBaron, 1989:310-337). Between the periods of chaos, intervals of discernible non-randomness occur. In principle, these are predictable, making share market behavior recognizable enough to be exploited often, and making the periods of randomness identifiable (Hsieh, 1991:1840-1847).

The application of neural network techniques has the potential, by fitting a nonlinear model into the form of a simple or difference equation to the estimated value of the coefficients, to provide information on the cyclical state of the system and to predict near-term share price magnitude and direction (Mulieri, 1991:28-34; Scheinkman and LeBaron, 1989:310-337; White, 1988:1-5; Stein, 1991:289; Jones, Lee, Barnes, Flake, Lee, Lewis and Qian, 1989:54-60). This study will take advantage of neural networks to check for the existence of nonlinear predictors of share price direction. Neural networks have the ability to aapproximate arbitrarily and closely, any measurable function, without having to specify the exact form of the function beforehand.

1.3 OBJECTIVES

The objectives of this study can be summarized into primary and secondary objectives. The primary objectives are:

- To develop and implement a neural network model for the forecasting of share prices.

- To identify and investigate the factors that affect the performance of the neural network forecasting model.

- To determine the applicability of a neural network as a forecasting model in comparison with the Box-Jenkins model.

- To determine whether or not the Johannesburg Stock Exchange exhibits chaos.

The secondary objectives are:

- To demonstrate that neural networks can be applied to nonlinear and chaotic share data to project the magnitude and direction of share prices on the Johannesburg Stock Exchange with a greater degree of accuracy than present time series analysis methods and techniques are able to do.

- To gain new insights into the application of neural networks as a method of exploiting nonlinear time series with low correlation dimension estimates.

- To demonstrate the potential applications of neural networks in the disciplines of economics, econometrics and management sciences. One of the aims of this study is to indicate the effectiveness of neural networks when applied to classification, associative memory and clustering.

- To provide an alternative methodology to present share price forecasting models and methods. Although still relatively new, the neural network methodology offers exciting possibilities in the science of prediction, both in the particular case of chaotic data series, and more generally across a wide range of applications.

1.4 METHODOLOGY

1.4.1 The sample

Industrial shares listed on the Johannesburg Stock Exchange served as the sample. The share population size comprised 128 eligible industrial shares listed on the Johannesburg Stock Exchange from December 31, 1986 to December 31, 1992. Based on a stratified random sampling process, 45 shares were found to be eligible candidates for the neural network model. A neural network model was constructed, based on 63 inputs, each forming part of one of the following groups:

- Fundamental inputs;
- technical inputs;
- Johannesburg Stock Exchange indices;
- international indices;
- gold price and foreign exchange rates;
- interest rates; and
- economic statistics.

The result of the model is the prediction of 1 output, which was the cumulative closing price of the 45 shares (reasons for a cumulative closing price are addressed in Chapter 5).

1.4.2 The study

Encouraged by evidence of nonlinearities in share price data found by studies done in the United States of America, by applying correlation dimension analysis on selected individual shares and indices (Mulieri, 1991:28-34; Dutta and Shekhar, 1988:20-21) it was felt that these techniques could be applied to selected daily Johannesburg Stock Exchange industrial shares, for the period 1986-1992. However, in order to determine whether the application of neural networks as a measuring instrument was valid, testing of the time series of daily share prices was required to ascertain whether the sample contained nonlinear dependencies. To establish this, the differences for each of the time series of daily share price data were calculated, resulting in a time series of daily share price changes. An estimated model for each of the time series of daily share price changes, using a Box-Jenkins Autoregressive Moving Average, was then constructed in order to remove long term linear dependency due to share price appreciations. Using this estimated model and the associated time series, a residual time series was calculated for each of the cumulative daily share prices. The residuals were then checked for significant autocorrelation coefficients. These residual values were then compared to a "scrambled" residual series to determine whether nonlinear dependencies exist.

Share price data and variables (macro-economical data, technical data and fundamental data for the period 1986-1992) were used to develop a neural network. The neural network was trained, using backpropagation, which involves repeatedly presenting a set of share price data and variables to the network, resulting in an output value. On completion of this, the result was compared to that of a Box-Jenkins model, and then further tests on the nonlinear dimensions of the Johannesburg Stock Exchange were made.

1.4.3 Research hypotheses

In terms of this view, as supported by the foregoing, the specific research hypotheses that this study sought to address are:

- H_1 - Neural networks can forecast share prices seven days ahead.
- H_2 - The forecasting accuracy of a neural network model is related to the architecture of the network model.
- H_3 - Neural networks represent superior forecasting models relative to Box-Jenkins models.
- H_4 - Fluctuations in share prices observed on the Johannesburg Stock Exchange are not the result of purely stochastic processes but, rather, include a nonlinear dynamic process.

1.4.4 Recording, analysis, interpretation and presentation of the results

The Information Network (I-Net) Pty (Ltd) was used to gather all the relevant data for the specific period under review. The technical indicators on the cumulative closing price were generated using *Excel* by Microsoft. *Statistica* by StatSoft was used to construct the Box-Jenkins model, as well as in the recording and processing of the data, gained from both the neural network model and the Box-Jenkins model. *Brainmaker Professional* by California Scientific Software was employed in the development of the neural network model.

1.5 LIMITATIONS AND DELIMITATIONS

The statistics employed in the achievement of the objectives of this research are deemed to be sufficient. However, others may be considered for the purpose of augmenting the inferential statistics employed in this study. Analyses performed were relevent to data covering the period 1986 to 1992. As such, any conclusions drawn from the data should be considered within the context of this study.

This is largely attributable to the multitude of factors which affect share prices. Furthermore, the results obtained in the study should be interpreted within the framework of the following additional criteria:

- Takeover bids;
- economic structural changes;
- annual reports and dividend announcements;
- socio-political structural changes;
- tax implications of trading; and
- brokerage costs.

1.6 ASSUMPTIONS

The study is based on the following assumptions:

Assumption 1: The markets are chaotic. This is one of the strongest assumptions related to financial markets. If the markets are random, a prediction is essentially an equivalent to a guess. Fortunately, evidence has indicated that the Johannesburg Stock Exchange is predictable. The studies are:

- Boshoff (1983:256): "This study established the nature of non-random behavior in [share] prices. It further made an objective appraisal of all the technical tools available and so determined which techniques have the ability to utilize such non-random behavior profitably. Finally, it demonstrated the ability of various technical trading rules to substantially improve on returns achieved by intermediate buy/hold strategies."

- Du Toit (1986:9.3): "The final conclusion of this investigation is therefore that the market at times assumes the properties of a totally efficient market but at other times prices deviate from underlying equilibrium values."

- Terespolsky (1991:48): "This report affirms the existence of long-term persistence in stock price time series on the JSE... .The H coefficients of stock price time series have been shown to be unstable over time."

  However, it is important to note that Du Toit's viewpoint confirms the assumption that markets do go through transitions. During these transitions, the market becomes temporarily random and, therefore, unpredictable.

Assumption 2: Technical indicators enhance market data - The underlying assumption for preprocessing financial data is that human traders believe that these transformations provide useful insight into how the market will continue to trend, and when the market will change direction. Assuming that technical analysis indicators do actually enhance signals, it is presumed that they should improve the ability of a neural network to predict future trends and direction changes, since neural networks have the ability to "fuse" data together.

Assumption 3: Encompassing the two previous assumptions, it is further assumed that investors are rational in forming their expectations and that the markets are informationally efficient so that share prices serve as aggregators of the information available in the market. Consequently, investors can infer the state of the market framework from the observed share prices. It is thus possible for a nonlinear model to optimally estimate the unobserved parameters from the underlying share price.

1.7 DEMARCATION OF THE RESEARCH

The study is divided into five chapters. Each will be discussed subsequently:

- Chapter 1 explains the scope of the study and the methods used in this work.
- Chapter 2 provides an overview of neural networks and addresses fundamental issues of the backpropagation neural network.

- Chapter 3 provides an overview of the contemporary schools of thought in the forecasting of share prices with specific reference to technical analysis, fundamental analysis, and traditional statistical methods, as well as providing an introductory overview on chaos theory.

- Chapter 4 offers an overview of the research methodology employed in this study.

- Chapter 5 presents a summary of the research as a whole, offers recommendations, and ends with suggestions for further research.

1.8 CONCLUSION

The application of neural networks in the disciplines of economics, econometrics and the management sciences remains relatively new. One of the aims of this study is to demonstrate potential applications of neural networks in these disciplines. In particular, it will indicate the effectiveness of neural networks when applied to classification, associative memory and clustering. Finally, the methodology of neural networks, although new, offers exciting possibilities in the science of prediction, both in the particular case of chaotic data series, and more generally across a wide range of applications.

Chapter 2 provides an overview on neural networks and addresses fundamental issues of the backpropagation neural network.

CHAPTER 2

NEURAL NETWORKS - FOUNDATIONS AND PARADIGMS

First seek to understand, then to be understood.
-- S.R. Covey

2.1 INTRODUCTION

For many decades, it has been a goal of science and engineering to develop intelligent machines, which were envisaged to perform all cumbersome and tedious tasks. The technologies that have emerged to meet these challenges include machine learning[1], automata, bionics, mathematical biophysics, general system theory, cybernetics[2], self-organizing systems, artificial intelligence[3], cognitive science[4], and artificial neural networks (ANS).

Artificial neural networks or neural networks are mathematical models of theorized mind and brain activity. Neural networks have been referred to as connectionist systems, adaptive systems, adaptive networks, artificial neural networks, neurocomputers, and parallel distributed processors. Neural networks exploit the parallel local processing and distribution representation properties that are believed to exist in the brain.

This chapter will explore the relationship between real neural systems and artificial neural systems, provide an overview of foundational ideas, constructs and terminology used to describe

---

1 Luger and Stubblefield's (1989:21) definition of machine learning is that it is a process whereby programs are written for machines to learn on their own, either from experience, analogy, examples or being "told" what to do.

2 Felsen (1975:43) believes that cybernetics is the science of general laws of data transformation, used in complex control systems and information-processing systems. However, broadly speaking, cybernetics can be defined as being primarily concerned with goal-seeking and purposive systems.

3 Hong (1988:20) explains artificial intelligence as the computer simulation and emulation of the human cognitive process with specific reference to thinking and perceiving.

4 Lawrence (1991:157) is of the opinion that cognitive science is a branch of psychology which originally dealt with the mechanisms of learning and memory. However, it now attempts to link mental states with underlying brain functions.

neural networks, and provide an overview of neural networks technology, and several of its key paradigms[5].

2.2 DEFINING NEURAL NETWORKS

An artificial neural network is a model that simulates a biological neural network. Hecht-Nielsen (1988:131) views a neural network as a parallel distributed information-processing structure, consisting of processing elements[6] interconnected with unidirectional signals called connections[7]. These processing elements have a single output connection that branches into as many collateral connections as necessary. These processing elements depend on the current values of the input signal arriving at the processing element by means of intruding connections and upon values in the processing element's local memory (Schmitt, 1991:38). However, Aleksander and Morton (1990:1) feel that neural network technology is concerned with the study of networks' adaptable nodes, i.e., through a process of learning from task examples, experimental knowledge can be stored and made available for use.

A simpler, but less rigorous, definition of a neural network, as understood by Simpson (1990:4), is that an artificial neural network is a nonlinear directed graph with weighted[8] edges that can cache patterns by changing the edges weights and can recall patterns from incomplete inputs. Based on this definition, it is evident that mathematics is the backbone of neural networks theory, an idea best expressed by Arbib (1964:2) "We apply mathematics to derive extensive conclusions from clearly stated premises. We can test the adequacy of a model of the brain by expressing it in mathematical form and using our mathematical tools to prove general theorems

---

5 A network paradigm is a network architecture that specifies the interconnection formation of a network.

6 A processing element is an artificial neuron in a neural network, consisting of a small amount of local memory and processing power. The output from a processing element is fanned out.

7 A connection is a signal transmission pathway between processing elements, corresponding to the axons and synapses of neurons in a human brain, that connects the processing elements into a network.

8 The weight is the strength of an input connection expressed by a real number, according to Obermeier and Barron (1989:219). Furthermore, the weight determines the intensity of the connections.

and experiments. We may return to our premises and reformulate them, thus gaining a deeper understanding of the workings of the brain. Further, such theories can guide us in building more useful and sophisticated machines." In mathematical terms, a neural network model is a directed graph with the following properties:

- A state variable n_i is associated with node[9] *i;*
- a real-valued weight w_{ik} ,with each link (*ik*) between two nodes *i* and k;
- a real-valued $\ddot{\upsilon}_i$ is associated with each node $_i$; and
- a transfer function $f_i\,[n_k,\, w_{ik},\, \ddot{\upsilon}_i,\, (k{\neq}i)]$ is defined for each node *i*, which decides the state of the node as a function of its bias (Muller and Reinhardt, 1990:12).

The mathematics most often used in neural networks technology includes differential equations, dynamical systems, linear algebra, probability and statistics.

Guez, Protopopsecu and Barhen (1988:80) believe that a neural network is a network of many neurons, like subsystems that are dynamically coupled and exhibit, by way of their collective behavior, useful computational features. Lippmann's (1987:4) definition corresponds with Guez, Protopopsecu and Barhen's definition. In addition, however, Lippmann also perceives that all neural networks attempt to achieve good performance through the dense interconnection of simple computational elements, structured on the present understanding of biological nervous systems.

The financial discipline perceives neural networks differently. Katz (1992:59) considers neural networks as heuristic[10] pattern recognizers. Fishman, Barr and Loick (1991:18) suggest that neural networks mimic the brain's most powerful ability, which they feel is pattern recognition. That is, neural networks, trained on previous data samples, are able to make decisions or predictions based on new data samples. Xenakis (1990:41), Stein (1991:89), Tazelaar (1989:214), and Sondak and Sondak (1989:241) all confirm Fishman, Barr, and Loick's viewpoint.

Given the definitions just described, the following sub-definitions and restrictions can be applied (terms are defined throughout this chapter):

---

9 A node is also known as a neuron.

10 Heuristics are computational rules of thumb. Distinct from algorithms, which are programs guaranteed to generate correct results under all circumstances, heuristics may only turn out to be correct a certain percentage of the time.

- The nodes of a neural network are called processing elements;
- the links of a neural network are called connections. Each connection functions as an instantaneous, unidirectional signal-conduction path (Hecht-Nielsen, 1990:22);
- each processing element can receive any number of input connections;
- each processing element can have any number of outgoing connections, but the signals in all of these must be the same;
- processing elements can have a local memory;
- each processing element possesses a transfer function, that can use local memory and input signals, which produces the processing output signal;
- input signals to the neural network arrive by way of connections that originate in the outside world; and
- output signals from the network to the outside world are in the form of connections that leave the network.

Neural networks represent a technology that has been inspired by studies of the brain and nervous system. Neural networks are best at doing some things that biological systems are good at:

- Pattern classification; and
- functional synthesis.

- Pattern classification occurs at several levels. At a very low level, it is the ability to detect edges and connected areas in a picture, or to differentiate between the sounds of a bell and a whistle. Other pattern classification problems include differentiating between very similar sounds, classifying propeller noises from ships, and recognizing speech and written language. At a higher level, pattern classification enables individuals to make "gut-level" judgements about the quality of a particular investment, or the risks involved in pursuing a particular activity. Most of these decisions are based on previous experience. Neural networks have been applied to several similar problems. These include credit application evaluation, loan approval, and industrial inspection systems.

- Functional synthesis consists of establishing relationships between several continuous-valued inputs and one or more continuous-valued outputs. This involves learning several complex nonlinear continuous-valued relationships. Neural network applications of functional synthesis include forecasting natural gas consumption and prices, and estimating error in feedforward servo systems.

2.3 THE BIOLOGICAL NEURAL NETWORK

2.3.1 Introduction

The fascination of neural networks arises in part from their having been inspired by the brain. The approach of neural computing is to capture the guiding principles that underlie the brain's solution to problems and to apply them to computer systems. Alexander (1991:17) confirms this by explaining that a neural network is an information processing system that is modelled upon the human brain's interconnected system of electrically-activated neurons. A description of a neural network's architecture could not be complete, therefore, without describing the biological neural system. Similarities between these two types of systems are important to observe and provide the basis for comparison of artificial neural networks with their biological counterpart. Subsequent sections will examine the way in which the brain operates and explore the brain's biological structure.

2.3.2 The structure of the brain

The brain is a very complicated organ with many diverse functions. This discussion will thus be limited to that part of the brain which is significant to neural network studies, namely, the cerebral cortex[11]. The cerebral cortex is a continuously folding layer which forms the outside of the brain. The human cortex is a pleated sheet of some 2000 centimeters square, and is about two to three millimeters thick (Lawrence, 1991:39). Most human cortexes are made up of many layers of neuron cells[12], which are densely interconnected in each layer. In effect, the characteristics we generally call intelligence, interest, awareness, interaction with the environment, and the abilities to adapt and learn are decided by the functioning of the cerebral cortex (Beale and Jackson, 1990:9). The cerebral cortex is thus the seat of the higher order functions of the brain, and the core

---

11 The cerebral cortex is also known as the neocortex, meaning the newest part of the cortex.

12 Discussed in section 2.3.3.1.

of intelligence. According to Dayhoff (1990:117), the size and the complexity of the cerebral cortex determines the critical difference between humans and lower animals.

2.3.3 The components of the brain

2.3.3.1 The neuron

As stated in section 2.3.2, the human cortex is made up of many layers of neuron cells. The brain contains over one hundred billion computing elements; according to Wassermann (1989:190), these elements are called neurons. A neuron, is a nerve cell that has become specialized, in the sense that it transmits information to other neurons or to muscle or gland cells (Thompson, 1985:29).

These neurons communicate throughout the body by nerve fibres called synapses. This network of neurons is responsible for all the phenomena that we call thought, emotion, and cognition. The exact manner in which this is accomplished is little understood, according to Wassermann (1989:191).

The brain also contains a dense network of blood vessels that provides oxygen and nutrients to the neurons and other tissues. This blood supply is connected by a filtration system called the blood-brain barrier. The blood-brain barrier is essential to the safety of the brain.

However, the neuron remains the fundamental building block of the nervous system and of the human brain. A neuron is made up of three parts (refer to Figure 2.1):

- the soma;
- the dendrites; and
- the axon.

Figure 2.1 - A biological neuron

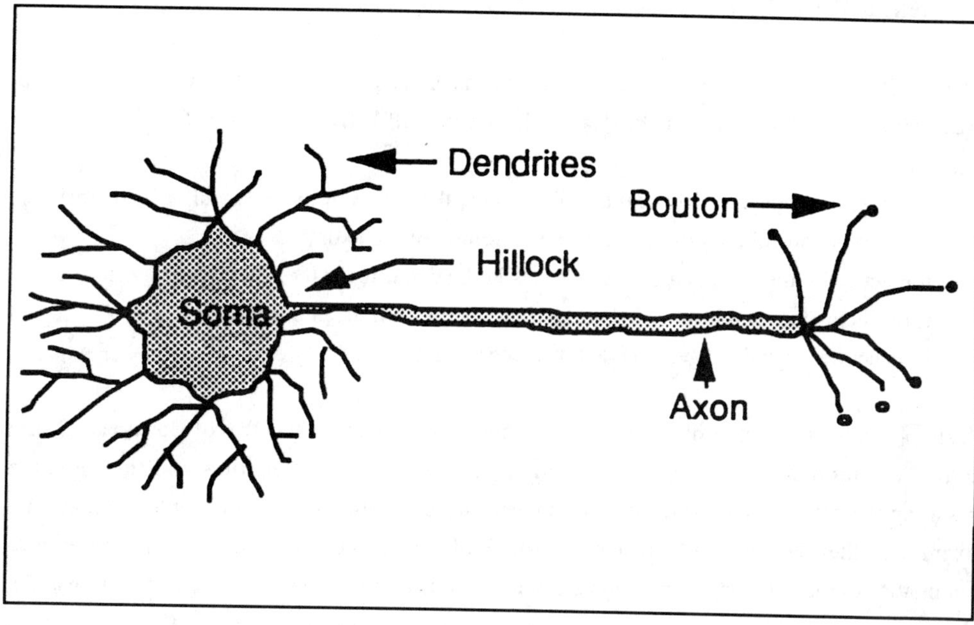

- The soma[13]: Each neuron has a body, called a soma, which contains the cell nucleus, various biochemical factories and other components that support the on-going activity. In the soma, the incoming signals are added up over time, resulting in the process during which the soma decides when and how to respond to inputs.

- The dendrites: Surrounding the somas are dendrites, which are receptors for signals generated by other neurons. According to Hawley, Johnson and Raina (1990:65), each neuron may be connected to one thousand or more neighbors by way of a network of dendrites.

- The axon: This is the outgoing connection for signals emitted by the neuron (Davalo and Naïm, 1991:4). When a neuron fires, an electrical impulse is generated. This impulse starts at the base (called the hillock) of a long cellular extension, the axon. The tip of the axon is

---

13 The soma is also referred to as the cell body in certain literature.

split into multiple ends called boutons, which are connected to the dendrites of other neurons (refer to Figure 2.2).

The specific function performed by a neuron depends on the properties of its external membrane. According to Davalo and Naïm (1991:4-5), the neuron fulfils five functions:

- It serves to propagate electrical impulses along the length of its axon and of its dendrites;
- it releases transmitter substances at the extremity of the axon;
- it reacts with these transmitter substances in the dendrites at the cell body;
- it reacts to electrical impulses that are transmitted from the dendrites; and
- it generates or fails to generate a new electrical impulse.

A simpler and less rigorous description of the operation of a neuron than that of Davalo and Naïm is that a neuron processes the electric currents that arrive on its dendrites and transmits the resulting electric currents to other connected neurons, using its axon. According to the literature examined, the classical biological explanation of this process is that the cell performs a summation of the incoming signals on its dendrites. If this summation exceeds a certain threshold, the neuron responds by issuing a new impulse that is propagated along its axon. If the summation is lower than the threshold, the neuron remains inactive. The pulse that is propagated between different neurons is therefore an electrical impulse.

The membrane of a neuron serves to maintain a potential difference between the interior of the neuron and the external world (Davalo and Naïm, 1991:5). In the resting state, chemical processes within the neuron keep the concentration of positive ions inside the cell lower than in the region surrounding it.

Figure 2.2 - A neuron firing

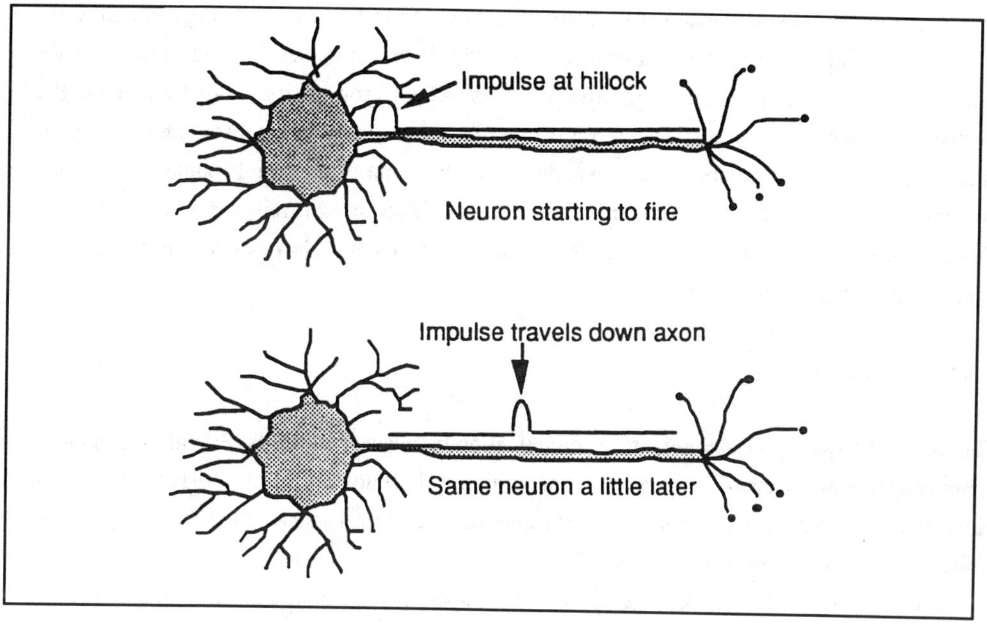

According to Lawrence (1991:33), in this state, the potential difference across the membrane is between forty and eighty millivolts. The propagation of impulses by the body of the neuron cell takes place using the mechanism of ion pumps and channels present in the axon membrane. The ion balance across the cell membrane can be disturbed by applying voltage across the membrane or by changing the ion concentrations. The membrane's electrical impulse is changed a little each time it receives an impulse. The membrane potential is thus gradually changed by several impulses until it reaches a threshold of about seventy-five millivolts (Wassermann, 1989:192). Once this threshold is reached, the electrical potential rapidly increases at that point on the membrane, starts an impulse down the axon, away from the soma, and returns to the resting level.

When a neuron fires, it sends an impulse down its axon. The electricity of the impulse generated at the hillock is greater than the threshold value of the adjacent area of the membrane and therefore excites this area. In a similar manner, each exited area stimulates the region next to it. Thus the impulse travels along the axon away from the soma. The impulse travelling down the axon is called an action potential. Lawrence (1991:34) explains that the action potential is initiated by activity at the synapses. After the action potential has been generated, the neuron's membrane cannot be excited for a short time, and this resting time is called the refractory period.

Neuroscientists usually measure the activity of a neuron in terms of its firing frequency, the number of impulses per second (Lawrence, 1991:35). These impulses form the output of the neuron and are continually affecting other neurons, which monitor its firing frequency. The electrochemical effects of each synapse on the membrane potential of a neuron are summed up in each dendrite. The dendrite effects are added up in the soma. If the sum is equal to or greater than the threshold for the neuron, then the neuron fires. The ease of transmission of signals is altered by activity in the nervous system. This ability to adjust signals is a mechanism for learning (Nelson and Illingworth, 1992:39).

2.3.3.2 Synapses

The role of the synapses is essential to communication between nerve cells. Signals propagating along cells may be electrical by nature, but according to Davalo and Naïm (1991:7), there is no direct connection between two nerve cells; they are separated by a space called the synaptic gap, which the electrical impulses cannot cross directly.

The inception of the synaptic operation is based upon the arrival of an action potential at one of the extremities of the terminal network, called the terminal button. The terminal button releases a chemical substance called a neurotransmitter; this substance then diffuses into the synaptic gap and attaches itself to a specific receptor sited on the terminations of the target neuron. This attachment causes the opening in the ion channels that causes a new electrical signal in the receiving dendrite.

2.3.3.3 How the human brain learns

To distinguish between human and artificial learning, it is imperative that human learning be classified and that the theories of how the human brain learns, be discussed. However, much is still unknown about how the brain learns and trains itself to produce information (Hinton, 1992:145). According to Rocha (1991:115), to learn is to model the observable world in order to understand it. To qualify this definition, Rocha (1991:115) states "A model is a set of relations between the data performed by a set of effectors. Understanding requires the model to fulfil some defined purpose which may be simple survival or a complex subject like pleasure. From a general point of view, to understand is to provide a set of adequate responses to adapt the system to the surrounding world, in other words, to maintain its identity in a changing environment."

According to Lawrence (1991:44), learning can be classified into two major types:

A) Associative learning - this involves learning the relationships between pairs of stimuli. This type of learning is a model for supervised neural networks.

B) Nonassociative learning - in this type of learning, there is no second stimulus to associate with the first one. In this type of learning, the repetition of a stimulus provides the opportunity to learn about its properties. This type of learning is a model for an unsupervised neural network.

Psychologists have many different theories of learning. It becomes evident from the literature that the following theories are worth noting:

- The traditional problem[14];
- theory of dualism;
- theory of reduction;
- connectionism theory; and
- cognitive theory.

Each of these schools of thought are briefly discussed below:

- The traditionalist view is that the traditional guise of the problems of neurobiology is that of any mental phenomena of the brain. In other words, these theorists maintain that the human brain learns because of mental states and not states of the physical mind.

- The theory of dualism's view is that the brain is a ghost machine and that it is not composed of physical material obeying physical laws but, according to Churchland and Sejnowski (1992:18), "soul-stuff" with which the brain operates. The basis of this theory is in

---

[14] Also known as materialism.

psychology, and the question might arise as to whether this psychological theory can be reduced to neuroscience. Works cited show that this is impossible for the following reasons:

A) Neuroscience is too hard, according to Churchland and Sejnowski (1992:19-20); the brain is too complex, and there are too many neurons and connections, thus making understanding the human brain a hopeless task.

B) Psychological states have intentionality.

- The theory of reduction believes that the workings of the brain should be explained by the integration of psychological and neurobiological theories. According to Churchland and Sejnowski (1992:2), reductions are explanations of phenomena described by one theory, in terms of the phenomena described by a more basic theory.

- The connectionism approach treats learning as a matter of making connections between stimuli and responses. A response can be any behavior and a stimulus can be any externally supplied input that affects behavior (Wassermann, 1991:93).

- The theory of cognition views the brain and the workings of the brain as a connectionist model, characterized by connections and differential strengths of connections between processing units. Connectionist models are designed to perform a task by specifying the architecture.

  Neural networks can be used to test cognitive theory. Part of the motivation for building neural networks is to test some current ideas about cognition that are based on biological research and mathematical theories (Lawrence, 1991:47).

However, it is interesting that a strong school of thought in artificial intelligence (AI) feels that the study of the brain is not the most efficacious road to understanding learning. They feel that the brain only represents one way of making a machine think. Traditional AI sees thought as a series of problems to solve, and believes strongly that there is no philosophical reason why computers cannot solve them. Zeidenberg (1987:237-238) feels that the basis for this belief lies in the Church-Turing thesis, which roughly stated, says that if a function is computable, a computation can be made with a conventional computer. Zeidenberg further states that this thesis cannot be proved, but is widely accepted, because to date no one has come up with a counter example.

Neural network researchers think that their models, by being most faithful to what we know about the brain, will show the most success in artificial intelligence. It can therefore be argued that the study of the human brain can be used for the study of neural networks, as neural networks are inspired by the human brain. Hertz, Krogh, and Palmer (1991:1) feel that the brain has many features that are desirable for artificial systems. These features are:

- The brain is robust and fault-tolerant. Nerve cells in the brain die every day without significantly affecting its performance;
- the brain is flexible. It can easily adjust to a new environment by "learning"- it does not need to be programmed;
- the brain can deal with information that is fuzzy, probabilistic, noisy, or inconsistent;
- it is highly parallel; and
- the brain is small, compact, and dissipates very little power.

In summary, the brain is a parallel, distributed information processing system, the basic processing unit of which is called the neuron. The neuron operates by firing pulses down the axon when sufficient input has been received from the dendrites. Connections take place through the chemical junctions called the synapses. Learning efficacy increases at the synaptic junction.

2.4 ARTIFICIAL NEURAL NETWORKS

2.4.1 Introduction

Neural networks have been hailed as the greatest technological advance since the transistor. They are predicted to become common household items by the year 2000 (Lawrence, 1991:3). However, the financial press and financial literature have largely confined their coverage of artificial intelligence applications to expert systems. While expert systems have been successfully employed in some business applications, Hawley, Johnson and Raina (1990:63) have shown that there are many applications that are beyond the scope of expert systems technology. Many of these problems can be overcome with another product of artificial intelligence research, namely, the artificial neural network system. Neural networks exploit the parallel local processing and distribution representation properties that are believed to exist in the brain.

In the disciplines of finance and marketing, some potential areas of application of neural networks, as identified by Hawley, Johnson and Raina (1990:63), are the assessments of bankruptcy risk, the identification of arbitrage opportunities, target marketing and technical and fundamental analysis. Askew (1990:435) feels that, in general, the task of neural networks is formidable, however, researchers applying neural network technology must separate the esoteric from the rational, and, in doing so, focus upon applications where neural networks provide a reasonable probability of utilization. It is imperative that some ways of directing neural network technologies toward the benefit of future business are found (Hong, 1988:19-21).

2.4.2 A brief history of neural networks

This section will discuss the history of neural networks, from their conception to their current state. The history of neural networks can be divided into the following periods:

- Conception;
- gestation;
- birth;
- stunted growth; and
- late infancy.

- Conception (1890-1949) - This period was characterised by attempts to understand the human brain. In 1936, Turing first used the brain as a computer. Today, Turing is widely regarded as the forebear of artificial intelligence as we know it. In 1943, a neurobiologist, McCulloch, and a statistician, Pitts, published a watershed paper entitled *A logical calculus of ideas imminent in nervous activity* (McCulloch and Pitts, 1943). This paper is regarded as the inspiration that helped to launch three diverse fields, namely:

  - The development of digital computers;
  - the development of macroscopic intelligence; and
  - the development of expert systems.

  McCulloch and Pitts proposed the following model: An artificial neuron forms a weighted sum of the action potentials that arrive at it; the artificial model then starts itself, depending on the value of the weighted sum. If this value exceeds a certain threshold, the neuron is started and transmits a response, the value of which is equal to the value of its activation. If the neuron is not started, it transmits nothing. The model is based on the operation of a biological neuron (refer to section 2.3.3.1). The McCulloch and Pitts model can be formulated as follows:

$$S = F\left(\sum_{i=1,n} W_i e_i\right) \qquad \text{...(2-1)}$$

Where: e_i = 1, n - inputs.
S = Output.
β = Threshold.
Wi = Weights.
F = Threshold function.
$F(x) = 1$ if $x > \beta$; $F(x) = 0$

In 1949, Hebb wrote a book, entitled *The Organization of Behavior,* in which he pursues the idea that classical psychological conditioning is ubiquitous in animals because it is a property of individual neurons (Hecht-Nielsen, 1990:15). It is evident from other literature that this idea was not in itself new, but Hebb extended it further than anyone had before, in that he proposed a specific learning law for the synapses of neurons. This law is known as Hebb's rule[15]. Hebb then used this learning law to build a qualitative explanation of experimental results from psychology. According to Lawrence (1991:67), Hebb's work served to inspire many other researchers to pursue the same theme - which further laid the groundwork for the arrival of neurocomputing. Many present neural network paradigms have their origin in this mechanism.

- Gestation (1949-1956) - This period was characterized by improvements in hardware and software, and ushered in the age of computer simulation. The first software simulation of a

---

15 Hebb's rule states that whenever two neurons are excited at the same time, the connections between the two neurons should be strengthened. According to Lawrence (1991:68-69), modern variations of Hebb's rule check that the neurons represent compatible concepts, and often use all inputs to decide exactly how much to strengthen the connections.

neural network was masterminded at the International Business Machines (IBM) research laboratories in 1953. Their first attempts failed, but after the collaboration with Hebb, successful adaptations were made.

- Birth (1956 to the late 1960s) - The Dartmouth summer research project on artificial intelligence, held in the summer of 1956, provided the necessary momentum for both the fields of artificial intelligence and neural computing. In the year following the Dartmouth project, Von Neumann produced material in which he suggested imitated the simple neuron functions by using telegraph relays or vacuum tubes (Nelson and Illingworth, 1992:28). However, in the 1950s, the dominant figure in neural network research was Rosenblatt, who invented a class of neural networks called "perceptrons". The perceptron was designed to resemble a biological sensory model, and used a combination of different layers of threshold neurons, in a variation of Hebb's rule of learning. He discussed (Rosenblatt, 1958: 386-408) the perceptron as a neural network pattern classification system that could identify both abstract and geometric patterns. The first perceptron was capable of some learning, and possessed a great deal of plasticity. Rosenblatt (1958:388) defines plasticity as "the process whereby the perceptron can be retrained to a point of no error after some cells had been destroyed."

  In addition, the perceptron was capable of making limited generalizations[16], and could categorize patterns properly despite noise[17] in the input. It is interesting that, according to Davalo and Naïm (1991:30), this type of neural network is still used today in various forms, for applications such as character recognition.

---

[16] One of the characteristics of a neural network, refer to section 2.4.3.

[17] Refers to the following, namely:

- Irrelevant or imprecise data present in input patterns;
- random values added to all weights to prevent the network from getting stuck in local energy minima (Lawrence, 1991:169); and
- imprecise information data purposely put in during the initial state to improve a network's accuracy.

Another major player in neural network research in the 1960s was Grossberg. He did a considerable amount of research which led to the development of neural network models (Nelson and Illingworth, 1992:29). Grossberg spent much of his time devising neurally inspired mechanisms in perception and memory. He also translated an associative rule for a synaptic model into explicit equations (Grossberg and Gutowski, 1987:200-235). Grossberg's innovation resulted in fundamental breakthroughs in neural network theory.

- Stunted growth (1969-1981) - This period can be characterized by criticism of neural networks which resulted in a halt to much of the funding for neural network research. This can largely be attributed to the following factors:

  - Some observers were disappointed by neurocomputer researchers being carried away by their enthusiasm in their statements and writings (Hecht-Nielsen, 1990:16). This so-called 'hype' discredited the field and angered people in the field of artificial intelligence, while still others felt threatened by the thought of "intelligent machines"; and
  - Minisky and Papert began work on an in-depth critique of Rosenblatt's perceptron. The book, called *Perceptrons*, was a detailed mathematical analysis of an abstract version of Rosenblatt's perceptron. The main result of this paper was Minisky and Papert's conclusion that:

    A) The perceptron could not handle inputs that were visually nonlocal.

    B) Neural networks were basically not "interesting" subjects to study.

    This drastically decreased the amount of funds being made available for neural network research (Minisky and Papert, 1969:120-140). At the time, Minisky and Papert's work appeared to have destroyed the perceptron and inadvertently, neural networks. Little attention was paid to the fact that Minisky and Papert had directed their criticism at a single-layered perceptron.

    According to Zeidenberg (1987:240), the computational power of the perceptron rises abruptly if more layers are added between the input and output layer; consequently, Zeidenberg asserts that Minisky and Papert's critique no longer applies.

However, this period was dominated by serial processing, with specific reference to both psychology and artificial intelligence. During this period, Anderson and Kohonen simultaneously developed the linear associator that used neurons that could fire in varying frequencies in response to incoming signals, instead of simply turning off or on as did the perceptron (Lawrence, 1991:68). In 1976, Grossberg became one of the first people to analyze some properties of competitive learning. His mathematical analysis led him to many insights that have since only been appreciated through extensive computer simulations (Finkbeiner, 1988:5). Furthermore, the influential work of Anderson, during this period, helped McClelland and Rumelhart to develop the parallel distributed processing theories, which form the basis of the present neural network theory.

- Late infancy (1982 - Present) - By 1982, the time was ripe for a renewed interest in neural networks. Several events converged to make this a pivotal year (Lawrence, 1991:30). In 1982, Hopfield presented a paper to the National Academy of Sciences, this being the first paper on neural computing to have been presented since the 1960s. Hopfield presented a neural computing system consisting of interconnected processing elements that seek an energy minimum. Hopfield's model represented neuron operation as a thresholding operation, and illustrated memory as information stored in the interconnections between neuron units. This paper not only showed that neural networks are capable of exhibiting very interesting behavior, but even provided some mathematical underpinnings for the theory (Lawrence, 1991:68). Hopfield's paper both stimulated a new round of neural network research and gave much-needed credibility to the neural network field. The two key ideas which he described in his 1982 paper were the addition of nonlinearities (such as feedback) to the system and the concept of global energy functions (Hopfield, 1982:2554-2558). The increasing attention the field was receiving also opened many sources of funding necessary for the pursuit of neural computing research.

  In the years since the first Hopfield paper, many university groups have started performing research in neural networks. Several important new models and learning rules have been developed, proving some startling capabilities (Lawrence, 1993:95).

2.4.3 The characteristics of a neural network

The general interest in neural networks arises from their fascinating characteristics which enable them to exceed the limitations of traditional information processors (Davalo and Naïm, 1991:105). The following are the characteristics of an ideal neural network:

- A neural network is composed of several processing elements that communicate through a set of interconnections with variable weights or strengths.

- Neural networks are one of the few artificial intelligence related technologies that have a rigorous, mathematical foundation (Nelson and Illingworth, 1992:59). The weights, summations, transfer functions, and learning algorithms all rely heavily on mathematics. These equations effect inputs, memory and recall, determination of energy levels, convergence, and stability within the neural network. The kinds of mathematics employed by neural networks are differential equations, linear algebra, and covariance matrices.

- Memories are stored or represented in a neural network in the patterns that variable interconnection weights create among processing elements. Information is processed by a spreading, constantly changing pattern activity, distributed across the processing elements. Consequently, the memory is distributed over many units, giving it the ability to resist noise[18]. Supplementary advantages of neural network memories, according to Davalo and Naïm (1991:105), are:

    - The loss of one individual component does not mean the loss of a stored data item. In a neural network, the destruction of one memory unit will change the activation map of neurons marginally; and
    - when one piece of knowledge corresponds to one piece of data stored in a particular place, the problem of managing full sets of knowledge arises. In order to find or use a particular fact, it is necessary to know its precise location, either its address or its precise contents. This technique cannot, therefore, take account of noisy data, and thus the preprocessing of data should be used to eliminate the noise. This limitation is overcome in distributed memories such as those of neural networks, in which it is possible to start

[18] Refer to footnote 17 for a definition of noise.

with noisy data and still make the correct data appear from the network's activation map without noise.

- A neural network is taught or trained rather than programmed. Typically, a neural network is presented with a training set consisting of a group of examples from which the neural network can learn. These examples, known as training patterns, are represented by vectors, and can be taken from sources such as financial data and diagnostic information. Because neural networks learn by example, it should be noted that neural networks have the potential for building computing systems that need not be programmed. According to Dayhoff (1990:10), this reflects a radically different approach to computing as compared with traditional methods, which involve the development of computer programs. In a computer program, every step that the computer executes is specified in advance by the programmer, resulting in a process that requires both time and personnel (Dayhoff, 1990:10).

- The operation of a neural network is controlled by three properties:

  - The transfer function[19];
  - the details of the structure of the connections among the processing elements; and
  - the learning law that the system follows.

- A major feature of a neural network is its ability to generalize, that is, successfully learn the characteristics of a general category of objects, based on a series of examples from the category. According to Beale and Jackson (1990:89), multi-layered neural networks generalize by detecting features of the input pattern that they have been taught, that are significant, and so coding them into the internal units. Thus an unknown pattern is classified with others that share the same distinguishing features.

  In general, neural networks are good at interpolation, but not good at extrapolation. They are good at detecting patterns that exist in the inputs that they are given, as an effect of generalization, and at allowing intermediator states not to be seen. However, inputs that are extensions of the range patterns are less well classified, since there is little with which to compare them.

---

[19] Also known as the squashing function.

- Dynamic stability is the ability of the neural network to remain within its functional boundaries and reach a stable state[20] (Lawrence, 1991:60). A neural network can be inputed with an extreme value of data and it will still be able to return to a stable state.

- A neural network innately acts as a processor for time-dependent spatial patterns, or spatio-temporal patterns (Caudill and Butler, 1990(a):8).

2.4.4 Neural network structure

Simulated neurons serve as the basic functional units of an artificial neural network. An artificial neuron is called a processing element (PE) or a node (refer to Figure 2.3). An artificial neuron may be defined by the following five elements, which are derived from the McCulloch-Pitts model:

- The nature of inputs;
- the input function, which defines the preprocessing which is carried out on its inputs;
- the activation function of the neuron, defining its internal state as a total of inputs;
- the output function, which determines the output of a neuron as a function of its activation state; and
- the nature of the output of the neuron.

---

[20] A stable state is the pattern a feedback neural network settles into after the neurons have stopped changing.

Figure 2.3 - An artificial neuron processing element

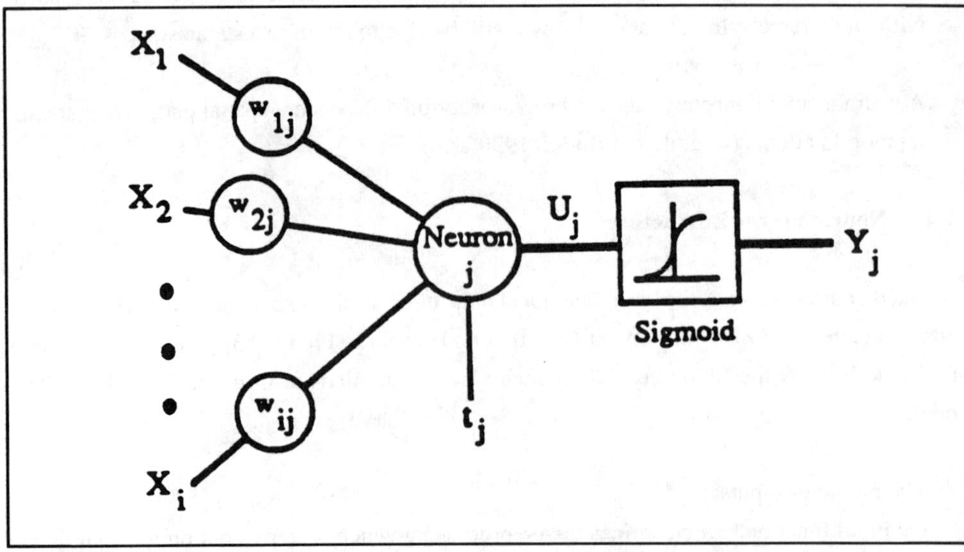

The structure of the neural network is defined by the interconnection architecture between the processing elements, the rules that decide whether a processing element will fire, and the rules which govern changes in the relative importance of the individual interconnections to a processing element's input. However, there are several ways of organizing the computing elements in neural networks. Typically, the elements are arranged in groups or layers (Anderson, Wisniewski and Viscuso, 1988:28). A single layer of neurons that connects internally (to itself) is called an auto-associative system (Kohonen, 1977:200). Two layer systems, with only an input and an output layer, are both fruitful to analyze and useful, despite some limitations, such as the inability to model certain functions (Anderson, *et al.*, 1988:28).

The advancement of learning algorithms available in neural network technology has made it possible to teach a multi-layered network to develop appropriate connection strengths. However, it became evident from the literature that most processing elements are normally arranged in three layers (refer to Figure 2.4).

Figure 2.4 - A three layered artificial neural network architecture

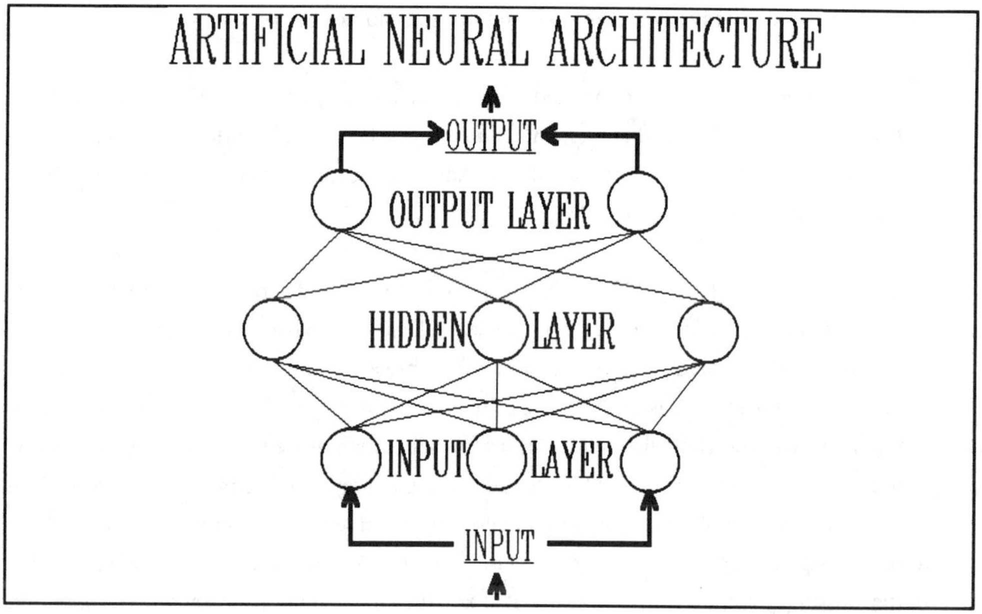

These three layers are:

- An input layer[21] - The input layer represents the layer where the neural network receives its data. The number of neurons in the input layer is determined by the number of categories, where each category of input data requires one input neuron. For the purposes of this study, relative numerical input data will be used. The reason for this is that neural networks train much better with relative numbers, which provide the known relevant relationships explicitly, rather than forcing the systems to discover them.

- A hidden layer - Between the input and output layers, there may be additional layers of units, called hidden layers. The hidden layers are analogies to the brain's interneurons, and, according to Finkbeiner (1988:10), the hidden layer is where the network records the input data in a form that captures the hidden correlations. This allows the network to generalize

---

[21] Also known as NET.

from previously learned facts to new inputs. Through learning, the neural network creates an internal mapping of the input data, which discerns the underlying causal relationships that exist within it, allowing the system to be intelligent and predictive.

The learning takes place within the hidden layer. Anderson (quoted in Finkbeiner, 1988:10) states that: "On the whole, what happens in the hidden layer(s) is a little mysterious. Loose thinking about the hidden units has always haunted the field of learning systems. It's a mysticism I'm not happy with."

Touretzky and Pomerleau (1989:227-233), in contrast with Anderson, view the prospects of finding out what is inside the hidden layers less bleakly: they feel that hidden units should really be called "learned-feature detectors" or "representation units" because the activity pattern in the hidden layer is an encoding of what the network thinks are significant features of the input. To understand the hidden layer representations that a neural network develops, Touretzky and Pomerleau (1989:234) looked at two examples of geometric problems. The first was a binary classification problem; the second involved driving a robotic vehicle along a road through a park. Touretzky and Pomerleau (1989:232) concluded that reducing the size of the hidden layer not only increases the rate at which a computer can simulate the network, but can also improve the network's performance. With too many hidden units, a network can simply memorize the correct response to each pattern in its training set. This is known as overcorrecting, which replaces the learning of a general solution. The importance of a hidden layer is obvious, but whether one or more hidden layers is preferable for a network to solve forecasting problems is not so obvious. That is why this study looked at the behavior of a neural network with different hidden layers.

The number of neurons in the hidden layer, and the appropriate number of hidden layers, is determined through experimentation. Too few neurons will prevent the neural network from correctly mapping inputs to output. Too many neurons will impede generalization by allowing the network to "memorize" the patterns presented to it without extracting any of the salient features. Thus, when presented with new data, the network is unable to process it properly, because it has not discovered the underlying relationships. However, Touretzky and Pomerleau (1989:233) state: "...while, we have removed some mystery concerning the representations that neural networks develop, the hidden layers have yet to give up all their secrets."

- An output layer[22] - The output layer is considered a collector of the features detected and the producer of the response that may be connected to a word, value or a machine. Thus, the output layer holds the response of the network to a given input.

2.4.5 The operation of a neural network

This section describes the seven steps that generally occur during the operation of a neural network:

- Computation of the net weighted input;
- conversion of the net input signal to an activation level;
- transfer of the net weighted sum;
- computation of the competition function of the output function;
- computation of the current error and error function;
- estimation of the backpropagated "error" value; and
- learning and adaptation.

2.4.5.1 Computation of the net weighted input

A neural network processes inputs to create outputs; to achieve this, each processing element takes in the output from many other neurons. Once inside the neuron, the weighted signals are summed to a net value. Each of the processing elements is then connected to other processing elements through weighted connections; these connections may be excitatory (with positive weights) or inhibitory (with negative weights). To date, there are four different kinds of weights, each with slightly different characteristics:

- Variable weights - these weights can adapt or change according to the learning rule for the processing element.

- Fixed weights - these are weights that do not learn, but are the same as variable weights with respect to calculating the effective input.

---

22 Also known as OUT.

- Modified weights - these weights do not learn, and are similar to fixed weights. However, they are further modified by mod factors from the current column in the recall portion of the application layer's learning of a recall schedule.

- Set weights - this type of connection usually acts identically to modified weights. Rather than using the mod factor, however, these weights are multiplied by the input value.

Each input will be given a relative weight or weighting. Weights are adaptive coefficients within the network that determine the intensity of the input signal (Nelson and Illingworth, 1992:45). These weights can be thought of as measures of connection strength. The initial weight for a PE can be modified in response to various inputs and according to the network's own rules for modification. In mathematical terms (refer to equation 2-2), this is achieved by computing:

$$U_i = \sum_{J=1}^{n} (X_i \times W_{ij}) \qquad \text{...(2-2)}$$

Where: U_i = The result of the summation function or the net weighted input.

i = The current processing element.

j = A processing element that is connected to i.

W_{ij} = The weight connecting processing element j to processing element i. For notational convenience, it may be assumed that the modified or set weight has already been multiplied by the appropriate factor.

X_i = The processing element from which the connection originates.

In this expression, U_i is the net weighted input received by processing element i from a total of *n* processing elements in the network. The incoming signal from the jth processing element is designated by W_{ij}. Once U_i has been computed, all information about which input signals were strong, and which were weak, will be lost. A strong input signal arriving over a weaker weighted connection may have less effect than a weaker signal arriving over a strongly weighted connection (Caudill and Butler, 1992(b):5). Thus, it is the net stimulus that matters, not the value of any particular one. In the same way, a processing element with two incoming signals has a two-dimensional weight vector and a two-dimensional input vector associated with it. The dimensionality of the weight vector and the input vector are always the same. It is noteworthy that the outputs and corresponding input signals can either be excitatory or inhibitory. An excitatory input means that the signals tend to cause the processing element to fire, while an inhibitory input means that the signal tends to prevent the processing element from firing.

2.4.5.2 Conversion of the net input signal to an activation level

The second step of the translation operation is to convert the net input to the activation level for the processing element. The activation level of the processing element is equivalent to the level of excitement of a biological neuron (Caudill and Butler, 1992(b):5). The activation function is a sigmoid, that is, the activation is expressed by an S-shaped curve.

The purpose of introducing this function is to allow the outputs to vary as regards time (Nelson and Illingworth, 1992:46). However, the activation function slowly decays over time and the excited state gradually returns to an inactive level (Lawrence, 1991:58). The state of activation is always the state of the neural network at any given time. Each neuron has an individual activation value. The activation value specifies what the neuron is to do with the signal after the weights have had their effect. On completion of the conversion of the net input signal to an activation function, the activation is passed through a transfer function.

2.4.5.3 Transfer of the net weighted sum

The transfer function determines the dynamic state of the neural network, the result being that the product of the weighted sum is transformed into a working output or a transfer output. Additionally, the transfer function of a neuron defines how the activation value is converted to an output value. This is achieved after the weighted sum of the effective inputs has been computed, and then transformed by a transfer function. The most common transfer functions, according to the literature, are:

- Threshold function - if the activation value is greater than some fixed amount known as the threshold, the neuron will output a one. If the activation value is below the threshold value, the neuron will output zero. Thus, the neuron activation must reach a certain level before the neuron contributes to a new total network state (Lawrence, 1991:58).

- Sigmoid function - also known as an S-shaped, semi-linear, or squashing function, this is one in which the output is a continuous, monotonic function of the input. Both the function itself and its derivatives are continuous in all cases. According to Lawrence (1991:202), the sigmoid function asymptotically approaches the low and high values (refer to equation 2-3). The center value of the input is the point at which the output jumps between low to high.

$$T = (1 + e^{-1_{gain}})^{-1} \qquad \textbf{...(2-3)}$$

Where: T = Result of applying the transfer function to the sum I.

Gain = The value for the gain parameter taken from the recall portion of the appropriate learning and testing.

e = The error function.

- Linear function - The linear function is the function where the output has a constant slope. The center of the value of the input is the point at which the output is equal to zero, therefore the gain is the slope of the line (refer to equation 2-4).

$$T = I \qquad \textbf{...(2-4)}$$

- Sine function - The sine function is the function that takes the trigonometric sine of the input (refer to equation 2-5).

$$T = \sin\ (I \times Gain) \qquad \textbf{...(2-5)}$$

Research done by Lapedes and Farber (1987:1-20), in an attempt to forecast the closing price of the Standard and Poor 500 for ten consecutive weeks, established that when a sine function is used instead of a sigmoid, the learning procedure seems to do a mode decomposition, in that it discovers the important frequency components of the function, as described by the discrete set of input or output examples.

After the transformation has been computed, the result is then scaled and limited. The transfer function is then post-processed into the following linear transformation (refer to equation 2-6):

$$\textit{Scale factor x Transformed value} + \textit{Offset} \qquad \textbf{...(2-6)}$$

The product of applying the transfer function to the sum computed by the weighted function is then reduced to upper and lower value limits. Refer to equation 2-7 for the operation performed:

$$T = \begin{bmatrix} High\ limit,\ if\ T > High\ limit \\ Low\ Limit,\ if\ T < Low\ limit \\ T,\ otherwise \end{bmatrix} \qquad \text{...(2-7)}$$

2.4.5.4 Computation of the competition function of the output function

This computation provides a way of allowing processing elements in a layer to compete with each other. This process, which is called learning, determines the final output value. Learning is discussed in detail in section 2.4.6. There are two different kinds of competition, namely:

- Output competition - When processing elements compete to determine which will be active, there can only be one or two winners. All the other processing elements in the layer will have an output of zero. The one or two winners will be chosen on the basis of the highest value of the product of applying the transfer function to the weighted sum value. Even if, for example, the transfer function is negative for all of the processing elements, the least negative will still be the "winner".

  When processing elements compete for output, only the first winner will learn to adapt; no other processing elements in the layer will adapt their weights.

- Learning competition - Under certain circumstances, it is desirable for processing elements in a layer to compete to determine which one will learn and adapt (Aleksander and Burnett, 1987:123).

2.4.5.5 Computation of the current error and error function

If a difference between the current output and the desired output is calculated, a raw error exists. This raw error is transformed by an error function; the resulting value is referred to as the current error.

2.4.5.6 Estimation of the backpropagated "error" value

Depending on the network paradigm used, the information may be backpropagated to a previous layer. The backpropagated value is either the current error[23] or the desired output, depending on the network type. The backpropagated "error" value is determined by multiplying each of the incoming connection weights by the backpropagated value and adding it to the error field in the source processing element.

2.4.5.7 Learning and adaptation

Variable connection weights are then modified according to the learning rule. The process of changing the weights of the connections to achieve the desired result is called "learning" or "adaptation". If some form of competition for learning is in effect, only weights belonging to the "winning" processing element will be updated. Learning rules use one or more of the learning coefficients from the learning and recall schedules.

2.4.5.8 Summary of the operation of a neural network

The processing element receives the input stimuli along its input connections and translates those stimuli into an output response, transmitted along the PE's output connection. The point at which the input connections meet the PE is usually called the synapse. The mathematical expression that describes the translation of an input stimulus pattern to an output response signal is called the transfer function. In mathematical terms, sections 2.4.5.1 - 2.4.5.7 can be described in three steps:

A) Computation of the net weighted input

Each input will be given a relative weight or weighting. Weights are adaptive coefficients within the network that determine the intensity of the input signal (Nelson and Illingworth, 1992:45). These weights can be thought of as measures of connection strength. The initial weight for a PE can be modified in response to various inputs and according to the network's own rules for modification. In mathematical terms (refer to equation 2-8), this is achieved by computing:

---

23 Current error is scaled by the derivative of the transfer function.

$$U_i = \sum_{j=1}^{n} (X_i \times W_{ij}) \qquad \text{...(2-8)}$$

Where: U_i = The result of the summation function or the net weighted input.

i = The current processing element.

j = A processing element that is connected to i.

W_{ij} = The weight connecting processing element j to processing element i. For notational convenience, it may be assumed that the modified or set weight has already been multiplied by the appropriate factor.

X_i = The processing element from which the connection originates.

B) Converting the net input signal to an activation level

The second step of the translation operation is to convert the net input to the activation level for the processing element. The activation level of the processing element is equivalent to the level of excitement of a biological neuron (Caudill and Butler, 1992(b):5). The activation function is a sigmoid, that is, the activation is expressed by an S-shaped curve (refer to equation 2-9):

$$f\ (I) = \frac{1}{1+e^{-I}} \qquad \text{...(2-9)}$$

C) Converting the activation level to an output signal

The final step is accomplished by the transfer function (refer to equation 2-10). This is achieved by using net a weighted value which is then biased by a previously established threshold value and sent through a threshold function. The threshold function is usually the sigmoid function, which has an input-to-output mapping, resulting in an output (Lawrence, 1991:57).

$$Y_j = F_{th}(U_j + t_j) \qquad \text{...(2-10)}$$

Where: Y_j = Output signal.

F_{th} = Threshold function.

U_j = Net weighted value.

t_j = Threshold value.

2.4.6 How neural networks learn

The underlying assumption in the analogy between neural network models and the real cortex[24] is that both structures learn to recognize patterns (Maddox, 1989:403). This requires neural networks to discover what pattern of coupling strengths between different pairs of elements will embody a learned pattern in a stable fashion. Similarly, the neurons in the cortex should make appropriate synaptic connections.

Neural networks learn to solve problems. That is, they are not programmed to do so. Learning[25] is thus fundamental to a neural network. Strictly speaking, training and learning are not the same processes: training is the procedure by which the network learns, and learning is the end-result of that procedure (Caudill and Butler, 1992(b):8). However, in this study the terms may be used interchangeably.

Learning implies that the processing element changes its input/output behavior in response to a training set of data or to external input. If a processing element has to adjust to the correct response to an input, the processing element itself has to make the changes. As previously mentioned, the output is computed because of the transfer function of the weighted input[26]. The processing element thus takes this value and applies the transfer function to it to compute the resulting output. The only way in which to change the weighted input is to modify the values of the weights on the individual inputs. Consequently, the neural network learns by changing the weights of the inputs. The learning law is discussed in subsection 2.4.6.2. However, in short, it is the process by which the neural network modifies its weights in response to external input. The equation that determines this change is called the learning law.

---

24 Refer to section 2.3.2 for a discussion of the cerebral cortex.

25 Also called adaptation or self-organization.

26 The net input is computed by multiplying the value of each individual input by its corresponding weight, or by taking the dot product of the input vectors.

2.4.6.1 Types of learning modes

There are two learning modes by which neural networks learn:

- Supervised learning; and
- unsupervised learning.

Each will be discussed subsequently

- Supervised learning - In this mode, the neural network is provided with an input stimulus pattern with a corresponding desired output pattern. Weights, which are generally randomly set to begin with, are adjusted by the network so that the next iteration or cycle will produce a closer match (Nelson and Illingworth, 1992:132). The purpose of the learning procedure is ultimately to minimize the error between the desired output and the current output sample by continuously modifying the weights.

  In supervised learning, it is necessary to train the neural network before it may become operational. Training (the procedure by which the network learns) consists of presenting input and output data (known as the training set) to the neural network (Nelson and Illingworth, 1992:132). Training a neural network is similar to fitting a curve to a set of points on a graph (Geake, 1990:18). The best curve will pass through many points and will generalize the trend of the data, while a curve that goes through all the points but wiggles about between them has generalized badly. During supervised learning, the neural network is consistently corrected by the values of the training set inputs. The neural network takes each input and produces an output, which it then compares to the correct output (provided by the user in the training set). This causes the neural network to construct an internal representation which captures the regularities of the data in a way which is distributed and may be generalized (Lawrence, 1993:86).

  According to Lawrence (1991:75-76), in a one-layered neural network, in which the stimulus-response can be controlled closely, this is easily accomplished by monitoring each neuron individually. However, in a multi-layered neural network, supervised learning is more difficult because it is harder to correct the hidden layers. Supervised learning is generally used in neural networks to decide, to map associations, to memorize information, or to generalize.

- Unsupervised learning[27] - Here, the neural network uses no external influences to adjust the weights during training and thus there is no training set to tell the neural network whether its input was correct. In this learning mode, the neural network looks for regularities or trends in the input signals, and makes adaptations according to the function of the network. Although it is not told whether it is right or wrong, the network must still have information on how to organize itself. There are two ways in which the neural network can achieve this:

  A) Organization can be maintained through emphasis on co-operation between clusters of processing elements (Nelson and Illingworth, 1992:133). In such a configuration, the clusters would work together and try to stimulate each other. If, for example, the external input were activated in the cluster, the cluster activity in the whole area could increase. Similarly, if an external input were decreased, this could cause an inhibitory effect on the entire cluster.

  B) Competition between processing elements also functions as a basis for learning (refer to 2.4.5.4). In this learning mode the processing elements are trained to compete with each other to determine which of the processing elements will learn and which will adapt. The rationale behind this is that the training of competitive clusters could apply the response of specific groups to specific stimuli and associate those groups with each other and with a specific appropriate response (Hecht-Nielsen, 1988:15). Two network types in particular make use of unsupervised competitive learning: Madaline and spatio-temporal pattern recognition. Each will be discussed briefly:

     a) Madaline competition - In this type of competition, one must keep track of the two processing elements with the sum closest to zero, one being positive and the other, negative. When the error in the output layer is computed, it is communicated back to the prior layer. The processing element closest to zero, but of the opposite sign to that of the error, wins and is adapted.

---

27 Also known as self-supervised learning.

b) Spatio-temporal recognition competition - the processing element in the current layer is connected to an output processing element with a desired output value of one. The processing element with the highest prior input wins.

Lawrence (1991:78) feels that, while unsupervised learning schemes are fascinating, they are not very well understood at present. This lack of understanding has, in part, precluded the incorporation of unsupervised networks into useful applications. Simplistically stated, unsupervised learning is the procedure by which the neural network is presented only with a series of input patterns and is given no information or feedback at all about its performance levels. According to Caudill and Butler (1992(b):8), this type of training procedure is often used for categorization or statistical modelling applications.

2.4.6.2 Learning laws

Neural networks determine the relationship between input and output data by looking at the training set. Knowing what output is expected from each input, the neural network learns by automatically adjusting or adapting to the strengths of the connections between the processing elements. This adjusting process is called the learning law.

According to Nelson and Illingworth (1992:136-137), many learning laws are in common use, most of these being some sort of variation on the Hebb rule (discussed in footnote 15). For the purposes of this study, only the learning laws actually utilized in the study will be discussed, namely:

- Hebb's rule;
- the Delta rule; and
- Kohonen's learning law.

- Hebb's Rule - The first learning law was introduced by the description which appeared in Hebb's book *The Organization of Behavior* in 1949 (Hebb, 1949:1-30). The rule stated that, if a processing element receives an input from another processing element, the weight between the processing elements should be strengthened (refer to equation 2-11).

$$w_{ij} = w_{ij} + C_1 \times [d_i]^1 \times [x_{ij}]^1 \qquad \textbf{...(2-11)}$$

Where: W_{ij} = Connecting weight from the jth input to the ith processing element in the current layer.

C_1 = Learning coefficient one.

d_i = Desired output of the ith processing element in the current layer.

x_{ij} = These are the outputs of the processing elements to which the current processing element is connected.

- The Delta rule[28] - The Delta rule says that, if there is a difference between the actual output pattern and the desired output pattern during training, then the weights must be changed to reduce the difference. According to Jones and Hoskins (1987:155-162), the Delta rule essentially assigns a pattern to the input units according to their activation levels; the more active an input is, the more responsible it is for the current distribution of activation among output units. The effect is that the connections pointing from the more active input units of a trail will undergo the largest modification in their weights. The same will occur among connections that point to output units with larger associated Deltas. The Delta rule is described in the following mathematical terms: the processing elements are modified so that they can monitor their own output. The output is then compared to an output signal (I_o). The error value (E) is computed for the input pattern (X) by subtracting the actual output (y), from the desired response (I_o):

$$E = I_o - y \qquad \text{...(2-12a)}$$

Finally, the changes in weights are calculated by the Delta rule:.

$$W_{new} - W_{old} = \frac{\beta E X}{X^2} \qquad \text{...(2-12b)}$$

Where: X = Input.

W = Weight.

β = The constant that measures the speed of the convergence of the weight vector.

---

28 Also known as the generalized Delta rule or the Least Mean Square learning rule.

Glover and Greenberg (1989:121-123) state that the Delta rule is a vector, and not a scalar equation. The error and the β values are scalar values, and only weights of the modified inputs are changed, while the weight and the training set inputs are always the same. However, according to White (1988:451-458), who employed neural networks to predict the IBM daily stock returns, a major defect of this method is that, because of the constant learning rate and the presence of a random component, this method will never converge to a useful set of weight values, but instead is doomed to wander.

A variant introduced to alleviate the problem, which is generally referred to as the problem of structured presentation of the training set, is to accumulate the weight changes over several training presentations and apply them all at once. This can be achieved by the Cumulative Delta rule:

$$m_{ij} = m_{ij} + C_1 \times e_i \times x_{ij} \quad at\ each\ iteration \qquad \textbf{...(2-13a)}$$

$$\begin{bmatrix} w_{ij} = w_{ij} + m_{ij} + C_2 a_{ij} \\ a_{ij} = m_{ij} \\ m_{ij} = 0 \end{bmatrix} \quad if\ learn\ Aux\ 1 = 0 \qquad \textbf{...(2-13b)}$$

Where: m_{ij} = The memory of the last change in weights for the ith processing element in the current layer.

w_{ij} = Connecting weight from the jth input to the ith processing element in the current layer.

a_{ij} = Auxiliary weight field.

e_i = The error for the ith processing element in the current layer.

x_{ij} = The jth input to the ith processing element in the current layer.

C_1 = Learning coefficient one.

C_2 = Learning coefficient two.

Aux 1 = General purpose counter.

The weight changes for the Delta rule are accumulated in standard term. When learning reaches an integer multiple of the accumulation period in Aux 1, the accumulated weight changes are applied to the connecting weight, and the weight and the weight accumulator are reset to zero. However, the Cumulative Delta Rule does not solve the problem of linkage between the learning coefficient and the epoch[29] size, which means that if the epoch size has adjusted, the learning schedule of a neural network must be adjusted too, which is cumbersome (Ver Duin, 1990:68). This can be overcome by employing the Normalized Cumulative Delta rule which gets around the problem by dividing the learning coefficients by the square root of the epoch size.

In short, the Delta rule is based on the reduction of the error between the actual output of a processing element and its desired output by modifying incoming connection weights.

- Kohonen's learning law - In this procedure, the processing elements compete for the opportunity of learning. The processing element with the largest output is declared the "winner", gaining the abilities to inhibit its competitors and excite its neighbors. Only the winning processing element is permitted an output, and only this PE plus its neighbors are permitted to adjust their weights. The Kohonen learning law is designed on the biological model using the interlayer interconnections to moderate this competition. Each processing element in the output layer is activated, and this acts as an inhibitor to each of the following inputs. These inhibitory inputs tend to reduce the activation of the other processing elements, which thus reduce their corresponding inhibitory inputs to one another. The effect of this is wholly inhibitory; but for the winning processing element's immediate neighbors, or those physically close to the processing neuron, the effect is actually positive, resulting in every processing element firing for itself, and, if this is not possible, influencing its neighbors. Thus, if any of the processing element's neighbors win, they are still allowed to change their weights, even though they cannot output. As the competing outputs circulate within the layer, the influence of the processing element eventually settles down to such a small part of the neural network that the largest overall excitation generates an output, and the remainder of the layer is quiescent. Refer to equation 2-14 for the Kohonen learning law.

---

[29] "Epoch" refers to the number of sets of training data presented to the network, in other words, the number of learning cycles.

$$W_{new} = W_{old} + \alpha(X - W_{old}) \qquad \text{...(2-14)}$$

Where: W = Weight vector.
X = Input.
α = Learning constant.

To reiterate, the winning input is the weight that generates the largest product, with the winning weight being the closest to the input. In Kohonen's learning law, both the difference between the inputs and a fraction of this difference are added to the original weight. Therefore, not only does the winner get its weight adjusted, but processing elements in the winner's neighborhood perform similar adjustments. They adjust their weights using the same learning rule by applying it to their own weight vectors. The complete effect of this presentation is that the winning processing element outputs a positive one signal, and its neighbors move closer to the input vector.

2.4.6.3 Learning difficulties

According to Beale and Jackson (1990:91-95), the neural network occasionally settles into a stable solution that does not provide the correct output. In these cases, the energy function of the neural network is in local minimum, also called local minima or overtraining[30]. This means that the energy level is higher in every direction in which the network could move in a certain energy landscape, than it is in the current position. However, learning is accomplished by following the energy function down in the steepest direction, until it reaches the bottom of a valley, at which point there is no direction in which to move to reduce the energy. Wassermann (1989:57) perceives local minima as the type of gradient descent employed; that is, the network follows the slope of the error surface downward, constantly adjusting the weights towards the minimum. The error surface of a neural network is highly convoluted, full of hills, valleys, folds, and gullies in high dimensional space. The network can get trapped in a local minimum (a shallow valley) when there is a much deeper minimum nearby.

Simply stated, overtraining occurs as the neural network is forced to match the target values more and more exactly. During this process, the neural network devotes its capacity to learning

---

30 "Overtraining" is the term used in this study.

the exact values of training data, rather than to drawing generalizations from it. The learning capacity is based on the size of the network, and, more specifically, on the number of connections in the network. If insufficient capacity is available, then the training tolerance will not be achieved and the neural network will never stop training. However, if sufficient capacity is available, then the testing tolerance will be achieved, though testing or running accuracy may tend to suffer. An alternative definition of overtraining is the state which occurs when the neural network has memorized the training data, resulting in a lack of generalization.

There are other approaches to minimize these learning difficulties. They are outlined as follows:

- Lowering the learning rate - If the amount of adjustment made by the learning rate to the weights (connection strengths) is altered, with the weights being progressively decreased, either by the learning rate or the learning coefficient ratio[31], then the gradient descent algorithm can achieve a better solution (Beale and Jackson, 1990:91). As the learning rate is decreased, the network settles into a minimum configuration, without overshooting the stable position, as the gradient descent takes smaller downhill steps. This approach enables the network to bypass local minima at first, and settle into a deeper minima without oscillating widely. (Beale and Jackson, 1990:91). An envisaged problem with a reduction in the learning rate is that it will take the neural network longer to converge.

- Addition of neurons - Overtraining can be considered to have occurred when two or more different classes are categorized as the same. This amounts to a poor internal representation within the neurons; thus adding units to the hidden layer will allow for better recording of inputs and lessen the occurrence of overtraining. However, Fishman (1993:interview) warns that adding neurons to the hidden layer will result in overtraining. The justification for this can be explained by comparing a single neuron to human biological memory, that is, the more neurons are added to the hidden layer, the greater the ability of the network to memorize the data; this results in tabular learning and, consequently, in overtraining.

---

[31] The learning coefficient ratio sets the amount by which to divide the learning coefficient value for the first transition. This defines the exponential decay, which is sampled at subsequent transition points.

Fishman suggests that the amount of neurons in the hidden layer should be about one third in relation to the amount of inputs.[32]

- Changing the momentum - The connection strengths' changes can be given some "momentum" by introducing an extra term into the weight adaptation equation. This will produce a large change in the weight if the changes are currently large, and will decrease as the changes decrease (Beale and Jackson, 1990:92).

  Thus, learning difficulties can be reduced by changing the momentum (refer to equation 2-15). This means that any weight adjustment because of an error from the training case will have a continuing effect with an exponential decay. For example, consider a training case *t*, with the momentum set at 50%. The weight adjustment will be made based on the current error, and 50% of the weight adjustment will be applied to the previous case. In the next training case, 50% of the weight adjustment results from the error at t+1, 25% from the error at *t*, and the remaining 25% from errors of previous cases. As each case is considered, the effect on the weight adjustment of each previous case is halved or reduced proportionately, as determined by the momentum setting.

$$w_{ij}\ (t + 1) = w_{ij}\ (t) + \alpha\ (w_{ji}(t) - w_{ij}(t - 1)) \qquad \text{...(2-15)}$$

Where: α = Momentum factor, $0 < \alpha < 1$.

  Momentum is of great assistance for speeding up convergence along shallow gradients, allowing the path which the neural network takes toward the solution to pick up speed. However, setting the momentum to a higher value helps smooth out the training process and prevents unusual cases from throwing the neural network off track, while continuously correcting for consistent errors. Setting the momentum lower may be appropriate for data that is smoother and more regular, or data for which the relationships to be learned are relatively simple.

- Addition of noise (refer to footnote 17) - Random noise disturbs the gradient descent algorithm from the line descent, and often this noise is enough to force the neural network

---

32 A rule of thumb, also known as a heuristic.

out of overtraining. According to Beale and Jackson (1990:92), this approach has the advantage of taking a little extra computation time, and so is noticeably slower than the gradient descent algorithm.

- Checking results - Overtraining can be measured by periodically checking the results of the test data set. Early stages of a training session should yield lower error measurements on both the training and the test data. This should continue, unless there are too few data sets in the training set. However, if at some point during learning the test data begins to produce worse results, even though the training data continues to produce improved results, overtraining has occurred, and the neural network has memorized the training data and was unable to generalize.

Another learning difficulty that can be encountered is called neural network paralysis. Under certain circumstances, as the network trains, the weights can become adjusted to very high values (Wassermann, 1989:57). This can force all or most of the neurons to operate at high values, in a region where the derivative is very small. Since the error which is sent back for training is proportional to this derivative, the training process will come to a standstill. Paralysis occurs when a large percentage of the neurons have acquired weights so large as to produce high values. According to Wassermann (1989:89), "There is no theory that can predict whether or not a network will become paralysed during training. Experimentally, small step sizes have been found to produce paralysis less often, but a step that is small for one problem may be excessive for another."

A learning problem which generally occurs during the first data representations is referred to as PE saturation. Every hidden layer and output layer PE processes data during its feed-forward pass in three steps: summation, transformation and output. For argument's sake, it is necessary to reiterate these steps briefly. The summation function is simply a sum of products, where each incoming weight is multiplied by the output value from the connection's source PE. Having performed the summation function, the resulting Internal activation value (I) is transformed, commonly by using a hyperbolic tangent (TanH). The resulting transformation value is then processed through the output function to produce the PE's output value. However, PE saturation occurs when the summation value is outside the effective range of the transfer function. This range is approximately ± 3.0 for TanH, and ± 6.0 for sigmoid. The problem resulting from PE saturation is twofold: Not only is the sensitivity of the data lost, but, during the error propagation pass, where the derivative of the transfer function is calculated, the PE's error becomes zero, which results in no learning taking place. Saturation is dependent upon the following factors:

- The scale of the data;
- the weight values and their initial random range; and
- the learning coefficient and momentums employed.

The following approaches can be employed to overcome PE saturation:

- Change (increase or decrease) the input range in which the data is scaled;
- change the initial random weight range between the input layer and the first hidden layer; and
- change the learning coefficient on the first hidden layer (Everly, 1992:19).

2.4.7 The classification of neural networks

The foundations of neural networks study consist of an understanding of the nomenclature required and a firm comprehension of the rudimentary mathematical concepts used to analyse neural network processing. In a broad sense, neural networks consist of three principal elements (Simpson, 1990:4):

- Topology - how a neural network is organized into layers and how the layers are connected;
- learning - how the information is stored in the network (refer to 2.4.6); and
- recall - how the stored information is retrieved from the network.

The element to be discussed in this section is topology. A neural network's topology evolves from the patterns, connections, and processing element functions that have already been described. The arrangement of the processing elements, connections, and patterns into a neural network is referred to as the topology of the network. Neural networks are classified by topology, according to different criteria.

The most general form of classification is the division of neural networks into single-layered perceptrons and multi-layered perceptrons.

- Single-layered perceptron - The minimal neural network topology found is a single-layered interconnected neural network. The single-layered neural network accepts input patterns in one of three ways:

  - Processing initialization only - the input pattern is used to initialize the input layer's processing elements, but, from then on the input pattern does not influence the processing;
  - processing element's initialization and constant bias - the input pattern is used to initialize the input layer processing element, and the input remains a constant-valued input bias throughout processing; and
  - constant bias only - the processing elements are all initialized to all zeroes, and the input pattern acts as a constant-valued bias throughout processing (Simpson, 1990:9).

The input may be binary or continuous (Rahimian, Singh, Thammachote and Virmani: 1993:164). Single-layered neural networks are used to perform four types of pattern processing: pattern completion, noise removal, optimization, and contrast enhancement.

- Two-layered networks - These neural networks consist of an input layer of processing elements fully interconnected to an output layer. There are three common types of two-layered neural networks: feedforward pattern matches, feedback pattern matches, and feedforward pattern classifiers (Simpson, 1990:10).

- Multi-layered perceptron - A multi-layered perceptron neural network consists of more than one layer. There are usually three layers of neurons. The neurons in the input layer do not perform weighting or nonlinear transformation. They simply send inputs from the world outside the network to the hidden-layer neurons (Berry and Trigueiros, 1993:104).

However, Lawrence (1991:69) feels that neural networks should be classified according to their neuron transfer functions, rather than by the number of layers. She distinguishes two classes, namely:

- Linear neural network models - The neurons of a linear model respond to changes in their inputs by changing the firing rate of their outputs. This was the first model to use neurons with linear transfer functions[33] rather than with logic units.

- Nonlinear neural network model - The output of the neuron is a nonlinear function of the sum.

Lawrence (1991:70-71) also asserts that neural networks can be classified according to the learning algorithm, which is usually either supervised or unsupervised (refer to section 2.4.6.2).

However, I found no single optimal classification procedure for neural networks. For this study, neural network architectures were classified in terms of the simple classification: dividing neural networks into feedback and feedforward networks, with appropriate branches.

2.4.7.1 Simple classification

Refer to Figure 2.5 for the simple classification of neural networks. It can be noted that the diagram is split into two sections:

- Feedback neural networks - Feedback neural networks can be constructed or trained. In a constructed model, the weight matrix is created by adding the outer product of the input pattern to itself, or to an associated input (Hertz, Krogh and Palmer, 1991:123-126). After construction, a partial or inaccurate input pattern can be presented to the network, and, after a while, the network will converge to one of the original input patterns. Examples of constructed feedback neural networks are Bidirectional Associative Memories (BAM) and Hopfield. In a trained feedback neural network, weight adjustments are made, which affect the signals as they move forward, as well as when they feed back to previous neuron inputs. An example of a trained feedback model is the Adaptive Resonance Theory (ART).

---

[33] A linear transfer function is one in which the output is equal to a gain value times the difference between the net input value less the center value. The center value is the value of the net input at which the output is equal to zero. (Anderson, 1988:20).

Figure 2.5 - Simple neural network classification

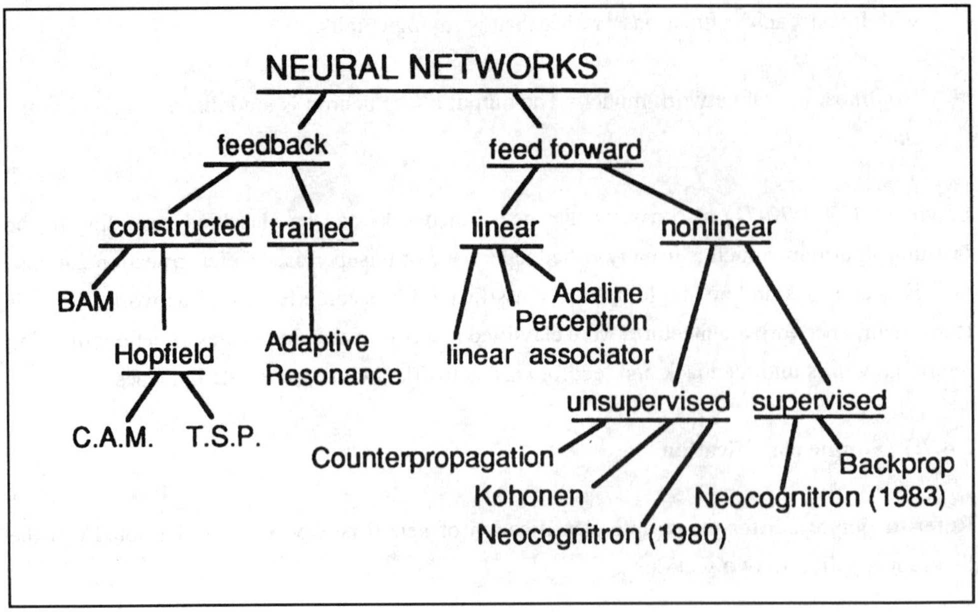

- Feedforward neural networks - The second main category of neural networks is the feedforward network. Feedforward neural networks are divided into linear and nonlinear feedforward neural networks (refer to section 2.4.7 for discussion). Nonlinear feedforward neural networks are further subdivided into unsupervised and supervised neural networks (refer to section 2.4.6.2).

2.4.7.2 The network paradigm selector table

A problem with the aforementioned classifications is that they do not clearly indicate what type of neural network paradigm should be employed for a certain application. This problem may be overcome by classifying neural network paradigms in terms of their appropriateness for a certain application (refer to Table 2.1).

Table 2.1 - Network paradigm selector table

Application	Purpose	Supervised	Neural network paradigm
Prediction	The use of input data to predict an output value	Yes	• Backpropagation • Digital neural network • Self-organizing map into backpropagation • Cascade correlation • Adaline • Madaline • Perceptron
Classification	The use of input data to predict a categorical output value	Yes	• Categorical learning • Counter propagation • Learning vector quantization • Probabilistic neural networks • Self-organizing map into categorization
Data association	Neural network learns association of error-free or ideal data, then classifies or associates data that contains the error	Yes	• BAM • Boltzmann pattern completion • Boltzmann input/output • Hamming • Hopfield
Conceptual-ization	Neural network analyzes data and determines conceptual relationships	No	• Adaptive Resonance Theory I • Self-Organizing map

Application	Purpose	Supervised	Neural network paradigm
Optimization	Neural network determines optimal values	No	• Hopfield
Data filtering	Neural network smooths the input signal	No	• Recirculation

2.5 THE NEURAL NETWORK PARADIGM

The primary network used for prediction is the feedforward network with nonlinear elements. There are many ways in which to train this type of network; however, most of them are related to backpropagation (the topology used in this study which is discussed in section 2.6). The related backpropagation paradigms include:

- Directed Random search - A neural network that is not based on backpropagation, but instead incorporates a random aspect, while keeping track of previously successful directions.

- Backpropagation with recirculation - The number of outputs equals the number of inputs since the network smooths its own signal.

- Adaline - A simple one-neuron network that uses bi-polar inputs and outputs.

- Madaline - First multi-layered predictive network.

2.5.1 Introduction

The backpropagation neural network is probably the best known and most widely used among the types of neural network systems currently available. This network is an offshoot of earlier work on the perceptrons, with the addition of a hidden layer and the use of the generalized Delta rule for learning (Maren, Harston and Pap, 1990:92).

In essence, the backpropagation network is a perceptron with a different transfer function in the artificial neuron, along with a more robust and capable learning rule.

2.5.2 The topology of a backpropagation network

2.5.2.1 The structure of a backpropagation network

The backpropagation network requires at least three layers, whereas the original perceptron could function with only two layers. The layers of a backpropagation network are referred to as the input, hidden, and output layers. The hidden layer is crucial, in that it allows the backpropagation network to extract features and to generalize (Maren, Harston and Pap, 1990:94). However, if the hidden layer is too large, it will encourage the network to memorize the input patterns, rather than to generalize the input into features. This reduces the network's ability to handle unfamiliar input once training is complete. On the other hand, a hidden layer that is too small dramatically reduces the accuracy of recall. The connections between the layers are only feedforward connections. Furthermore, all connections are typically between adjacent layers; the input layer neurons connect only to those of the hidden layer, and hidden layer neurons connect only to the output layer.

2.5.2.2 The transfer function employed

The sigmoid transfer function is employed by a backpropagation neural network. Refer to section 2.4.5.3 for a discussion on the sigmoid transfer function.

2.5.2.3 The learning algorithm

The algorithms governing the operation of backpropagation are[34]:

Step 1: Initialize weights and offsets (Lippmann, 1987:17). Set all weights and neurons to small random values.

Step 2: Present the backpropagation network with input vector ($X = {}_{x}\cdots{}_{x-1}$) and desired outputs ($T = {}_{t}\cdots{}_{t-1}$). The backpropagation network is thus presented with a continuous-valued

---

[34] Assume that a sigmoid transfer function is employed.

input and specified the desired outputs. If the network is used as a classifier, then all desired outputs are typically set to zero, except for those corresponding to the class which the input forms (Lippmann, 1987:17).

Step 3: Calculate actual outputs. The connection weights between the hidden and output layers are adjusted, along with the activation thresholds in the output neurons. The difference between the actual value and the desired value of the output neuron(s) is used to drive this stage.

Step 4: The connection weights between the input and the hidden layers are adjusted, along with activation thresholds in the hidden layer (Maren, Harston and Pap, 1990:99). Refer to equation 2-16 for weight adjustment.

$$W_{ij}\ (t+1) = W_{ij}(t) + \eta\delta_j x_i \qquad \textbf{...(2-16)}$$

Where: $W_{ij}(t)$ = The weight from the hidden neuron i or from an input of neuron j at time t

X_i = The output of neuron i or an input.

η = The gain term.

δ = Error term for neuron j.

However, if neuron j is an output neuron, then refer to equation 2-17.

$$\delta_j = y_i(1-y_i)(d_i-y_i) \qquad \textbf{...(2-17)}$$

Where: d_i = The desired output of neuron j.

y_i = The actual output.

If neuron j is an internal hidden neuron (Lippmann, 1987:17), then refer to equation 2-18.

$$\delta_j = x_i(1-x_i)\sum \delta_k \; W_{jk} \qquad \text{...(2-18)}$$

Where: k = Overall neurons in the layers above neuron j. The internal neuron thresholds are adapted in a similar manner by assuming they are connection weights on links from auxiliary constant-valued inputs (Lippmann, 1987:17).

Step 5: Repeat from step 2. Repetition of these steps will lead the network to converge to a set of connection weights that minimizes the error for reorganizing all the patterns in the training set. This can also be expressed by the learning rule in terms of a function, Delta, or the generalized Delta function (refer to equation 2-12 and section 2.4.6.2 for a detailed discussion of the generalized Delta rule). However, according to Maren, Harston and Pap (1990:100), a problem can arise if the value of the error does not monotonically decrease as the weights between the input and output neurons approach a minimum value.

The operation of the backpropagation neural network can be summarized as follows:

- Select the training pair from the training set by applying the input vector to the network input;
- calculate the output of the network;
- calculate the error between the network output and the desired output;
- adjust the weights of the network in such a way as to minimize the error; and
- repeat the four previous steps in the training set until the error for the entire set is small.

2.5.2.4 Caveats

Backpropagation, despite its recognized performance, is not free of problems. Possible problems include overtraining, network paralysis, and long training times (Kang, 1991:28). As discussed previously, the error surfaces of multi-layered perceptrons, unlike those of the single-layered perceptrons, have flat areas and shallow troughs, and hills and ravines in high-dimensional space (Hecht-Nielsen, 1990:593-605). In general, such an error surface may contain local minima, and the network can get trapped in any of them. Although some researchers have actually been able to discover a local minimum after a lengthy experiment, experience has shown that a local minimum does not cause serious problems (Hinton, 1989:185-234). Alexander (1991:17) points out that backpropagation is inadequate for larger tasks in its current form, because of the time it takes for the learning process to converge to a solution.

Another problem is that the desired output is usually defined in terms of 0 and 1, values which actually need an infinite potential using equation. In other words, they will never be achieved. According to Carling (1992:147), this can be overcome by accepting values within some limit of 0 and 1, for example 0.1 and 0.9.

The most critical problem concerning the implementation of backpropagation is the slowness of the training process (Hagiwara, 1990:617-620). Numerous studies have attempted to improve the convergence speeds. Suggested ideas include the use of conjugate gradients, the use of the Quasi-Newton algorithm (Webb, Lowe and Bedworth, 1988:4157), careful selection of the learning parameters (Stevens, 1985:287-297), the use of higher order derivatives (Himmelbau, 1990:631-634), and the use of the self-constructing network.

2.6 FACTORS INFLUENCING SUPERVISED LEARNING IN NEURAL NETWORKS

An objective of this study was to investigate the major factors that influence the way in which neural networks are organized, which in turn affects the performance of the neural network model when applied to share market forecasting. The following factors were noted:

- Number of processing elements;
- number of hidden layers;
- number of inputs; and
- training set.

In general, the evaluation of the performance of a neural network forecasting model is based, according to Kang (1991:44), on the following criteria of success:

- The training time;
- the ability to learn and generalize; and
- the ability to predict.

In this section, the theoretical background of the four factors influencing neural networks' organization will be discussed. The scope of this study, however, did not include experimentation with different network paradigms; therefore, a network paradigm discussion will not be presented here. Furthermore, the performance of forecasting methods is often dependent upon the type of data utilized (Makridakis, Wheelwright and McGee, 1984:132). However, the data pattern in a time series is a condition already given to implementors of neural network forecasting models (Kang, 1991:44) and can therefore not be controlled by them. Thus, no discussion of such difficulties will be included here. The subsequent sections will deal with a discussion of two design factors.

2.6.1 Number of processing elements

The number of processing elements needed in a neural network for the input and output layers is directly determined by the number of inputs and outputs of the system. The number of processing elements is an important factor that influences the abilities of the neural network. A well-structured neural network should not only learn the training patterns, but also respond correctly to new patterns.

Some of the literature stresses the assumption of an infinite number of hidden processing elements. On the other hand, a large number of hidden processing elements will slow down the training time, which is a serious drawback of any feedforward neural network model running on a serial computer (Kang, 1991:45). The use of a large number of processing elements has also been criticized because of the memorization effect.[35] Even though there are no definitive rules regarding the number of neurons to use, some suggest the following guideline (refer to equation 2-19).

$$Number\ of\ hidden\ processing\ elements = \frac{(inputs + outputs)}{2} \qquad \text{...(2-19)}$$

2.6.2 Number of hidden layers

The role of the hidden layers and the effect of hidden processing elements are of particular importance because of their substantial impact on the neural network's ability to learn. Since the Minisky and Papert paper proved that a single-layered perceptron cannot represent arbitrary functions, a number of researchers have explored ways in which to overcome this problem. A

---

35 This refers to the phenomenon which occurs when a neural network starts memorizing the data, resulting in perfect predictions on the training set, but not on the critical testing set.

typical supervised feedforward neural network is multi-layered. As explained, the architecture consists of an input layer, one or more hidden layers and an output layer. There have been several studies that have proven that one hidden layer is both necessary and sufficient[36]. Irie and Miyake (1990:641-648) proved that a two-layered neural network can represent a continuous function if the input or the output functions are absolutely integrable within bounds. On the other hand, Hornik, Stinchcombe and White (1989:359-366) reported that neural networks with as few as one hidden layer can be perfect approximators. According to Kang (1991:48), this proof requires an unlimited number of processing elements. A study done by Stinchcombe and White (1989:613-617) reported similar findings to those of Kang; however, their findings are more general, in that the activation function or transfer function of the processing elements in the hidden layer can also be any nonlinear function.

Advocates of a single hidden-layered neural network structure assume either that an unlimited number of hidden processing elements are available, or a different transformation function is used for each continuous mapping to be approximated, both of which are unknown in practice. Having realized this problem, Chester (1990:265-68) explained the advantages of creating two hidden layers. Each layer, consisting of a few processing elements, can achieve the same degree of accuracy as a network with a single hidden layer with many processing elements can. He further claims that a neural network with two hidden layers is better because the second hidden layer reduces interference among processing elements, something that tends to worsen the overall approximation capability of a neural network. His view is supported by Arai (1989:419-423), who suggests the addition of more than one hidden layer, with an appropriate reduction of the number of processing elements. A study done by Chang (1992:60), indicates that the object is to use as few hidden layers as possible. He advocates this because each additional hidden unit adds to the load of the central processing unit (CPU). However, he hesitates to offer specific guidelines, except to say that, for a neural network of a reasonable size, the hidden layer need only be a relatively small fraction of the size of the input layer. If the network fails to converge to a solution, it may be necessary to add more processing elements, not layers.

The importance of a hidden layer is emphasised in the literature, but whether one or more hidden layers is preferable for a neural network to be able to solve a problem, is not obvious. This is why the behavior of the neural network with different hidden layer structures must be observed.

2.7 LIMITATIONS OF NEURAL NETWORKS

---

[36] Arai (1989:419-423), Hornik (1989:359-366), and Irie and Miyake (1988:641-648).

The rapid increase in neural network research activities has resulted in many successful applications. The development of more powerful multi-layered networks, combined with more complex learning mechanisms, has provided the necessary theoretical background upon which successful applications of neural networks may be based. It has been demonstrated that neural network computing is particularly suited to special types of tasks for which conventional computing is not appropriate; however, there are a number of problems that neural networks cannot deal with well. The following limitations exist:

- Neural networks cannot provide precise answers - One of the characteristics of a neural network is its ability to generalize. Consequently, the network will indicate a certain tendency or a certain range.

- Neural networks cannot count - A neural network converts the input data into an output by exploiting the parallel processing capabilities of a computer. Currently, computers are unable to count in a parallel mode. Even if the computer should count in a parallel mode, the nature of a neural network will result in generalization, making precise counting impossible (Nelson and Illingworth, 1992:75).

- Neural networks cannot justify their answers - They have no facility to match the "how" or "why" found in expert systems (Nelson and Illingworth, 1992:75).

- The development of training materials - Even after a neural network system has been initially designed, there is still much to be done regarding the selection of appropriate training materials. The quality of training material provided for neural network development is ultimately related to the quality of the decisions the neural network will make.

  Implementation and technology issues will need to be addressed in order to overcome the limitations mentioned above.

2.8 NEURAL NETWORKS IN COMPARISON WITH OTHER TECHNOLOGIES

The subsequent sections will provide a brief discussion of the available technology which may be compared with neural networks. These include the following technologies:

- Expert systems[37];
- fuzzy logic; and
- statistical techniques.

2.8.1 Expert systems

Expert systems and neural networks both provide methods for formalizing qualitative aspects (Zahedi, 1991:25). While neural networks and expert systems have the common goal of claiming to model human reasoning artificially, they use different methods. Expert systems assume the brain is a black box which initiates the human reasoning process. An expert system processes knowledge sequentially, represents it explicitly, and typically employs deductive reasoning. According to Zahedi (1991:25) learning takes place outside the system[38].

Contrary to expert systems, neural networks treat the brain as a black box and imitate its structure and function, using a parallel approach to simulate human intelligence. They represent knowledge implicity within their structure and apply inductive reasoning to process knowledge.

2.8.1.1 The differences between expert systems and neural networks

A comparison between expert systems and neural networks can be made from a number of perspectives. However, to accomplish the mission of endowing computers with human qualities, researchers have pursued two fundamental approaches. According to Newell and Simon (1981:41), the expert system group chose to concentrate on simulating and formalizing human reasoning and logic processes, based on the hypothesis that a symbolic system has the necessary and sufficient requirements. Zahedi (1991:34), further claims that human logic and reasoning formed the foundation of the expert systems approach and that expert systems thus focus on how

---

37 An expert system is a program that uses rules and facts to solve a particular problem.

38 A system is a group of elements which operate as a whole to achieve a desired result.

a person logically justifies actions and decisions, and attempt to give the machine a similar logical and reasoning capability.

On the other hand, neural network researchers have opted for simulating human intelligence according to how the brain functions. Hence, neural networks have focused on simulating human intelligence by modelling the brain. Refer to Table 2.2, which indicates the differences between expert systems and neural networks.

According to Lawrence (1992:36), expert systems are good at procedural types of problems such as scheduling, and teaching. However, a major weakness of expert systems is that they rely entirely on precise, up-to-date rules.

The question might arise as to why so few expert systems have been developed for business applications. One possible explanation for this lack of development is that business applications require more behavioral variables, which can slow down the acceptance of such systems. The heuristic knowledge that leads to good judgement in human behavior is hard to define. This line of reasoning can also be followed as to why expert systems have not been successfully employed in the forecasting of share prices.

Table 2.2 - The differences between neural networks and expert systems

Comparison	**Expert systems**	**Neural networks**
Processing method	Inherently serial	Inherently parallel
Knowledge stored	Explicit manner in the form of production rules, frames, objects, or semantic nets[39]	Network interconnection weights in an implicit manner
Learning	Takes place outside the system; the knowledge is obtained outside the machine and then coded	Takes place according to a static set of rules

[39] Zahedi (1991:35).

Comparison	Expert systems	Neural networks
Form of reasoning employed	Deductive reasoning - knowledge and facts are given to the system	Inductive approach - the system is driven by data
Theoretical basis	Mathematical logic, including predicate logic, and predicate calculus	Inherently statistical approach, which assumes the existence of error and ambiguity in its underlying foundations

2.8.2 Fuzzy Logic

Fuzzy logic allows vague information to be processed in a logical fashion. The concept of fuzziness (Lawrence, 1993:65) may be explained as follows:

- Fuzziness refers to vagueness, rather than probability;
- fuzzy data can be expressed in varying degrees.
- fuzziness is a way of working with fuzzy variables which involves steps and special operations;
- fuzzy systems use fuzzy logic to define and handle data; and
- fuzzy systems do not, in themselves, usually comprise the entire solution, rather, they are used as a problem solving method within a computing method.

Neural networks and fuzzy logic systems are similar in that they both deal with uncertainty using continuous values. Both the fuzzy logic systems and neural networks are different from traditional forms of artificial techniques in that they do not require any specific formulas to solve a problem, other than the mathematics inherent in the neural networks or the fuzzy logic system. However, neural networks can employ fuzzy principles in several ways. The neural network can be constructed so that it can interface to fuzzy logic systems through the interpretation of a fuzzy output. According to Lawrence (1993:71), this can be achieved if the outputs are not distributed. A fuzzy response might be interpreted as a probability, depending on the design. Lawrence illustrates this with an example of a neural network designed to diagnose a disease. Either a patient has a disease (output is a 1) or doesn't (output is a 0). When the neural network is given some new patient data which is somewhat similar to the examples on which it has trained, it might output 0.8. This means that the network is fairly certain of a diseased conditioning and suggests that further testing should be done.

Furthermore, the data used to train the neural network can be a member of a fuzzy set. Neural networks can handle fuzzy data as naturally as any other data, therefore there is no need to round off or estimate the data to train the neural network. A large amount of research has been done whereby fuzzy logic techniques have been incorporated into neural network algorithms.

2.8.3 Statistical techniques

Statistics were developed from the scientific need to make sense of repeated measurement of phenomena and the desire to investigate the nature of relationships between different measurements. The question might arise as to whether neural networks are alternatives to existing statistical techniques. White (1992:81) feels that statistical methods can offer insight into the properties, advantages, and disadvantages of neural network learning paradigms. Conversely, neural network learning methods have a lot to offer in the field of statistics. One of the objectives of this study was to compare neural networks with an existing time series forecasting method. Consequently, all comparative results will appear in Chapters 4 and 5.

2.9 CONCLUSION

For many, neural networks still exist only in the realm of theory without having real, practical, everyday uses. However, neural networks have progressed from conception to actual products. The purpose of this chapter was to provide an overview of the structure and the operation of neural networks, with special emphasis on the backpropagation network.

Chapter 3 will provide an overview of the contemporary schools of thought in the forecasting of share prices.

CHAPTER 3

CONTEMPORARY SCHOOLS OF THOUGHT IN THE FORECASTING OF SHARE PRICES

The important thing is not to stop questioning.
Curiosity has its own reason for existing.
-- Albert Einstein

3.1 INTRODUCTION

The prediction of share price performance involves the interaction of many variables, making prediction very difficult and complex. This has served as a constant enticement to individuals who have hoped to earn fame and fortune by unravelling a price forecasting method and models based on a substantive predictive formula which would result in a superior trading strategy. However, most attempts to understand the stock market have been either model-driven, statistical, or both. Such models have been useful in expanding our knowledge of share price behavior. Nevertheless, many empirical financial anomalies have remained unexplainable, largely due to the partial equilibrium nature of these models.

Over the last century much research has been performed by statisticians, bankers, financiers and economists in the search of this lucrative formula. The research over the years has broadly identified five schools of thought in the analysis of shares in order to project a future share price:

- Technical analysis;
- fundamental analysis;
- traditional time series forecasting techniques;
- efficient market hypothesis; and
- chaos theory.

The implications of these studies have indicated:

- A conviction that shares were characterized by an underlying mass psychology; and
- shortage of mathematical and statistical adroitness for effective research in the field of projecting future share prices.

3.2 TECHNICAL ANALYSIS

3.2.1 Introduction

The most controversial school of thought in the analysis of a future share price is technical analysis. The skeptical attitude towards technical analysis has been the result of a mystique that has developed around concepts associated with the subject.

The predominant problem with the use of technical analysis is that the method makes use of a vast array of highly subjective tests in order to determine a future share price. Adversaries further claim that the stock market is efficient, which implies that technical analysis is without merit. Studies done by Botha (1978:61-65), Brown (1977:61-62), Bennett (1978:50-65), Gilbertson and Roux (1977:21), and Hadassin (1974:13-24) concluded that a form of the efficient market hypothesis does exist on the Johannesburg Stock Exchange, but there is no mutual feeling of what type of form exists, namely, either the weak-, semi-strong or strong-form.

Another perplexity in the use of technical analysis can be expressed by the random walk hypothesis, which basically states that shares move randomly and cannot be predicted. Therefore, according to this hypothesis no method exists which can accurately forecast a share price, thus the use of technical analysis is nullified.

The proponents of technical analysis indicate that it involves the study of internal stock exchange information and, thus, the methodology of technical analysis rests upon the assumption that history repeats itself.

Technicians believe that fundamental analysis is, at best, inefficient and futile. They claim that there are so many factors affecting the value of a company that fundamentalists can only analyze a relatively small sample of factors at any time. Proponents of technical analysis further claim that there are so many contradictory studies on the efficient market hypothesis and the random walk hypothesis that the use of technical analysis cannot be nullified on these two hypotheses alone. One might well ask whether technical analysis is useful at all. In a study done by Lovell-Greene, Affleck-Graves and Money (1986:9), it was found that 55.4 percent of the analysts in the Republic of South Africa used technical analysis. A study done previously by Paulo (1984:120) indicated that the number of analysts using technical analysis was between 40 and 50 percent. However, a study done by Van Eyden (1991:7) indicates that the use of technical analysis has increased to 95 percent, representing a 39.6 percent increase in the use of technical analysis in the five years following the study of Lovell-Greene, Affleck-Graves and Money.

3.2.2 Defining technical analysis

Pring's (1985:2) view on technical analysis is that it is a reflection of the idea that share markets move in trends which are determined by the changing attitudes of investors to a variety of different forces. However, Murphy (1986:1) notes that technical analysis is a market action study. The term "market action" includes three principal sources of information available to the technician:

- Price;
- volume; and
- open interest.

With the aid of the study of market action, the technician, through the primary use of charts, forecasts a future share price trend.

Edwards and Magee (1966:5) regard technical analysis as the science of recording, usually in a graphic form, the actual trading in a certain share and deriving from this the probable future trend. Sharpe and Alexander (1990:689) conclude that technical analysis is the study of internal stock exchange information. As such, Sharpe and Alexander (1990:689) imply that the word "technical" reflects a study of the market itself and those external factors which are reflected in the market. The Market Technicians Association's board of directors approved the following definition of technical analysis (1991:8) "Technical analysis is the study of data generated by the action of the markets and by the behavior of market participants and observers. Such a study is usually applied to estimating probabilities for the future course of prices for a market, investment or speculation by interpreting the data in the context of precedent."

In summary, it can be said that technical analysis is the use of historical share price information. It entails the plotting of this past information on a chart and deducing a future share price movement. The purpose is to weigh the influences of supply and demand in an effort to determine whether buying or selling pressure is gaining a predominant position. The result of this interaction between supply and demand will govern the direction and the possible extent of the subsequent price movement. Conclusions are based on the interpretation of patterns, trends, cycles, and formations that develop on the charts and are primarily concerned with the identification of major turning points in the market, as assessed by market factors. It must be noted that the interpretation of the various patterns, formations and cycles is by no means an exact science and it is quite possible that two technicians will interpret the same chart differently.

3.2.3 The assumptions of technical analysis

Pinches (1970:104-110) states that technical analysis is based on the following assumptions:

- The market value of a share is determined solely by the interaction between supply and demand;
- prices move in trends which persist for an appreciable length of time; and
- changes in trends represent shifts in the balance between supply and demand.

Technical analysis also assumes the following:

- The interaction of supply and demand is reflected by a share price and is discounted by the market; and
- history repeats itself.

Attention must be given to the last two of these assumptions as they can be difficult to understand.

- The interaction between supply and demand is discounted by the market. Technicians believe that anything which could possibly influence a share price, such as fundamental, political and psychological factors is reflected by a share price. The market discounts all pertinent information, which is the basis of fundamental and economic forecasting, through the interaction of supply and demand.

- The charts do not themselves cause markets to move up or down. A chart simply reflects the sentiments of the marketplace, and these sentiments are discounted by market action.

- Market participants typically anticipate future movements in economic and financial developments and take action by buying or selling so that the market will reach a major turning point well ahead of the occurrence of an actual development. Hence, Murphy (1986:3) states that the use of technical analysis is simply a technique which is used to aid the chartist in the process of studying the market.

- History repeats itself. Since technical analysis is a study of the stock market, which in turn is influenced by human psychology, it could be reasoned that human psychology tends not to change over time, as time is the dimension which measures both recurring cycles and investor psychology at length.

It could be concluded that history is bound to repeat itself. Writers in the field of technical analysis such as Gann, Elliot and Dow have identified recurring cycles in the financial markets.

3.2.4 The classification of technical analysis techniques

Technical analysis involves the basing of conclusions on different patterns, trends, cycles and formations by using different techniques. Therefore, it is necessary to categorize these techniques. It must be noted that this was achieved with great difficulty, due to the fact that certain techniques can fit into two or more categories.

Pring (1985:3) classifies technical analysis techniques into three categories:

- Sentiment;
- flow-of-funds; and
- market structure.

The problem with this classification is that Pring does not clearly define each of the categories listed.

Technical indicators can be classified according to the following categories:

- Filter indicators;
- momentum indicators;

- trend line analysis;
- cycle theory;
- volume indicators;
- wave analysis; and
- pattern analysis.

- Filter indicators

Filter indicators are indicators which make use of the two variables of time and price. The purpose of filter indicators is to remove short-term price movements in order to determine a longer term trend.

Boshoff (1983:146) points out that the desire to filter out shorter term movements implicitly indicates disbelief in the existence of short-term serial dependence and a belief or a suspected belief in the existence of long-term dependence or persistence.

- Momentum indicators

The objective of momentum indicators is to anticipate the beginning of a new trend or to identify a new trend after its inception.

Momentum indicators measure the rate of growth in a share price. That is, they measure the velocity of a share price's movements over a selected period, thus identifying any rate of change in a share price. The justification for the use of momentum indicators lies in the fact that buyers begin to dominate sellers in an up-trend. A point is reached where the buying power of the buyers slowly starts to diminish and the upward movement in share prices also starts to progressively diminish, in which case the momentum indicator would forecast a change in trend.

- Trend line analysis

  A trend line is a line joining two or more bottoms or tops. The objective of a trend line is to indicate the expected direction in which a share will move. In other words, a trend line is a line drawn on a chart, tangential to the trading bottoms of an uptrend, or to the trading tops of a downtrend.

- Cycle theory

  Cycle theory is based on the postulation that history repeats itself, and history specifically repeats itself in recurring cycles.

  Cycle theorists maintain that shares, share markets, sectors, commodities and almost every commercial data stream move in regular cycles. They maintain that cycles are repetitive and of relatively fixed duration, making them predictable. By definition, cycles are timing tools; however, they should not be used as an entry timing mechanism. The four principles which underlie the cyclic philosophy are:

  - The principle of summation;
  - the principle of harmonicity;
  - the principle of synchronicity; and
  - the principle of proportionality.

Attention is given to each of these principles:

- The principle of summation states that all share price movements are the simple addition of all the active cycles which have a specific influence on that specific share.

- The principle of harmonicity states that corresponding cycles are related to each other by small whole numbers.

- The principle of synchronicity states that cycles of different lengths will reach a trough position at a corresponding time.

- The principle of proportionality states that a certain proportion is applicable to the relationship between a cycle period and the specific amplitude of a cycle.

  The underlying factor which influences the length of a cycle is time, and time is a dimension which measures both the recurring cycles in investor psychology and their lengths. Cyclical theory implies that, in each market, these psychological forces will conform to an approximate time pattern.

  The technical analyst is concerned with the right time to buy and sell. The analyst aims to buy as near to the starting point of an upward cycle in a share's price as possible, and to sell as near to the top of the cycle as possible.

- Volume indicators

  Volume can be defined as the number of shares traded on a specific day. Technicians believe that volume precedes price, meaning that any upside or downside pressure actually shows up in the volume figures before it is manifested in a share price trend.

- Wave analysis

  The proponents of wave analysis theory propose that share prices move in specific wave sequences.

  In the 1930s, chartist R.N. Elliot developed the Elliot wave principle. This theory is based on the premise that a bull market comprises five waves and a bear market comprises three waves. According to this theory, a five-cycle bull run should be followed by a three-cycle downward correction. Since Elliot, a number of chartists, such as Edwin Coppock, have developed highly complex wave theories. The primary use of the different wave theories is to determine the future trend of a share's price. However, these theories should never be used as a timing mechanism.

- Pattern analysis

  Pattern analysis has often been dismissed as an unscientific method in the analysis of shares, the objective of pattern analysis being to identify specific patterns which signal that a share price will either continue to move in the same direction or change direction. Joubert (1989:2) feels that pattern analysis will always have a strong subjective element, since the development of a pattern can only be judged by the human eye.

3.2.5 The construction of a chart

Charts are the working tools of the technical analyst. The technician has to decide on the following factors which affect the construction of a chart:

- The type of chart; and
- the choice of scale.

3.2.5.1 The types of charts

- A **bar chart** is a series of vertical lines that depict the highs and lows of a share over a specific time period. This depiction could be a daily, weekly or monthly record. Bar charts are usually illustrated together with volume indicators, which indicate the volume over the period under review. The bar chart is primarily used by technical analysts in the study of trend lines, waves, patterns and in momentum analysis.

- A **line chart** is a chart on which the closing prices of a period of time are connected by a line. Boshoff (1983:141) feels that the major disadvantage of a line chart is that such a chart does not give any idea of the inter-period price variation. The line chart has similar uses as the bar chart.

- A **point and figure** chart is unique, in the sense that this chart is one dimensional. The chart does not incorporate time and only plots the price of a share. Because this chart has no time axis, it is capable of revealing the nature of the share price movement over an extended period of time.

The point and figure chart depicts the price levels where shares tend to oscillate for a long time before moving sharply to another level. This charting method primarily involves the study of support and resistance levels.

- A **candlestick chart** is a charting method, originally from Japan. The highs and lows are plotted as a single line and are referred to as shadows. The price range between the open and the close is plotted as a narrow rectangle and is referred to as the body. If the close is above the open, the body is white. However, if the close is below the open, the body is black.

3.2.5.2 The choice of scale

Two types of scales are most commonly used:

- An arithmetic scale occurs where the horizontal distance between the vertical lines is equal to the price of a share. For example, on an arithmetic scale, the distance between 10 and 20 on the vertical scale is exactly the same as that between 20 and 30, and between 30 and 40. The problem is that the chart is visually inconsistent, which could have an adverse effect on the analysis of shares.

- The semi-logarithmic scale is used to counter the problems of the arithmetic scale. It is necessary to convert the prices to their logarithm so that the price percentage move is equal to the price percentage move in the vertical magnitude at any price range. Thus, the distance between the vertical lines is a percentage change and not a price change. For example, on the arithmetic scale, the distance between 10 and 20 on the vertical scale represents an increase of 100 percent, which is the same distance as that between 20 and 40, or between 40 and 80. In each case, the distance represents another 100 percent. The semi-logarithmic scale permits direct comparison of any two areas on a graph. In other words, equal distance is equal to map percentage. This type of scaling also facilitates the placing of stop-loss orders.

3.2.6 The various technical analysis indicators used in this study

The various indicators are:

- Moving averages;
- momentum oscillators;
- relative strength index;
- stochastic indicator;
- on balance volume;
- price volume trend;
- moving average convergence divergence;
- log delta; and
- rate of change.

The choice of indicators will be discussed in Chapter 4.

3.2.7 Moving averages

3.2.7.1 Introduction

Moving averages are the tools used on a price or indicator to generate a simple trading system, or to confirm the data obtained from other indicators. Moving averages (MA's) smooth the data, allowing trends to be seen more easily, and so provide the benchmark for determining whether a reversal in a trend has begun.

3.2.7.2 Defining the moving averages technique

Three different types of moving averages are in popular use:

- The simple moving average;
- the linearly weighted moving average; and
- the exponentially weighted moving average.

- The simple moving average

The simple moving average is the sum of a number of values, divided by the number of values that were added to obtain the sum. Refer to equation 3-1.

$$\frac{MA_{tn} = (P_t + P_{t\text{-}1} + \dots\ P_{t-(n+1)})}{n} \qquad \text{...(3-1)}$$

Where: MA_{tn} = The n-term simple moving average at time t.
n = The term length of the simple moving average.
P_t = The share price at time t.

- The linearly-weighted moving average

The simple moving average makes use of equal weights assigned to share prices. In the calculation of the simple moving average, the last day receives the same weight as the first day.

In an attempt to correct this, a linearly-weighted moving average is constructed, where a greater weight is given for the most recent closing share price. Refer to equation 3-2.

$$\frac{LMA_{tn} = P_t + (n\text{-}1)P_{t\text{-}1} + \dots + (1)P_{t\text{-}n} + 1}{n + (n\text{-}1) + (n\text{+}2) + \dots 1} \qquad \text{...(3-2)}$$

Where: LMA_{tn} = The linearly-weighted average for term n at time t.
n = The length of the linearly-weighted average.
P_t = The share price at time t.

However, the linearly-weighted average still does not overcome the problem of including the price movement covered by the length of the average.

- The exponentially-weighted moving average

An exponentially-weighted moving average essentially incorporates all past price data into the current moving averages by assigning exponentially smaller weights to each past data point.

The exponentially-weighted moving average takes the entire price history of a contract into account and assigns weights according to equation 3-3.

$$EMA_D = \alpha PR_D + (1-\alpha)EMA_{D-1} \qquad \textbf{...(3-3)}$$

where: EMA_D = The exponential-weighted moving average for day D.
PR_D = the price on day D.
α[40] = A smoothing constant, which can be estimated as $\frac{2}{(n+1)}$, where n is the simple moving average length.

The greater the value D is, the more weight will be given to the recent price data in the computation of the moving average and vice versa. The smaller the weight associated with each data point, the smoother the moving average, because an extreme price would only have a small impact on the resulting moving average.

Many technicians choose to make use of exponentially-weighted moving averages, because they incorporate more prices into the calculation than do simple moving averages. Many technicians also prefer to give a greater weight to recent prices as opposed to giving equal weight to all the data points.

3.2.7.3 Trading rules determined by moving averages

The basic use of a moving average is as a trend indicator. By changing the period of the moving average, one can attempt to observe different trends.

---

[40] The α constant approximates a value for a simple moving average. Its value is determined by the formula $\frac{2}{(n+1)}$, where n is the number of days for a simple moving average. For example the approximation for a 10-day moving average would use an $\alpha = \frac{2}{(10+1)} = 0.18$.

The choice of the required period is problematical and subjective. However, the criteria for the selection of a term's length should be as follows:

- If any evidence for correlation or serial dependence, either long- or short- term, exits, then the extent of this dependence should dictate the period length of the moving average.

  Boshoff (1983:152) notes that a moving average should give one buy and one sell signal. This characteristic can be enforced by simply lengthening the term of the moving average. The danger of Boshoff's view on the lengthening of the term of a moving average is that the moving average becomes insensitive.

- The use of one moving average

  The moving average is plotted on a bar chart or line chart on its appropriate trading day, along with the price action of that specific day. When the closing price moves above the moving average, a buy signal is generated. A sell signal is produced when the price moves below the moving average. This is illustrated in Figure 3.1.

  In Figure 3.1, the price is represented by the thick solid line on the chart, while the moving average is represented by the thinner, dotted line. When the moving average line cuts below the price line, a buy signal is generated, and *vice versa.*

  The disadvantage of using one moving average is that it can generate false signals through the formation of whipsaws. To reduce the number of whipsaws that occur when using a single moving average, filters are imposed on the moving average. The following are examples of filters which can be used:

  - Time filters are imposed in order to place a certain time delay before any action is taken. For example, for a particular moving average, a filter might require a closing time penetration of three days.

- Trading bands or envelopes are lines drawn a certain percentage above and below a moving average line. These are used as filters for moving average buy and sell signals. Instead of buying when the price rises above the moving average, the price first has to rise above the upper band before a buy signal is generated.

Figure 3.1 - The 144th day, exponential moving average for Iscor

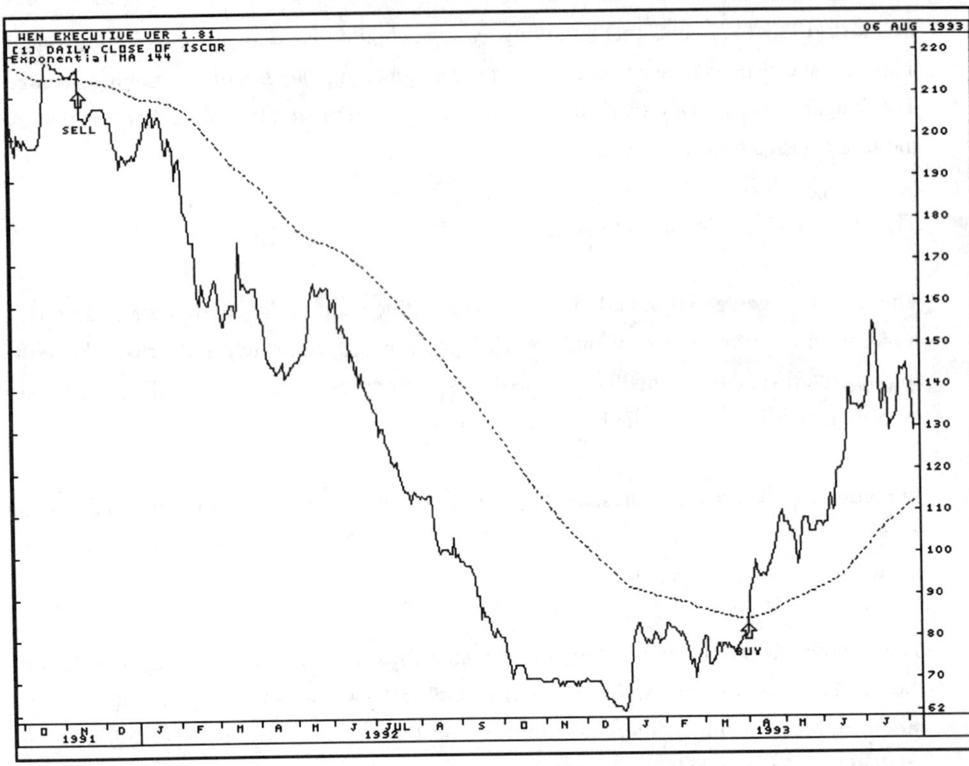

- The use of two moving averages

The use of a single moving average usually produces a large number of whipsaws and false signals, necessitating the use of filters. To improve the performance and reliability of moving averages, many technicians prefer to use two or three moving averages.

When two moving averages are employed, the longer one is used for trend identification, and the shorter one for timing purposes. It is the interplay between the two averages and the price itself that produces the price and the trend signal.

When the shorter term (more volatile) moving average crosses over the longer term (smoother) moving average, then some traders assume that a change in the trend has occurred.

This is known as the double moving average crossover. In general, it can be said that when the shorter moving average crosses the longer moving average, a buy signal is generated.

The period of time chosen for the use of the two moving averages employed depends on the trading risk preferred by the trader. The shorter the term, the greater the risk. However, the major drawback in using a longer term (smoother) moving average is that what is gained in risk control is lost in timeliness.

- The use of three moving averages

Triple moving averages are used when a trader is looking for the overall trend in the market, as well as a buy or sell short-term trading strategy.

A short-term average is imposed upon a medium term average which in turn is imposed upon a long-term average. When all three are moving in the same direction, then some traders assume that a definitive market trend exists.

A buy alert is given when the short-term moving average rises above the medium and long-term averages. For the buy alert to be confirmed and converted into a buy signal, the short-term moving average must remain above the medium- and long-term moving average for the period of the delay.

The three moving average technique tends to produce superior results. This method is more difficult to define because not only must the three moving average periods be determined but the delay period, which has the effect of changing the moving average periods, must also be determined.

The critical element in a moving average system is the length of the time periods used in the calculation of the averages. Table 3.1 depicts the required time length of a moving average in comparison with a required market cycle or trend.

Table 3.1 - Moving average length compared with market trend

Trend	Moving Average
Very short-term trend	5 - 13 days
Short-term trend	14 - 25 days
Minor intermediate trends	26 - 49 days
Intermediate trends	50 - 100 days
Long-term trends	100 - 200 days

Any set of trading rules should be dictated by the nature of the dependence of the share price and the time series used. In essence, the best strategy for using moving averages is to determine an optimum time period, the desired penetration requirement, and the optimal combination of moving averages.

3.2.7.4 Criticisms against the use of moving averages

This section addresses a selection of caveats regarding the use of moving averages.

- Moving averages tend to signal all major trends, resulting in false signals. The accumulation of these false signals can generate a whipsaw effect on the moving average. It must be noted that whipsaws seldom occur at the top of a cycle. Most are usually found at the bottom of, or halfway up or down, the cycle.

  Whipsaws can be overcome by charting the rate of change (ROC) in a moving average. The rate of change in a moving average is captured by a moving average convergence divergence (MACD) indicator.

- Moving averages, as a basic trend-following system, tend to assume an equal unit size position. As a result, given an extended trend, the best a moving average can do is to indicate a one unit position in the direction of the trend.

Schwager (1984:424) feels that the following inadequacies exist in the use of moving averages:

- A parameter shift can occur when the optimal variation of moving averages is based on past data. However, one may then discover that the same variation performs poorly during the ensuing period.

- The moving average can surrender a large percentage of profits. For example, because of the unavoidable lag of the moving average behind the price, a rapid change in price direction, from a downtrend to an uptrend, will carry the price well along the new trend before the average reacts. The buy signal is generated once the price has already moved away from its reversal by a significant fraction of the total move due to the moving average.

3.2.7.5 Conclusion

One of the basic assumptions of technical analysis is that shares move in trends. Since moving average trends consist of minor fluctuations in price, these underlying trends can become more visible with the aid of moving averages.

Inherent shortcomings do exist in the use of moving averages. However, moving averages still provide a means for objective evaluation of shares, incorporating the human psychological factors of fear and greed. The success rate with the use of moving averages is largely determined by the optimal moving average combination of period length, filter method applied and the moving average type. Studies performed by James (1968:315-326) and Boshoff (1983:60) have shown that averages can be used as a successful trading strategy. However, when dividends are taken into account, their use of moving averages would have been less successful.

3.2.8 Momentum indicators

3.2.8.1 Introduction

Momentum (or rate-of-change indicators) measure the rate of growth in a share price over a certain time period of time.

This strategy is based on the premise that the second differential of a share price starts to decline or rise before a selling or buying turning point. Boshoff (1983:169) points out that the justification for the momentum concept lies in the fact that as buyers start to dominate sellers in an up-rally, a point will be reached where buying power will slowly start to diminish and the rate of upward progression in prices will slow down.

3.2.8.2 Construction

To generate a momentum chart, the percentage gain or loss in a price over a selected period must be shown in order to measure the velocity of a price movement. Refer to equation 3-4.

$$Momentum = \frac{Share\ price\ today\ -\ Price\ n\ days\ ago}{Share\ price\ n\ days\ ago} \times 100 \quad \textbf{...(3-4)}$$

3.2.8.3 Interpretation

A positive rising momentum indicates not only that the price trend is rising, but also that it is accelerating. This indicates that the price is ensconced in a strong trend. However, a falling momentum in the positive area indicates that, although the price trend is still rising, it is decelerating. It is during this phase that the momentum indicator warns that the price is ready to fall (refer to Figure 3.2).

Figure 3.2 - The 100 momentum for Iscor

- A divergence between the momentum and the price action exists when the momentum is in an extreme position. This is usually an important warning signal.

- The trader should be buying when the momentum line is in the lower end of a momentum band and selling when it is in the upper end of a momentum band.

3.2.8.4 Conclusion

The momentum indicator measures the rate of change in a share price, making it sensitive to any changes in a price trend. However, it is perhaps more subject to the effects of noise on the price than any other indicator, unless a very long momentum is used. This often results in a long time lag. To overcome this problem, a moving average can be imposed on the momentum indicator.

The main function of the momentum indicator is to identify an early change in the direction of the market.

3.2.9 Relative strength index (RSI)

3.2.9.1 Introduction

The Welles Wilder "Relative Strength Index" measures the internal or relative strength of the upward and downward movements of a share price.

The relative strength index is intended to give an early warning that a share price is about to change the direction of its trend. The relative strength index is thus a momentum indicator which shows the relationship between a specific set of upward movements and a set of downward movements.

3.2.9.2 Construction

The relative strength index is a normalized indicator, which is generated in such a manner that the values of the indicator are limited to a predefined range, usually between 0 to 100. Refer to equations 3-5 and 3-6.

$$Relative\ strength\ index = 100 - \frac{100}{RS} \qquad \text{...(3-5)}$$

$$RS = \frac{Average\ of\ n\ days\ up\ closes}{Average\ of\ n\ days\ down\ closes} \qquad \text{...(3-6)}$$

3.2.9.3 Interpretation

As with all momentum indicators, the relative strength indicator tends to generate false signals during the deceleration of the current trend. The relative strength index chart is typically a line chart, with 0 and 100 at the lower and upper limits, respectively. Horizontal lines are typically placed at the points representing readings of 30 and 70.

The relative strength index indicates overbought and oversold levels and tends to identify support and resistance areas better than the price itself. It is customary to regard any break downward from above the 70 level as a sell signal and any break upward from below the 30 level as a buy signal. Murphy (1986:300) states that the relative strength index, used in conjunction with various chart patterns, is useful for indicating support and resistance levels. To summarize, it can be said that this indicator can be used in the following ways:

- When the indicator breaks 30 points going down, and then reverses direction and breaks 30 points going up, a buy signal is generated;
- when the indicator breaks 70 points going up, and then reverses direction and breaks 70 points going down, a sell signal is generated;
- if divergence exists between a share price and the RSI, this indicates an impending reversal; and
- trend line analysis can be used for the same purpose.

3.2.9.4 Conclusion

The relative strength indicator is useful as an indicator of support and resistance levels. As with all other momentum indictors, false signals are generated during a deceleration of the current trend (refer to Figure 3.3). The leeway provided by the 30-70 levels solves this problem to a certain extent. The relative strength index is not suitable for use as a single indicator, mostly because of its volatility. However, it can play a role in a two-tiered or staggered trading system. Trading with the guidance of the relative strength index by itself is risky. However, if the correct time period can be selected, the relative strength index can be a good indicator for the short-term trader.

Figure 3.3 - M-Net 21-day relative strength index graph, April 1990 - August 1993

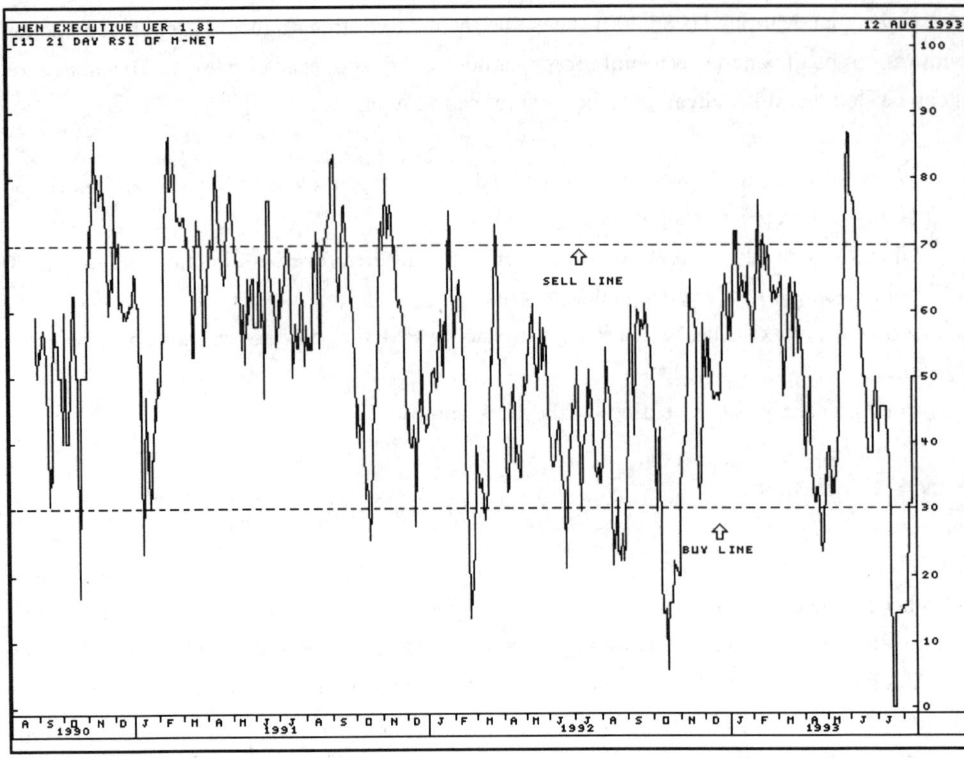

3.2.10 Stochastic indicators

3.2.10.1 Introduction

The stochastic indicator is a momentum indicator which converts the daily high and low for shares into a percentage scale and measures the close between the high and low on this scale.

3.2.10.2 Construction

The stochastic indicator was developed by George Lane and is based on the premise that closing share prices tend to accumulate near the top of each period's trading range during upward trends, and near the bottom during downward trends. The stochastic indicator consists of two lines - the percent K line and percent D line.

- Percent K line

  This indicates the number of time periods used in the stochastic calculation. This value controls the internal smoothing of the stochastic indicator. A value of one is considered a fast stochastic, while a value of three is considered a slow stochastic though these values can vary. Refer to equation 3-7.

$$\%K = 100 \times \frac{C_n - L_n}{H_n - L_n} \qquad \text{...(3-7)}$$

Where: C_n = Latest closing price.
L_n = Lowest price for period n.
H_n = Highest price for period n.

- Percent D line

  This parameter is the number of time periods used on the moving average percent K. The moving average is thus referred to as percent D and is plotted on the top of percent K. Refer to equation 3-8.

$$\%D = 100 \times \frac{(\, n \times (C_n - L_n)}{(\, n \times (H_n - L_n)} \qquad \text{...(3-8)}$$

Where: C_n = Latest closing price.
L_n = Lowest price for period n.
H_n = Highest price for period n.
n = Period n which must be shorter than period n for %K

3.2.10.3 Interpretation

The standard stochastic is calculated in a fast or a slow form. The fast stochastic will typically have a period of 5 to 6 days, while the slow stochastic will be calculated for about 11 days. Analysis, using the stochastic indicator, is usually performed on the average, or percent D, chart. Interpretation is exactly the same as for the RSI, with the exception that horizontal lines, in this case, are sometimes drawn at 25 and 75 points. A sell signal is thus generated when the stochastic breaks down from the upper region through the 75 point line, while a buy signal is generated when a share breaks up through the 25 point line. While the stochastic indicator remains between the 25 and 75 point lines, the signal is indeterminate, indicating that the trend will be sideways.

Murphy (1986:304-306) suggests the following strategy to generate buy and sell signals using the stochastic indicator:

- Buy signal - A buy signal is generated when the percent K line crosses above the percent D line, after the percent D line has already bottomed and turned up; and
- sell signal - A sell signal is generated when the percent D line has already crested and turned down before it is crossed by the percent K line.

3.2.10.4 Conclusion

The stochastic indicator can be valuable as a timing signal generator, either in its own right, or as a means of examining cyclical patterns in a share price. However, because of its volatility, it may not be as useful an indicator for long-term decision making.

Joubert (1989:5) notes that it is not acceptable practice to use standard periods for the share under examination. The volatility of the price must be considered in the selection of the most suitable parameters for the calculation of the stochastic indicator.

3.2.11 On balance volume (OBV)

3.2.11.1 Introduction

Volume or turnover represents a second dimension of technical analysis. Initially, chartists were only interested in the price and, for a long period of a time, volume was graphed simply as a bar chart. It was up to the analyst to relate price changes to changes in the level of turnover.

Volume analysis only came into being after Joe Granville formulated the on-balance volume indicator.

3.2.11.2 Defining on-balance volume

Granville (1976:276) defines on-balance volume as an indicator which generates buy and sell signals after subtracting downside volume from upside volume, resulting in positive or negative readings. Granville (1976:145-170) bases his indicator on a number of assumptions regarding the market and its behavior. The three initial assumptions are:

- When the price of a share increases from the previous close, this indicates that demand exceeds supply;
- when the price of a share drops, this indicates that the supply exceeds the demand; and
- when the price of a share remains unchanged from one day or week to the next, the level of demand matches the supply.

In addition to these basic assumptions, Granville introduced two other assumptions:

- The volume of shares traded on a day when the price rises can be used as a measurement of an excess of demand over supply; and
- the number of shares traded on a day when the price falls can serve as a measure of an excess of supply over demand.

Granville believed that the imbalance between supply and demand could be represented by a single indicator. Basically, the indicator forms an index of the net direction of volume movement over a certain time span.

3.2.11.3 Construction

Taveles, Harlow and Stone (1974:188) suggest that the on-balance volume be calculated as follows: if the latest day has a higher closing price, then all volume should be assigned a plus sign. However, if the latest day's close is lower than that for the previous day, all the volume should be assigned a minus sign. These positive and negative figures are then added to provide a cumulative total.

The construction of this indicator is accomplished by means of a very simple set of rules:

- Begin with an arbitrary large number, in order to avoid future negative cumulative totals;
- if the share price closes above the previous day's price, add the share turnover for the day to the cumulative total or on-balance volume;
- if the price closes below the previous day's close, subtract the share turnover for the day from the cumulative total or on-balance volume; and
- if the share price does not change at all, set the new value of the on-balance volume equal to the previous value.

It should be noted that Teweles and Jones (1987:181) regard the method of calculation for the on-balance volume as questionable. They point out that each day's price movement is determined by transactions on both the buying and selling side. Therefore, it does not seem reasonable to assign volume to both the plus or minus side simply because the close is higher or lower than that of the preceding day.

3.2.11.4 Interpretation

For the purpose of generating buy, sell or neutral signals, on-balance volume is interpreted by evaluating High - Low - High - Low or Low - High - Low - High sequences. $High_1$ and Low_1 represent the first high and low in a specific sequence, and $High_2$ and Low_2, the second subsequent sequence. The following rules apply:

- If $High_1 < High_2$ and $Low_1 < Low_2$, the signal is buy;
- if $High_1 > High_2$ and $Low_1 > Low_2$, the signal is sell; and
- all other sequences are neutral.

A sequence of higher highs and higher lows generates a buy signal, and a sequence of lower highs and lower lows generates a sell signal.

A second way of using on-balance volume is to compare the trends of a share price and the on-balance volume of an index over a period of time. Usually, both of these indicators adhere to the same trend. However, a discrepancy will occur when the share price is moving sideways, while the on-balance volume is distinctly up or when the price is consistently lower, and while the on-balance volume ranges sideways or upwards.

One method for interpreting on-balance volume is as follows: a rising line indicates the accumulation of shares by strong buyers, whereas a falling line indicates the distribution of shares by strong sellers. Any sharp movement in the on-balance volume may indicate the presence of a big buyer or seller.

The major criticism of on-balance volume is that, since each day's price change is determined by transactions on both the selling and buying sides, it is an exaggeration to assign all volume to the plus or minus side simply because the closing price for one day is higher or lower than that for the preceding day. Arnold (1984:76-77) feels that a more reasonable approach to the construction of on-balance volume is to ignore the previous day's close and to determine whether a share price rises or falls based on the present day's open relative to the present day's close. The problem identified by Arnold (1984:76-77) was overcome by Mark Chaiken, who developed the Chaiken volume accumulator.

A further problem with the use of on-balance volume is that no objective rules exist for interpretating the on-balance volume indicator nor have any been advocated by Granville. Granville presented many objective calculations, but failed to present a completely quantifiable set of decision-making rules. Rockwell (1967:107-130) concludes that the profit-making ability of successful traders is mainly based on short-run fluctuations. Rockwell's view thus nullifies the use of on-balance volume, which is based on long-term accumulation.

Figure 3.4 illustrates the on-balance volume indicator. Hexton (1990:125) points out that a bullish forecast is made when the price of a share and the volume agree in direction. However, when the direction of price and volume differ, a bearish signal is indicated.

Figure 3.4 - On-balance chart of Standard Bank Investment Corporation, 1985-1990

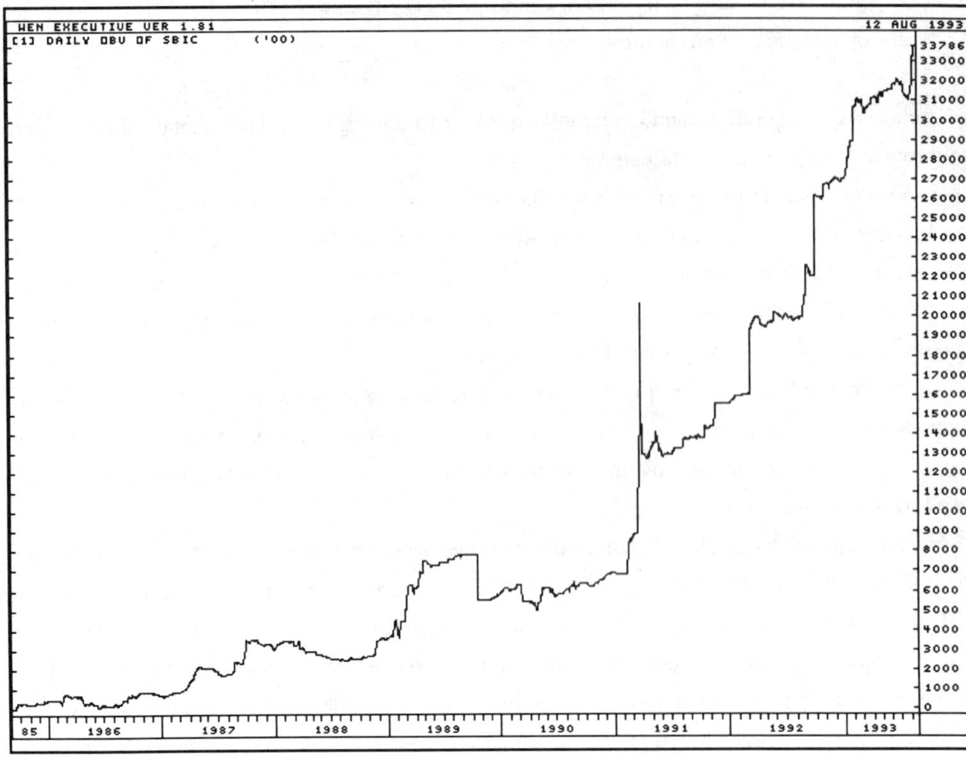

3.2.11.5 Conclusion

On-balance volume may help the analyst to identify the internal strengths and weaknesses of a specific share. Sometimes, volume divergences versus share price movements are the only indicators of future reversals. This indicator is embodied with many deficiencies and is capable of false signals, and thus should only be used to determine long-term movements. On-balance volume is a very useful tool in the identification of accumulation and distribution of shares. However, Du Plessis (1989:1-3) states that the on-balance volume indicator should be treated with extreme caution because it is notoriously unreliable. Whatever interpretation is used, on-balance volume can provide the analyst with a means for quantifying the volume of price moves.

3.2.12 Price volume trend (PVT)

3.2.12.1 Introduction

Two aspects of on-balance volume have drawn much criticism from analysts. The first is the fact that on-balance volume disregards the turnover on days when the price does not change. The second is the fact that the magnitude of the price change from day to day is not reflected in the calculation of the on-balance volume. Such problems have resulted in the need for another indicator which does not suffer from these perceived inadequacies. This has resulted in the creation of the price volume trend (PVT) indicator. This indicator seeks to overcome shortcomings of on-balance volume by calculating the magnitude of a share price change. It should be noted that price volume trend is also known as volume price trend in certain publications.

3.2.12.2 Defining price volume trend

Price volume trend is a cumulative line which indicates the current percentage change in a share price from the previous period, multiplied by the current volume. This figure is then added or subtracted from the previous price volume trend figure. Ryan (1988:125) explains that price volume trend is a technical indicator which calculates the volume of shares traded on a specific day times the percentage change in price for that specific period.

3.2.12.3 Construction

The following steps are involved in the construction of the price volume trend:

- Compute the percentage change in the price for the period under review;
- if the price goes down, the resulting percentage becomes negative; if the price goes up, the percentage will be positive;
- multiply the daily turnover by the percentage change in the price;
- calculate the cumulative total of the adjusted turnover; and
- add the result to the previous cumulative differential total.

The aim underlying this percentage difference is to measure the buying support or positive demand for a specific share. Therefore, the turnover on days when the price does not change should be taken into account in the calculation as this represents excess demand over supply.

It is assumed that the magnitude of any price change will be reflected by the difference or balance between the supply and demand, and that this change will be expressed as a percentage.

3.2.12.4 Interpretation

The interpretation of the price volume trend is the same as that for on-balance volume. A rising line indicates the accumulation of shares by strong buyers, whereas a falling line indicates distribution by strong sellers.

Markstein (1966:140-141) suggests that the price volume trend should be used in conjunction with support and resistance lines. He feels that when the price volume trend line has been moving down and suddenly moves upwards above the previous resistance top, a buy signal is indicated. After an upward movement in the volume price trend line, it may move downward to reach below the last support level, indicating a sell signal.

Markstein (1966:146) states the following trading rules:

- Never trade in shares which are in an up trend when the overall trend is downwards; and
- avoid trading on volume price trend signals within congested trading ranges.

In general, the price volume trend by itself does not seem to offer significant advantages over on-balance volume, except for those shares where the price remains unchanged for an extended period.

3.2.12.5 Conclusion

Price volume trend analysis can be an important adjunct to the analysis of a share price, particularly in the identification of possible support and resistance levels and of value in the estimation of the probability whether the support or resistance levels will be reached, obeyed or penetrated. However, the price volume trend is not explicit enough over the short-term to be of real value in the forecasting of a future share price.

3.2.13 Moving average convergence-divergence

In essence, the moving average convergence divergence indicator is an overbought/oversold type of oscillator which, in simple terms, measures the difference between two chosen moving averages.

3.2.13.1 Construction

The moving average convergence-divergence indicator calculates the exponential average of the difference between fast and slow exponential moving averages (refer to equation 3-9), and a third exponential moving average is used as a trigger line.

$$MACD = EMA_1 - EMA_2 \qquad \text{...(3-9)}$$

Where: MACD = Moving average convergence-divergence.
EMA_1 = Exponential moving average for period 1 (Fast).
EMA_2 = Exponential moving average for period 2 (Slow).

3.2.13.2 Interpretation

The basic buy signal is given when the oscillator line penetrates the trigger line on the downside, while a sell signal is given when the oscillator line moves above the trigger line.

An ideal buy signal occurs when there is bullish divergence accompanied by the oscillator moving above the trigger line and then crossing both lines above the zero line. An ideal sell signal is given by a bearish divergence and a move below the trigger line, which is then followed by a downward penetration of the zero line.

3.2.14 Log delta

3.2.14.1 Introduction

The rationale behind the use of log delta is not as a technical indicator *per se*, but rather a normalizer of data. It may happen that most share prices are distributed around a certain value and that a few share prices occur at an extreme end of the range. This can result in the distribution of raw data with long "tails." If this data is fed into a neural network during neural network training, the small percentage of examples will "crowd" the majority of the data into a small range. To overcome this, a log of the values is computed which compresses the distance between the extreme data values more than the majority of data values. A useful extension to the above is to first compute the delta between each current value and the previous value and to then compute the log of the delta.

3.2.15 Rate of change (ROC)

3.2.15.1 Introduction

The rate-of-change indicator is specifically used in determining the rate of change of the underlying trend, and not in the day-to-day changes of the price itself. The reason for using the rate-of-change indicator to the underlying trend, rather than the price itself, is that small fluctuations in the price may tend to conceal the trend when a graph is examined.

3.2.15.2 Construction

According to Murphy (1991:275), the rate-of-change indicator employs a price ratio over a selected span of time. He further states that to construct a ten-day rate-of-change indicator, the latest closing price is divided by a time-delayed closing price. The resulting value is then plotted above or below a value of 100.

3.2.15.3 Interpretation

A rate of change that reaches an extreme value in either the upper or lower end of the band may be interpreted as a share price that has also reached an extreme. At this point, the share price could consolidate or change price movement. Huang (1973:76) suggests the following trading rules:

A bullish signal is generated when:

- The rate of decline of the smoothed series has diminished by less than one percent; and
- the unsmoothed rate of change has already turned positive.

A bearish signal is generated when:

- the rate of increase of the smoothed series has dropped to a level of less than one percent; and
- the unsmoothed rate of change has already turned negative.

3.2.16 Review of studies done on the application of technical analysis to the Johannesburg Stock Exchange

The value of technical analysis as a security market forecasting tool has always been questionable, a situation which can largely be attributed to the internal contradictions of technical analysis and postulations of the efficient market hypothesis. However, to date, four empirical research studies have been undertaken to determine whether technical analysis can be employed in share market forecasting:

- J.H. Boshoff (1983)[41];
- S.B.S. Paulo (1984)[42];
- G.S. Du Toit (1986)[43]; and
- R.J. Van Eyden (1991)[44]

Refer to Table 3.2 for a comparison of the empirical findings of each of these studies.

---

41 *A critical appraisal of technical analysis on the Johannesburg Stock Exchange.*

42 *The impact of the efficient market hypothesis on the security investment practices of the South African life insurance industry.*

43 *Technical analysis and market efficiency on the Johannesburg Stock Exchange.*

44 *The evaluation of certain technical analysis techniques to determine the future market price of shares on the Johannesburg Stock Exchange.*

Table 3.2 - A comparison of empirical findings

Author	**Justification of the use of technical analysis as a forecasting technique**	**Methodology employed in empirical study**	**Research findings**
J.H. Boshoff	**Accept**	Statistical analysis of : ● weekly share prices data (196 top S.A industrial and mining shares) ● weekly shares indices data (41 S.A sectoral and overall indices) ● daily shares indices data (3 overall indices) ● commodities daily data (gold)	● Established that share prices on the JSE exhibited non-random behavior. ● Various technical trading rules can be employed
S.B.S. Paulo	**Reject**	Analysis of a questionnaire sent to registered members of the Life Offices Association of South Africa Firms (10 firms responded)	● Rejection of the efficient market hypothesis. ● Rejection of the use of technical analysis tools

Author	**Justification of the use of technical analysis as a forecasting technique**	**Methodology employed in empirical study**	**Research findings**
G.S. Du Toit	**Accepts - only when prices deviate from underlying equilibrium values**	An quantitative analysis of 180 shares.	• Technical analysis and the efficient markets are not mutually exclusive but a combination of both approaches provides a better description of the market processes than any one of the approaches individually
R.J. Van Eyden	**Rejects**	Analysis of questionnaire mailed to 239 members of the Johannesburg Stock Exchange and technical analysts (90 members and 10 analysts responded)	• The use of technical analysis is accurate in the confirmation of a trend, in other words merely confirming a form of the efficient market hypothesis

3.2.17 The disadvantages and advantages of technical analysis

3.2.17.1 The disadvantages of technical analysis

- Technical analysis assumes that the behavior of the stock market in the past is indicative of the behavior of shares in the future. However, Van Horne and Parker (1968:132) feel that a future share price cannot be forecasted on the basis of a comparison of present share prices with past share prices.

- Technical analysts tend to create patterns and trends which they claim have predictive significance. As Levy (1966:83-89) states: "The market action may be the reflection of the chart action instead of the reverse." Thus the interpretation of charts can become a self-fulfilling prophecy.

- If technical analysis is continually successful, the use of such a system will neutralize whatever profits may potentially exist.

- Technical analysis is subjective. Chart interpretation results from human subjectivity rather than mathematical objectivity.

- The major problem with technical analysis stems from the efficient market hypothesis. The belief in the use of technical analysis is in direct contrast to the EMH, which contends that the adjustment of share prices to new information is very rapid.

3.2.17.2 The advantages of technical analysis

- Many fundamental variables impact the share market at any one time, during which structural changes occur regarding the interaction of these fundamental factors. It may be impossible to weigh all of these fundamental factors. However, an evaluation does take place in the market place and, thus, technical analysis may be useful for identifying when the changes are to occur.

- Technical analysis incorporates human psychology into the projection of a future share price.

- Technical analysis is based on the premise that share price movements are caused by the interaction of supply and demand, and the flow of funds may be detected by an analysis of various technical indicators rather than by an analysis of fundamental economic and financial statistics.

3.2.18 Conclusion

The use of technical analysis in the investment world has gained popularity largely due to the advent of the computer. Despite its popularity, controversy exists regarding it validity and use. The subjective nature of technical analysis invariably causes prejudice. The use of technical analysis is based on the premise that, by tracking and smoothing past data, one can reach meaningful conclusions about future share prices.

In summary, it can be said that if the stock market is seen as a market for investments, the fundamental approach is more congenial. However, if the stock market is seen as a trading market, technical analysis is more plausible.

3.3 FUNDAMENTAL ANALYSIS

Fundamental analysis is the interpretation of financial statements, economic analysis of the appropriate sector, competition, and other variables which can affect a company, in order to determine the expected return, risk and intrinsic value of a share.

3.3.1 Defining fundamental analysis

Murphy's (1986:5) view of fundamental analysis is that it focuses on the economic forces of supply and demand which cause share prices to move higher, lower, or stay the same. The factors influencing supply and demand are:

- The inflation rate;
- the general level of interest rates;
- the exchange rate;
- the gross domestic product;

- sanctions;
- job unrest; and
- market sentiment.

The fundamental approach investigates all the pertinent factors affecting the price of a share in order to determine the intrinsic value of the share. The intrinsic value of a share is what the fundamentals indicate a share is actually worth, based on the law of supply and demand. If this value is below the current market price, then the share is overpriced and should be sold.

Oldert's (1989:313) perception of fundamental analysis is that it concerns itself essentially with the question of profitability. The basic question asked by the fundamental analyst is: "How good will this company be as a generator of profits in the future ?"

However, Gitman and Joehnk (1981:283) feel that fundamental analysis is merely the phase of share analysis which deals with assessing the investment merits of a specific company and is ultimately aimed at formulating expectations about a company's future prospects and the potential return and risk behavior of its shares.

Fundamental analysis thus asserts that a future trend in a share price can be predicted by examining all the factors which are likely to affect the performance of a company and its shares and by attempting to quantify these influences in order to provide estimates of a future cash flow accruing to the investor. Various techniques and methods of traditional analysis are used. The basic objectives of such techniques are to estimate the future intrinsic value of a share and to quantify this by placing a present value on the share. Fundamentalists base their projections on historical financial and company data in order to arrive at an assessed value. These values are influenced by the degree of risk and uncertainty in the discounting of a share. Bethlehem (1977:49) believes that the theoretical justification for fundamental analysis lies in the notion of intrinsic value and in the hypothesis that states that any departure of the market price from such a value will be corrected in time by the operation of the forces of demand and supply in the securities market.

3.3.2 The assumptions of fundamental analysis

The basic assumptions underlying fundamental analysis are the following:

- The profitability of a company will eventually determine the share price;
- share prices change as anticipations change, as a result of new information;

- the intrinsic value of a share is determined solely by the value of the company;
- the price of a share at any time equals the discounted value of the stream of income from the share; and
- the price of a share is a function of the set of anticipated returns and anticipated capitalization rates.

3.3.3 The methodology of fundamental analysis

In order to determine the intrinsic value of a share according to the fundamental approach, a detailed analysis of the following is required:

- The economic environment;
- the industry; and
- the company.

3.3.4 The economic environment

The first step in fundamental analysis is to determine the state of the economic environment. The analyst tries to determine the state of the economy, where it is heading, and the economic implications of these movements for investments and general share prices. This is done because share prices tend to turn before the general economy does. The economic environment is assessed through an analysis of the following:

- Cyclical indicators; and
- interest rates.

3.3.4.1 Cyclical indicators

The cyclical indicator analysis method (CIAM) is an approach used to forecast the general state of the economy using the principle that an economy experiences observable periods of expansion and contraction, which are generally referred to as business cycles. The behavior of the economy is captured in the business cycle, which is an indication of the change in the total general economic activity over a period of time. Cohen, Zinbarg and Zeikel (1987:15) postulate that substantial evidence exists to suggest that an ability to foresee business cycle turning points several months ahead improves the ability to foresee major turning points in the general level of share prices. The CIAM is subdivided into an analysis of the following:

- Leading indicators;
- coincidental indicators; and
- lagging indicators.

- Leading indicators are measurements of anticipation or new commitments. These indicators forecast the future trend of the economy, and are consequently highly sensitive to changes in the economic climate as perceived in the market-place. They usually reach their peaks and troughs before any of the other corresponding indicators reach them.

- Coincidental indicators consist of those economic indicators with peaks and troughs which roughly coincide with the peaks and troughs of the business cycle. They are comprehensive measures of economic performance which pertain to output, employment, income, and trade.

- Lagging indicators follow the movement of the coincidental indicators. Their peaks and troughs occur after the peaks and troughs of the general economy. Thus, they are useful in confirming a change of trend in the economy.

De Kock (1989:240) feels that the indicator approach does have the following limitations:

- The indicators can generate false signals;
- at times, indicators generate signals which are not conclusive,
- there are problems in the gathering and revising of data; and
- there are numerous political or international developments which can significantly influence the economy, but which cannot be encompassed in a statistical system.

3.3.4.2 Interest rates

The last part of the analysis of the economic environment is an analysis of interest rates. Changes in interest rates directly influence the economy and share market. Generally speaking, when interest rates rise, investors tend to invest in interest-bearing investments and not in shares. De Kock (1989:342) argues that changes in interest rates affect the share market for the following reasons:

- Fluctuations in the price charged for money influence the earnings or profits that companies are able to make and, therefore, the price which investors are willing to pay for shares;
- movements in interest rates alter the relationships between competing financial assets, of which the debenture market to share market relationship is the most important; and
- the number of equities which are purchased with borrowed money. This is generally referred to as marginal debt, which is influential in that any change in the cost of carrying debt resulting from changes in interest rates will have a definite effect on the desirability of holding securities.

Interest rates are determined by the following factors:

- The productivity of capital (The investor can increase the productivity of capital by using the optimal combination of time, return and risk);
- the riskiness of the environment;
- the willingness of the investors to take risks;
- the willingness of investors to wait;
- the interaction between supply and demand forces;
- the money and capital market;
- governmental monetary reserves; and
- the balance of payments.

3.3.5 Industry analysis

The second step involved in fundamental analysis is to evaluate other companies which operate in the same industry (or industries). This is done for the following reasons:

- To determine if a company and its shares are under-performing or over-performing, relative to others in the same industry.

- To classify a company according to the life-cycle stages of the industry. These stages can be classified as follows:

    - The growth stage;
    - the transition stage;
    - the mature stage; and
    - the stabilization or decline stage.

The industry life-cycle approach is totally dependent on business cycles which in turn are dependent on the general economy. This interdependence can cause an industry and the individual companies forming part of an industry to move back and forth between the different cycles, as categorized by the industry life-cycle.

The classification of the industries according to Francis (1986:495) can be particularly valuable to the analyst in estimating growth rates in sales, earnings and dividends. In order for the fundamentalist to categorize a specific industry, the analyst has to forecast the future growth rate based on historical data and expected earnings.

In the case of the Johannesburg Stock Exchange, an alternative method of estimation is to graphically evaluate a specific industry or an individual company in relation to the overall JSE actuaries' index. This method can also be used to determine whether an individual company forming part of an industry is under-performing or over-performing relative to its industry and in which category the company falls, namely; the growth, transition, mature or stabilized or declining stage.

3.3.6 The company

The final step in fundamental analysis is to identify the individual factors which are unique to each company and to determine how these unique factors in correlation with the previous two analyses influence the generation of revenue for the company.

3.3.7 The determinants of share prices

In the determination of the intrinsic value of a given share, the fundamentalist must continuously be aware of the fact that the value of a company, as reflected by its share price, is largely determined by the following factors:

- The expected volume of goods or services delivered to a company and its specific consumer market;
- the expected future retail price of the finished products;
- the present and expected costs of production;
- the present and expected future earnings per share; and
- the expected dividend policy of the company.

However, Eiteman, Dice and Eiteman (1966:504) feel that a share price is determined by the following two factors:

- The financial condition of the company in the future; and
- the behavioral response of the investors to its future condition.

Francis (1976:439) postulates that the determination of the intrinsic value of a share is influenced by the following factors:

- The variation in a share price attributed to changes in the level of the whole stock market; and
- the changes peculiar to each company which are assumed to come from within the company.

To summarize, the fundamental determinants of a share price are:

- The expected growth rate;
- the expected dividend payout of the share;
- the degree of risk; and
- the level of market interest rates.

3.3.8 The valuation of common shares

The nucleus of fundamental analysis is to eventually determine the intrinsic value of a share. In order to do this, a valuation of the specific share has to be completed. The following methods of valuation can be used:

- The capitalization of the income -- this determines the intrinsic value of a share based on the expected cash flow over an expected time period.

- The zero-growth model -- this model assumes that the amount paid out in dividends per share will remain the same from period to period. With this assumption in mind the intrinsic value can be calculated.

- The constant-growth rate -- this model assumes that dividends grow from period to period at the same constant rate indefinitely.

- The multiple-growth model -- this model primarily focuses on time. The focus is on a specific time period in the future, after which dividends are expected to grow at a constant rate.

- Finite holding period model -- this model combines the expected or present price of a share with the expected or future dividend and discounts into one cash flow.

3.3.9 Advantages and disadvantages of fundamental analysis

3.3.9.1 Advantages of fundamental analysis

- Fundamental analysis provides a systematic approach to analyzing shares.

- A company can be compared with others in its industry. This comparison can provide the analyst with insight into whether a company is under- or over-performing relative to its industry.

- Fundamental analysis provides additional information which may not be generally available to the chartist or technician.

- Fundamentals may sometimes indicate or anticipate a major price movement well in advance of any technical signals generated by charts.

- Fundamental analysis attempts to intimately acquaint the investor with a company's past operations and its present financial condition.

Schwager (1984:142) identifies the following additional advantages:

- A knowledge of fundamentals may permit a trader to adopt a more aggressive position in those cases where the fundamentals suggest the potential for a major move. The strictly technical trader, on the other hand, must treat all trading signals equally.

- An understanding of the underlying fundamentals can assist in deciding when to stay with a winning trade.

- The way in which a market responds to fundamental news can be used as a trading tool, even by the technical trader.

3.3.9.2 Disadvantages of fundamental analysis

The disadvantages of fundamental analysis are:

- The use of one-year comparisons is overly simplistic. However, such comparisons are fairly widespread because they offer a simple means for instant analysis.

- No matter how highly a fundamentalist rates a company, it will be of no avail unless other fundamentalists arrive at similar conclusions and, by so doing stimulate a demand for that company and its shares.

- The use of fundamentals for timing does not appear wise. Fundamental analysis is a method of determining the intrinsic value of a share under certain statistically given conditions. However, it is not a good idea to use supply-demand statistics to provide an instantaneous price signal, because they constantly change and are never stable.

- Companies' published financial reports provide the major source of information for the fundamentalist. In many cases, the information provided in the financial reports is inadequate. Reports may not contain all relevant information since some corporate authorities do not disclose certain information in their financial reports, thus making it impossible to make a fair assessment of the company.

- Nominal share price levels recorded are compared with share prices of previous years. In drawing comparisons with the past, it is necessary to adjust historical prices for inflation. However, in many instances, this is not done.

- Fundamental analysis ignores expectations, despite the fact that markets often place greater emphasis on expectations for the following year than on prevailing fundamentals. This is especially true in transitional periods when the supply situation is moving from surplus to tightness, or *vice versa.*

- It ignores seasonal considerations. Almost every share exhibits one or more seasonal patterns. Ignoring seasonal factors can easily lead to the misinterpretation of fundamental data. A comparison of production and consumption figures with the corresponding figures of previous years does not require any consideration of seasonal factors. However, if comparisons of fundamental data involve different time periods during the year, it is essential to examine historical data carefully for possible seasonal behavior and to make the necessary adjustments.

- Projecting earnings growth rates for future years is an extremely complicated and inexact task, but most difficult of all is the selection of a suitable price earnings multiple in a market that could, on average, double or halve its capitalization value over a certain period.

- Drawing conclusions on the basis of insufficient data is problematical. However, sometimes it is virtually impossible to construct a fundamental forecasting model for a market because of a lack of comparative historical data. After all, how can one interpret the price implications of a projected statistical balance if, for example, there are only two previous years of data available for making comparisons?

Schwager (1984:26) feels that a lot of confusion surrounds the concepts of demand and supply. Demand is probably one of the two most misused words in commodities literature and analysis. The confusion between demand and consumption is a matter of semantics. The two terms represent very different concepts, and their frequent usage as synonymous terms has led to many major analytical errors.

- As stated previously, a future share price depends on a company's future financial condition and the behavioral response of the investors to its future condition. It is clear that even the most thorough analysis of a company and its past financial statements reveals very little insight into these two factors which determine a future share price.

- One of the major problems of fundamental analysis is that it totally ignores the psychological make-up of investors. Malkiel (1985:105) states that fundamental analysts believe that the market is ten per cent psychological and ninety per cent logical, while chartists believe that the market is only ten per cent logical and ninety percent psychological.

Bethlehem (1977:49-51), cites the following additional disadvantages of fundamental analysis:

- Implicit in the notion of intrinsic value is the quality of stability relative to market prices. However, should it be possible to determine the intrinsic value objectively, the problem of market timing would still arise. Given that the share market prices fluctuate, a simple difference between market price and the intrinsic value would, in itself, be an indication to buy or to sell a particular share.

- Because intrinsic value is subject to change and because it may itself be influenced by changes in the market price, many practical difficulties arise in its calculation. The practical difficulties that arise in the estimation of the intrinsic value have to do, mainly, with the timing, receipt and the processing of information.

The implications of the efficient market hypothesis for fundamental analysis will be discussed in section 3.5.

3.3.10 Conclusion

Fundamental analysis is the phase of share analysis that deals with the assessment of the investment merits of a specific company and its shares, and is ultimately aimed at the formulation of a future projected intrinsic share value.

There are obviously certain advantages and disadvantages to this approach. However, for long-term stability and growth, this approach is far superior to technical analysis.

3.4 TRADITIONAL TIME SERIES FORECASTING[45]

3.4.1 Introduction

Real world data is often noisy, that is, it contains a substantial amount of random components.[46] In addition, data is possibly contaminated by inaccuracies, missing observations, and outliers. Even the selection of an optimal traditional forecasting method will not remedy the inaccuracy of forecasts generated from bad or noisy data (Chang, 1992:2).

Traditional time series forecasting can essentially be characterized as either objective or subjective. Subjective forecasting is based on the decision maker's experience in the field. Purely subjective methods of time series forecasting include juries of executive opinion, studies, and surveys, among others. However, such judgemental forecasts usually integrate complex information and the subjective experience of the decision maker into forecasts. Therefore, the subjective approach can be used for long-term forecasting. However, according to Goodrich (1989:120-134), purely subjective forecasts may only reflect individual biases.

Objective forecasting uses quantitative methods to extract statistical features that characterize the data. However, both subjective and objective forecasting can be oriented towards satisfying a certain opinion, rather than optimizing. Objective forecasting can be categorized into three sets of distinctions:

---

45 Time-series analysis deals with the methods of analysing past data and then projecting the data to obtain estimates of future values.

46 Also known as random error.

- Univariate versus multivariate forecasting;
- fixed versus adaptive parameter forecasting; and
- statistical versus empirical forecasting.

The objective approach considers, in it simplest form, a parametric set of recurrent models on data, such as that described by equation 3-10.

$$s_t = a_0 + a_1 s_{t-1} + \ldots + a_k s_{t-k} + w_t \qquad \textbf{...(3-10)}$$

Where: $a_0 + a_1 s_{t-1} + \ldots + a_k s_{t-k}$ = True model without uncertainty.

w_t = White noise.

$\{s_t\} t=1 \ldots T$ = Sample of S.

This type of quantitative model is well suited for series where the relevant information is quantitative and for which the time series is sufficiently regular. However, there are numerous financial time series, such as share prices, which do not have the characteristics as shown in equation 3-10.

For the purpose of this study, only univariate and multivariate forecasting will be compared and not the other two sets of distinctions, since an objective of this study is to compare traditional statistical methods with a neural network model. Traditional share market evaluation models can be divided into two groups:

- Univariate models; and
- multivariate models.

3.4.1.1 Univariate time series forecasting models[47]

Unlike the multivariate approach, univariate time series forecasting never attempts to discover the causal factors that affect the behavior of data (Chang, 1992:6). Parameters are allowed to vary in the adaptive approach in order to reflect the continuous changes in data structure. In contrast,

---

47 Also referred to as the self-projecting approach.

fixed parameter methods do not respond to further pattern changes. The statistical approach to forecasting maps a model to data, while empirical approaches attempt to evaluate several objective methods and make a selection according to some optimizing criterion. This represents the typical case in share market forecasting.

However, the main concern in univariate time series forecasting is, of course, to predict what will happen from what has happened. The following univariate times series forecasting models have been employed in share market forecasting models:

- Classical component model;
- exponential smoothing model;
- Box-Jenkins ARMA model; and
- state space model.

The reasons univariate models have been employed (Hoff, 1983:10) are:

- They can be applied quickly and easily;
- they provide a basis for comparison with forecasts developed through other methods;
- they require a minimum amount of data; and
- they can provide reasonably accurate short- to medium-term forecasts.

One of the objectives of this study is to compare neural networks to the Box-Jenkins model. The methodology involved in the construction of the Box-Jenkins model will be discussed in Chapter 4. However, to provide a theoretical justification for using Box-Jenkins, an overview will be provided in section 3.4.2.

3.4.1.2 Multivariate time series forecasting models

According to Chang (1992:70), a multivariate time-series forecasting model is merely a univariate model expanded to include the identification and estimation of the transfer function relating a dependent variable to multiple independent variable(s). The general objective of the transfer function is to estimate the dynamic response characteristics between a change in the level of the dependent variable and a change in the independent variable. The most common analyses for multivariate times series forecasting are:

- Regression analysis;
- correlation analysis; and
- multiple regression analysis.

3.4.2 Box-Jenkins forecasting[48]

3.4.2.1 Introduction

Classical time-series forecasting techniques are essentially descriptive methods that attempt to break down a time series into distinct components, representing effects of groups of explanatory factors (Hamburg, 1991:581). These components are:

- Trends;
- cyclical fluctuations;
- seasonal fluctuations; and
- irregular movements.

During analysis, all series movements are regarded as sequences of independent random variables. The assumption of independent random variables may be a pure approach to forecasting, but it may also be unnecessary. However, there are many cases in which the sequential elements in a series are highly dependent. Therefore, it would be inefficient to apply a solution that did not take advantage of all the available information. Box-Jenkins provides a forecasting tool that assumes measurable properties of these random variables.

The Box-Jenkins method of forecasting is different from most methods, in that it does not assume any particular pattern in the historical data of the time series (Hanke and Reitsch, 1986:355). Box-Jenkins uses the iterative approach of identifying a possibly useful model from a general class of models. This model is then checked by comparing the residuals between the forecasting model and the historical model. The data points will be small, randomly distributed, and independent.

---

48 The Box-Jenkins technique applies autoregressive and moving average methods to time series forecasting problems.

3.4.2.2 The construction of the Box-Jenkins model

The Box-Jenkins model captures the behavior of a time series in the following equation forms:

- Autoregressive model (AR(2)) - The Autoregressive model takes the following form (refer to equation 3-11):

$$Y_t = B_1 Y_{t-1} + B_2 Y_{t-2} + \ldots + B_p Y_{t-p} + e_r \qquad \textbf{...(3-11)}$$

Where:		
Y_t	=	Dependent variable.
$Y_{t-1}, \ldots, Y_{t-p}$	=	Independent variables that are dependent variables specific lagged time periods.
$B_1, \ldots, B_p$	=	Regression coefficients.
e_r	=	Residual term that represents random events not explained by the model.

- Moving average model (MA) - The moving average model takes the form of (refer to equation 3-12):

$$Y_t = e_t - W_1 e_{t-1} - W_2 e_{t-2} - \ldots - W_q e_{t-q} \qquad \textbf{...(3-12)}$$

Where:

$W_1, \ldots, W_q$ = Weights.

$e_{t-1}, \ldots, e_{t-q}$ = Previous values of residuals.

- Autoregressive moving average model (ARMA) - In addition to the AR and MA models, the two can be combined, providing a third class of general model. (refer to equation 3-13):

$$Y_t = B_1 Y_{t-1} + B_2 Y_{t-2} + \ldots + B_p Y_{t-p} + e_r - W_1 e_{t-1} - W_2 e_{t-2} - \ldots - W_q e_{t-q}$$

...(3-13)

The model identification process is based on matching the autocorrelation pattern of the observed time series with known patterns of various specific forms of the ARMA model.

ARMA models are often favored over other time series forecasting methods for the following reasons (Pankratz, 1983:150), namely:

- The Box-Jenkins models are based on a solid foundation of mathematical theories;
- an appropriate ARMA model yields optimal univariate forecasts; and
- ARMA models can handle a wide variety of forecasting conditions.

However, the forecasting derived from ARMA processes does have the following disadvantages:

- ARMA models are relatively complex and may require more experience and computing time to identify a useful model;
- at least fifty data points are needed to produce accurate forecasts (Kang, 1991:38);
- ARMA models are better suited for short-term forecasting; and
- the performance of ARMA forecasting can be impaired by the presence of repeated outliers (Pack and Downing, 1983:20-40).

Figure 3.5 - Box-Jenkins methodology

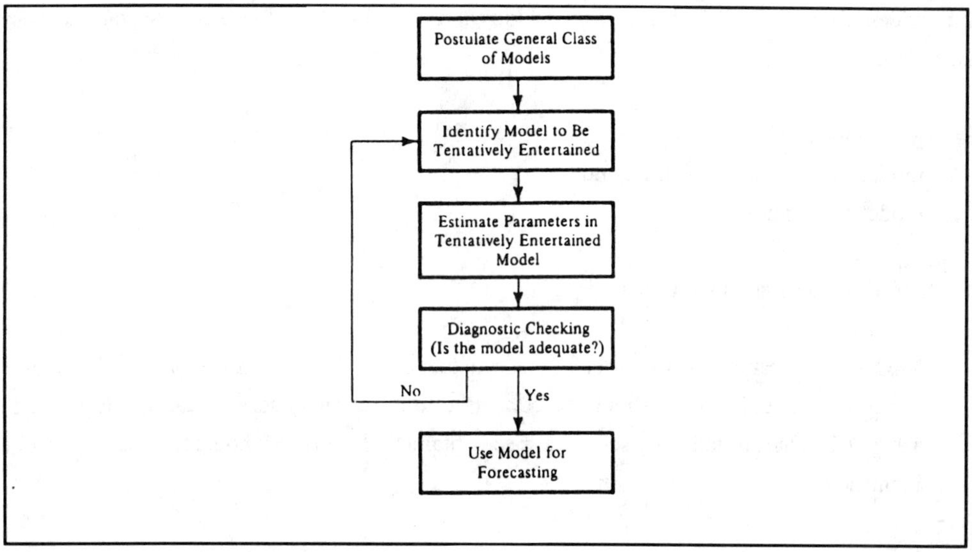

3.4.2.3 Applying Box-Jenkins methodology

It is evident from Figure 3.5, that the Box-Jenkins approach involves three separate stages. These stages are:

- Model identification;
- model estimation and testing; and
- model application.

Each of these steps are now discussed.

- Model identification - this step determines whether or not the series is stationary[49]. If the time series is non-stationary, it should be converted to a stationary series (Hanke and Reitsch, 1986:361). Once a stationary series has been obtained, the form of model to be used must be identified.

- Model estimation and testing - this step can be accomplished by comparing the autocorrelation and the partial-autocorrelation coefficients of the data to be fitted with the corresponding distributions for the various ARMA models.

  According to Hanke and Reitsch (1986:362-363), the following guidelines can be employed in identifying the appropriate model:

  - If the autocorrelation trails off exponentially to zero, an AR process is indicated;
  - if the partial-autocorrelations trail off, a MA process is indicated; and
  - if both trail off, a mixed ARMA process is indicated.

  By counting the number of autocorrelations and partial-autocorrelations coefficients that are significantly different from zero, one can determine the order of the MA and/or AR processes.

---

[49] Mean values change over time.

- Model application - once an adequate model has been found, forecasts can be made for one or several periods into the future.

3.4.2.4 Comparing Box-Jenkins to neural networks

Sharda and Patil (1990:491-493) provided a comparison between Box-Jenkins and neural networks, using seventy-five different time series. They concluded that a simple neural network could forecast about as well as a Box-Jenkins forecasting system. In terms of the MAPE (mean absolute percentage error), neural networks sometimes outperformed the Box-Jenkins approach by more than 100 percent. However, in other cases, the latter system proved much better. The authors did not provide any explanation as to when and why one approach is superior to the other.

Similar results were also noted by Tang, Almeida, and Fishwick (1991:303-310) in their paper, which provided a comparative study that was carried out to investigate the forecasting capabilities of neural networks and Box-Jenkins. They concluded that neural networks provide a promising approach to time-series forecasting. Furthermore, Tang, Almeida, and Fishwick (1991:309) state: "For time series with long memory, both the Box-Jenkins model and the neural network perform well, with the Box-Jenkins model performing slightly better for short-term forecasting. Neural networks proved to be better for long-term forecasting. For short-memory time series, such as the stock market, neural networks appear to be superior to Box-Jenkins models. By approximating the underlying mapping of the time series, a neural network provides robust forecasting in cases of irregular time series. The neural network model is more parsimonious in data requirements than the Box-Jenkins model."

Kang (1991:122) used a total of 140 simulated time series, each of which was composed of ninety-four observations. Every group of time series contained twenty replicates, each of which were generated with a different initial random seed regarding error components. Kang employed Box-Jenkins and a feedforward neural network, and compared the forecasting capabilities of both. The research indicates that the performance of the neural network was better than or equivalent to Box-Jenkins models in most cases. However, across the data patterns used in this study, on average it was found that neural networks produced more accurate forecasts than Box-Jenkins for longer forecasting horizons.

Research done by Chang (1992:79-90), in the forecasting of a rainfall series for the Dallas/Forth Worth area (U.S.), concludes that neural networks significantly outperformed Box-Jenkins, state space, and chronological network models.

One of the purposes of this study is to provide answers to unresolved issues and inconsistencies raised in the literature, particularly regarding the effects of the hidden layers and the number of processing elements on the implementation, and to obtain reliable results through a study that is based on both neural networks and forecasting theories, with emphasis on Box-Jenkins (refer to Table 3.3).

Table 3.3 - Comparing neural networks with Box-Jenkins

Researchers	Inputs	Hidden processing elements	Time series	Forecast horizon	Findings
Sharda & Patil (1990)	2,4	Two hidden layers, each with 10 `PE`	Chaotic time series	Up to 100 periods	Parsimonious, neural networks are better if more inputs are used and more processing elements are used
Tang, Almeida & Fishwick (1991)	2e+05	Not known	Chaotic time series	24 periods	Time series with long memory: Box-Jenkins performs better. However, if time series exhibits short-term memory, neural networks are better
Kang (1991)	4,8,12	Two hidden layers	50 actual	24 periods	Neural networks are far superior to Box-Jenkins for seasonal demand pattern with linear trend
Chang (1992)	7,48	One hidden layer 7 and 6	140 actual	24 periods	Neural networks significantly outperform Box-Jenkins

3.4.3 Conclusion

The review of the Box-Jenkins method in this section provides the basis for their comparison to neural networks. Since the objective of this section was to provide a theoretical foundation prior to exploring the effectiveness of neural networks in the forecasting of share prices, other modified univariate time series forecasting methods were considered beyond the scope of this study. These include: combined forecasting, dynamic regression, classical component models and space state methods.

3.5 THE EFFICIENT MARKET HYPOTHESIS (EMH)

3.5.1 Introduction

No concept in investment finance has been as widely tested and little believed as "efficient markets". Yet the concept remains the bedrock of the quantitative capital market theory (Peters, 1991:13). The implication of the EMH is that any forecasting technique, whether technical or fundamental, is called into question. In its stronger forms, the EMH casts doubts on the possibility of beating the stock market by successfully exploiting fundamental information. According to Laing (1991:12), "At best, market fundamentalists were guardians of market efficiency and rationality by collectively ensuring that current stock prices reflect true value. Mere actors in an absurdities drama, if you will."

There are several reasons for the popularity enjoyed by the EMH in the 1960s and 1970s:

- The EMH was rooted in a very strong theoretical foundation. This foundation began with Samuelson's work on the behavior of speculative prices, which shows that prices of shares follow a random walk (1965). This was further supported by Harry Markowitz's theory of portfolio selection (1959) and by William Sharpe's construction of the Capital Asset Pricing Model (CAPM), which describes the implications of optimal portfolio construction for asset prices in security market equilibrium (1964). The final contribution was Robert Luca's Rational Expectations Hypothesis (1978), which examines the implications of optimal forecasting for individual behavior and macro-economic performance.

- A second reason for the popularity of the EMH, according to Fortune (1991:18), was the hubris of the financial market practitioner during the 1960s. He clarifies this by saying that this period rested upon the notion that opportunities for unusual profit were abundant, requiring only a reasonable person and a little care to sort out the wheat from the chaff in financial markets. The EMH provided an antidote to this hubris, and argued that opportunities to make unusual profit were both rare and ephemeral.

  "Thus, the EMH counselled healthy skepticism in investment decisions... skepticism about a 'beat the market' strategy has led to the popularity of index funds, which allow investors to 'hold the market' without worrying about individual stocks" (Fortune, 1991:18).

The purpose of this study is to construct a neural network model, which *per se* could predict future share prices. The implications of this is that, if the null hypothesis is rejected, it could be concluded that a form of the efficient market hypothesis does exist on the Johannesburg Stock Exchange. However, it is not an objective of this study to test forms of market efficiency but, rather, to accept or reject the EMH, based on the forecasting capabilities of neural networks. Therefore, subsequent subsections will provide an overview of the efficient market hypothesis.

3.5.2 Defining the efficient market hypothesis

The EMH states that, at any time, the price of a security fully captures all known information about the share, resulting in price behavior that is like a random walk in time, except when there are changes in information. Therefore, asset prices reflect optimal use of all information, and the price of an actively traded asset is an optimal forecast of the asset's "fundamental values" (Fortune, 1991:19).
This statement can be converted into the following mathematical equation; refer to equation 3-14.

$$P_t = E(P_t^* | \Omega_t) \qquad \textbf{...(3-14)}$$

Where: P_t = Market price.
E = Expected fundamental value.
P_t^* = Fundamental value if a state number occurs.
Ω_t = Set of all the available information at time t.

However, stated formally, the simple efficient market hypothesis asserts the following: (refer to equation 3-15).

$$E(r_t|I_{t-1}) = r^* \qquad \textbf{...(3-15)}$$

Where: $E(r_t \mid I_{t-1})$ = Conditional expectation of r_t given publicly available information at time t-1.

I_{t-1} = The σ generated by publicly available information.

r^* = A constant consisting of the risk-free return plus a risk premium[50].

An implication of the EMH for the behavior of an asset price is that Ω_t contains all the relevant information available at time t, as well as current publicly available information on the company policies and prospects. Therefore, the market price of an asset should be uncorrelated with any information available at the time the price is observed. A second implication, which can be deduced from equation 3-14, is that the sequence of prices will be a random walk with drift; prices will vary randomly around a rising trend. The fact that new information is random, having no predictable components, forms the basis of the "random walk" test (Fortune, 1991:18-19).

---

50 I_{t-1} includes the previous share price history. The force of the simple efficient market hypothesis is that the previous history is of no use in the forecasting of r_t.

3.5.3 The origins of the efficient market hypothesis

The first documented work relating to the use of statistical methods for analyzing returns was published in 1900 by Bachlier. He contended that market returns are independent, identically distributed **IID** random variables, an idea which forms the basis of the random walk hypothesis (Bachlier cited in Cootner, 1964:17:19). From the 1920s to the 1940s, market analysis was dominated by the fundamentalists (followers of Graham and Dodd) and the technicians (followers of Edwards and Magee). According to Peters (1991:15), the 1950s added a third group, the Quants (followers of Bachlier). However, the claim that share prices follow random walks wasn't actually formalized by Osborne until 1964. The purpose of his paper, entitled *Brownian Motion in the Stock Market*, was to show that logarithms of common share prices can be regarded as an ensemble of decisions in a statistical state, each varying with time, and are equivalent to the movement of a particle in a fluid, which is known as the Brownian motion. His research was based on a number of assumptions (Osborne, cited in Cootner, 1964:101-110):

- Assumption 1 - Prices move in discrete units of 1/8.
- Assumption 2 - The number of transactions per day is finite and not important.
- Assumption 3 - Prices and value are related and their relationship is the prime determinant of market returns.
- Assumption 4 - Given two securities with different expected returns, the logical decision is to pick the share with the highest expected return[51].
- Assumption 5 - Buyers cannot have an advantage over sellers, or *vice versa*, if a transaction is to be accomplished.
- Assumption 6 - If decisions for each transaction in the sequence of transactions for a single share are made independently, then the distribution will be normal.

---

[51] 'Expected return' is the sum of the probabilities of a return times the associated return (Peters, 1991:16).

- Assumption 7 - Share price changes are independent and, thus, follow a random walk.

In summary, the random walk hypothesis states that, because investors are able to equate price and value (rational expectation[52]), they will trade at the equilibrium price using information available at that time (dissemination of market information). Therefore, share prices have no memory and, thus, all prices are serially independent. According to Peters (1991:17-18), "The founding fathers of the capital market theory were well aware of these simplifying assumptions and their implications. They were not trying to minimize the impact of these assumptions...they felt that the assumptions did materially affect the usefulness of the model, especially if certain assumptions about investor behavior were accepted. The concept of the rational investor was crucial to what became the EMH."

The vast majority of empirical studies on the random walk hypothesis, employing a multitude of statistical tests, have not produced any conclusive evidence that either supports or refutes the theory. These tests fall into two categories:

- Test for independence of price changes; and
- test for conformity to some probability distribution.

Research done by Fama (1965:34-105), using the correlation coefficient test, was unable to generate evidence for rejecting the random walk hypothesis. However, Fama conceptualized the rational investor in the random walk hypothesis, which was finally formalized into the efficient market hypothesis. Peters (1991:18) notes that the EMH, in its pure form, is similar to Osborne's assumption (*see* Assumption 5), which does not require independence through time or accept only **IID** observations. The random walk model does require those assumptions. If returns are random, then markets are efficient. However, the converse may not be true.

3.5.4 The three forms of the efficient market hypothesis

The efficient market hypothesis has been divided into three different forms:

- Weak form - This states that price changes are independent and may be a random walk, and

---

52 Paulo (1984:51).

that movements in share prices follow a sub-martingale pattern; consequently, past analysis of share prices is of no purpose. The difference between the weak form of the EMH and the random walk hypothesis, according to Tinic and West (1977:95), is that the latter contends that the expected value of a future price change is independent of past price changes, while the weak form only requires that the probability distribution of price changes is dependent on the distribution of past price changes and subject to the expected values of future prices being independent of past price changes. Refer to Table 3.4 for tests done to validate the weak form.

Table 3.4 - Tests to validate the weak form

Property	Test
Non-correlation	Serial correlation
	Run
Homogeneous distribution	Distribution
Fair game	Trading rule

- Semi-strong form - This asserts that share prices fully reflect all publicly available information regarding each share. According to Paulo (1984:58), at this level of efficiency, researchers are concerned with the speed of market reaction to significant new information, and the market is regarded as efficient if market prices adjust rapidly. Tests done to validate the semi-strong form are:

  - Speed adjustment tests.

- Strong form - This involves all known information including the previous sets and any other information known by insiders. According to Paulo (1984:59), tests of this form of the efficient market hypothesis attempt to measure the degree to which certain insiders can obtain a monopoly on information and then outperform the market. Tests done to validate the strong form are:

  - Mutual fund performance tests.

However, it is implicit in the above that if share prices are to reflect certain information sets fully, information will be impounded almost instantaneously in an unbiased fashion (Knight, 1981:32).

3.5.5 Relevant research on the efficient market hypothesis

For the purposes of this study, research will include only those tests performed on the predictability of share market returns, with general conclusions regarding overseas studies, and a general conclusion drawn from these. However, a brief survey of empirical evidence regarding the efficiency of the Johannesburg Stock Exchange will follow in section 3.5.5.1. Bodie, Kane and Marcus (1993:376-397) divide the tests into the following categories:

- Returns over short-term horizons;
- returns over long horizons;
- predictors of broad market returns;
- portfolio strategies and market anomalies;
- small-firm effect;
- neglected-firm effect and liquidity effects;
- market-to-book ratios;
- day-of-the-week effect;
- inside information;
- value line enigma; and
- mutual fund performance.

Comprehensive research by Bodie *et al* from 1965 to 1990 on the EMH concludes that markets are very efficient, though, given time, it may be possible for diligent, intelligent, or creative investors to make profits. They further feel that the issue is not whether or not the market is efficient, but how much efficiency the market seems to have. This, in turn, depends on the costs and benefits of information searches regarding particular securities. However, Fortune (1991:35) states: "Our fundamental conclusion is that the efficient market hypothesis is having a near-death experience and is very likely to succumb unless new technology, as yet unknown, can revive it."

Peters (1991:38) concludes that, if investors did react to information in a linear way (as the information arrives), it could profoundly change the nature of the markets. Instead, investors react in a nonlinear or delayed fashion. He contends that the assumption of the EMH that investors are rational, and therefore price changes are independent, cannot be endorsed without substantial empirical evidence. The literature overview on the EMH has indicated that no studies have convincingly either supported or rejected the EMH. However, the current capital market paradigm is based on efficient markets and linear relationships between cause and effect. It can, therefore, be concluded from a review of the literature that no clear-cut evidence for or against the EMH exists.

Many strict fundamental analysts were initially pleased by the random walk attack on technical analysis. However, through further development of the random walk hypothesis into the efficient market hypothesis, it became evident that market prices react so quickly to new information that share analysis will not enable investors to realize consistently superior returns on their investments. This is because of the extreme competition among investors, resulting in share prices seldom being far above or below their justified value levels. Fundamental analysis thus loses much of its value. It also follows that fundamental analysis can only be defended as long as it consistently produces results which are superior to those produced by a random selection of shares.

3.5.5.1 The efficient market hypothesis and the Johannesburg Stock Exchange

A few share market studies of the Johannesburg Stock Exchange have been performed. This section will examine the various studies undertaken to determine the efficiency of the Johannesburg Stock Exchange. They are:

- Affleck-Graves and Money (1975:382-388) tested the serial correlation of returns from fifty listed companies between 1968 and 1973. They used weekly data on ten lag categories, resulting in the calculation of 500 coefficients of correlation. They conclude that between 70 and 80 percent of the shares in the sample support the weak form of the EMH. However, they felt that the conclusion drawn from the research was dependent on the implicit assumptions which underlie the test (normally distributed returns and finite variances). The weak form of the EMH was thus **accepted**.

- Haddasin (1976:13-14) tested the serial correlation of returns from 30 shares using a difference interval of 1 day over the same period studied by Affleck-Graves and Money.

Haddasin concludes that the Johannesburg Stock Exchange is an inefficient market, and, therefore, technicians should be able to generate greater returns than those of the market. Therefore the random walk hypothesis was **refuted**.

- Scholsberg (1976:1-17) studied a sample of 6 highly traded shares and concluded that 5 of the 6 shares could best be described as having compound normal distribution returns, the distribution returns being symmetrical. The final conclusion was that highly-traded shares showed evidence of efficiency, therefore **accepting** the weak form of the EMH.

- Roux and Gilbertson (1976:1-19) applied 4 different trading rule tests to a sample of 24 shares. The results indicate that a buy-and-hold strategy outperforms the trading rules in each case. This result, they claim, constitutes evidence for the **acceptance** of the weak form of the EMH.

- Strebel (1977:15-21) reassessed the evidence reviewed by Roux and Gilbertson in 1976, from tests performed on 10 shares in each of two categories: highly and thinly traded shares. The study indicates that, at best, the efficient market hypothesis only applies to half the shares traded on the Johannesburg Stock Exchange, representing those shares with an average annual trading volume in excess of at least 250,000. Therefore, the study of Roux and Gilbertson was refuted, indicating an **inconsistent** acceptance of the weak form of the EMH.

- Gilbertson and Roux (1977:21-30) responded to Strebel's research by analysing his arguments against the assumption that the JSE is an efficient market. Their research indicates that the rejection of the CAPM for low trading volume shares was not justified, that Strebel's conclusions were based on results calculated from questionable data, and that his methodology was open to criticism. Consequently, they **accepted** the weak form of the EMH. In another study, Gilbertson and Roux (1978:223-233) found evidence which indicates that price changes are not completely independent but, in turn, shows that the deviations are not of a sufficient magnitude to permit traders to consistently outperform buy-and-hold strategies.

- Botha (1978:129-131) determined the validity of the random walk hypothesis with respect to the behavior of share prices on the Johannesburg Stock Exchange by studying weekly readings of the South African industrials group Index and the daily closing prices of seven ordinary shares. Botha's investigation rejects the random walk hypothesis and further **rejects** the efficient market hypothesis in its weak form.

- Knight (1981:230-243) studied the effect of market reaction to announcements of changes in the basis of valuation of company stocks from FIFO to LIFO. The results indicate that the price of a share rises, only to be followed by a negative trend. He concludes that the JSE is an inefficient market, therefore **rejecting** the EMH.

- Brümmer and Jacobs (1981:53-59) investigated the behavior of 94 quoted shares on the Johannesburg Stock Exchange over the period 1970 to 1977 by way of serial correlations and run tests. The results of the study indicated that the Johannesburg Stock Exchange does not statistically comply with the weak form of the efficient market hypothesis, therefore **rejecting** the EMH.

- Boshoff (1983:254-256), in a study of 200 shares, set out to establish whether share prices on the Johannesburg Stock Exchange exhibit any non-random behavior that could be utilized by technical analysts. The study concluded that share prices on the JSE exhibited a non-random behavior, and technical analysis can thus be employed to exploit this non-random behavior. Consequently, higher returns can be earned using technical trading rules compared with buy-and-hold strategies. He further concludes that the null hypothesis has to be rejected and an alternative hypothesis formulated, stating "...that the decision time series is effective and will produce results superior to an indeterminate buy-and-hold strategy." From this statement, it can be inferred that the study **rejects** the EMH.

- Paulo (1984:127-129) completed a study which set out to determine the relevance of fundamental and technical analysis and, in particular, the efficient market hypothesis regarding the South African life insurance industry. The study concludes that the EMH is to be **rejected** on the basis that all the respondents in the sample perceived the market in which they operated as inefficient.

- Knight and Affleck-Graves (1985:157-160) focused on the speed and the direction of the movement of share prices in response to the release of listed companies' preliminary results. Forty-one listed companies were analyzed from 1973 to 1980. The study indicates that the market reacts fairly rapidly to the earnings information reported. The study further indicates a **consistency** with the semi-strong form of the EMH.

- Du Toit (1986:9.3), undertook a study to prove that above-average returns can be achieved with a trading model that includes the principles and foundations of both technical analysis and the EMH. Du Toit concludes "...that the market at times assumes the properties of a totally efficient market, but at other times prices deviate from underlying equilibrium values...[this] implies that technical analysis and efficient markets are not mutually exclusive, but that a combination of both approaches provides a better description of the market process than any one of the approaches individually."

- Beechar (1986:80-90) studied share price movements prior to and following the announcement of share splits. The results of the study indicate that much of the share price change occurs before the actual split, which can be largely attributed to the increased dividend flow expected after the split. He concludes that there is support for the semi-strong form of the EMH, because the market adjusted to a new equilibrium within ten days. Therefore, it can be concluded that this study **accepts** the EMH.

- Ooms, Archer and Van Der M Smit (1987:187-197) studied the impact of dividend announcements on the market. Their findings indicate that knowledge of future dividend information does not generate significant returns different from those generated by the market. In conclusion, they **accepted** the EMH.

- Bhana (1987:198-202) investigated abnormal return behavior of 50 companies listed on the JSE over the period 1975 to 1985. He concludes that the JSE appears to be inefficient in reacting to the public announcement of a take-over proposal, with a significant market reaction occurring five days after the announcement date. Consequently, he **rejected** the EMH.

- Van Den Honert and Barr (1988:1-10) evaluated the asymmetry of returns that accrue to shareholders of acquiring and acquired firms by measuring the returns of both the acquiring and the target companies based on four identifiable features. The results indicate that acquiring companies tend to benefit in the short-term, while the target companies experience abnormally positive returns around the announcement date. Consequently, the results conclude that inefficiencies in the market exist, therefore **rejecting** the EMH.

- Jacobson's (1988:35-36) objective was to identify whether abnormal returns relative to the market may be generated prior to the issuance of a cautionary announcement. The results of the study indicate that the JSE does not appear to be efficient in reacting to new information contained within the cautionary announcement. The research further indicates that an equilibrium return of a share price can take up to two weeks to develop, resulting in a **rejection** of the EMH.

- Bhana (1990:129-135) set out to determine the economic value of secondary dissemination of share recommendations in newspapers and financial journals in South Africa. A sample population was stratified according to the original recommendations appearing in stockbrokers' and investment advisory service newsletters. The study concludes that share prices do adjust in response to analysts' recommendations. Bhana states that the findings of his study "may be interpreted as a contradiction of the strong form of market efficiency. However, the findings do not necessarily contradict the notion of an efficient market - publication of analysts' recommendations in newspapers make the market more efficient by passing new information to a large group of investors." Therefore the findings of the study do not clearly indicate an acceptance or denial of the EMH.

- Bhana (1991:33-40) examined share market response to substantial changes in dividend policies for a random sample of 40 listed companies between 1970 and 1988. The results **did not support** the semi-strong form of the EMH, since the market's reaction to dividend announcements continued for a period of up to 19 days after the event.

- Page and Way (1993:35-47) investigated the "over-reaction" hypothesis on the Johannesburg Stock Exchange, using data for the period 1974-1989. The study indicates that "the information contained in historical share prices is significant and investors could have achieved abnormal returns by studying past price movements only and then constructing and holding arbitrage portfolios for between two and three years." The results **support** the existence of a long-term weak-form of inefficiency over the period investigated.

- Bhana (1993:31-42) studied the relationship between growth in money supply and share prices in order to test the efficiency of the Johannesburg Stock Exchange. The Johannesburg Stock Exchange Overall Index was used to measure the growth rate of share prices on the Exchange. Quarterly data on the money market was used to determine money growth over the period 1980 to 1989. He concludes "...that past information about monetary policy was inefficiently processed by participants on the JSE...therefore, although the JSE appears to have been inefficient in the past, attempts by investors to outperform the monetary market could possibly render it more efficient." Therefore, the study indicates **inconsistent** findings with reference to the EMH.

3.5.5.2 Employing neural networks to test the efficient market hypothesis

In the economic literature reviewed, the standard method for testing the efficient market hypothesis is to embed a linear autoregressive model for asset returns into equation 3-15 with equation 3-16.

$$r_t = w_0 + w_1 r_{t-1} + \dots + w_{pr_{t-1}} + \varepsilon_t,\ t = 1,2\dots, \qquad \textbf{...(3-16)}$$

Where: $w = (w_o, w_1, \dots, w_p)$ = Column vector of weights.

p = A positive integer determining the order of the autoregression.

ϵ_t = Stochastic error assumed to be such that $E(r_t \mid I_{t-1}) = 0$.

According to White (1993:314-318), the efficient market hypothesis implies the restriction that that $w_1 = \dots = w_p = 0$. Therefore, any empirical evidence that $w_1 \neq 0$ or $w_2 \neq 0$ ... or $w_p \neq 0$, is evidence against the efficient market hypothesis. However, empirical evidence that $w_1 = \dots = w_p = 0$, while not refuting the efficient market hypothesis, does not confirm it either. However, the time series might exhibit a deterministic nonlinear process with no linear structure (Sakai and Tokumaru, 1980:588-590; Eckman and Ruelle, 1985:650).

White (1988:II-453) postulates that a linear autoregressive model of order p (AR(p)model) corresponds to a simple linear feedforward network. Given inputs $r_{t-1}, \dots, r_{t-p}$, the network output is given as $r_t = w^{53}_o + w_1 r_{t-1} + ... + w_p r_{t-p}$. Thus, it can be deduced that neural networks are appropriate models for determining whether an economic time series conforms to or rejects the efficient market hypothesis.

3.5.6 Conclusion

The results of the studies on the efficient market hypothesis regarding the Johannesburg Stock Exchange are neither conclusive nor extensive. Traditional tests of the EMH have involved the estimation of linear autoregressive models of asset returns and the testing of the null hypothesis, whereby the coefficients of the lagged returns are equal to zero (Tsibouris and Zeidenberg, 1993:interview).

Nevertheless, the inability to refute the null hypothesis does not imply an affirmation of the efficient market hypothesis: it may simply be that there are nonlinear patterns that are linearly undetectable. A new methodology, using chaos theory, has emerged. This theory can be employed to detect nonlinear patterns. Since neural networks are capable of approximating arbitrary Borel measurement functions according to Tsibouris and Zeidenberg (1993:interview), they are able to exploit non-parametric estimation methods.

3.6 CHAOS THEORY

3.6.1 Introduction

With advancements in computer and telecommunication technologies today, the world's major economies are becoming more globalized. As this trend accelerates, financial markets and economies are becoming more and more interrelated. Accordingly, fundamental factors will become increasingly significant to financial market analysis. However, in the global marketplace, prevailing statistical methods - in which a single market is modelled through historical simulation and back-testing of its own past price behavior - are rapidly losing their competitive advantage. This is largely due to the belicf that markets are complex systems embedding the paradox between:

---

53 Where w_o, w_1, ... , w_p are the network weights derived using a suitable learning procedure.

- The orderly deterministic nature of scientific law; and
- the chance events that occur all around us or in the global market place.

However, the various linear models that have tried to capture the complexities of the economic system have not always worked very well (Just and Rausser, 1981:197-208). In some cases of short-term forecasting, the success of time series and econometric models implies that a time series is not always generated by a random process. However, the long-term failure of these models to explain behavior indicates that they have not captured the true nature of the underlying generating process (Blank, 1991:711-712). A new methodology, called nonlinear dynamics or "Chaos theory", may offer an alternative explanation for the behavior of economic phenomena. Chaos theory, analyzes whether or not a process is a deterministic system, based on the assumption that at least part of the underlying process is nonlinear. According to the literature reviewed, there has been increasing interest among economists in a new field of study that may offer an alternative explanation for the seemingly random behavior of many economic variables. However, most economic research done in the past has focused on linear, statistical and single market methods that have been the mainstay throughout the past decade.

It must be clarified that the purpose of this investigation is not a study of chaos theory. Therefore, the literature overview of this concept will be limited. However, if neural networks do indicate that share prices can be predicted, tests using chaos theory should be considered.

3.6.2 Defining chaos theory

Before a definition of chaos theory is given, a brief description of the historical development of the theory will be presented. It is generally recognized that the work of mathematician Benoit Mandelbrot, who wrote a number of papers on economics between 1962 and 1972, laid the foundation of chaos theory in the article *The variation of certain speculative prices*, published in 1963. Mandelbrot (1963:308) studied cotton spot price data, and noted that the "histograms of price changes were indeed unimodal and their central 'bells' reminded one of the 'Gaussian ogive'." He further noted that there were so many outliers that ogives fitted to the mean square of price changes were much lower and flatter than the distribution of the data itself. The tails of the distribution of price changes were, in fact, so long that the sample second moments typically varied in an erratic pattern. Mandelbrot went on to conjecture that these prices were following a form of Paretian statistics, which could account for the long tails, price gaps and price peaks skewed beneath the main. However, Cootner (1964:333) voiced misgivings about Mandelbrot's conjectures, noting that a few theoretical and empirical defects existed in his evidence. Notwithstanding the harsh criticism, Mandelbrot's findings did not prove the normal distribution obsolete. According to Steidlmayer (1993:14), what his arguments did prove is that a strange relationship between the bell-curve and chaos theory exists. The oddly shaped distribution he found in cotton spot prices became the precursor to the so-called Mandelbrot set, one of the cornerstones of chaos theory. Mandelbrot's work thus provides the basis of chaos theory, which was expanded on by other authors of economics such as Grandmont, Day, Benhabib, Brock and Scheinkman, all of whom have attempted to import the insights of chaos theory into economics (Mirowski, 1992:289).

According to Hsieh (1991:1840), chaos is a nonlinear deterministic process which "looks" random. However, in a mathematical sense, the word 'chaos' does not mean randomness (Anders, 1989:31). In randomness, the values of a time series cannot be predicted, as no predetermined causal correlation exists. From the chaos viewpoint, time series values only appear random - in reality, they are predetermined by a formula. Griffith and Southworth (1990:55) state: "The chaos theory is an attempt to prove that there is an order to seeming randomness in financial markets."

As mentioned before, from the chaos viewpoint, time series values appear random while, in reality, they are predetermined by a formula. This is why mathematicians call chaos "deterministic chaos" which is based on a theory of nonlinear growth with feedback. Griffith and Southworth (1991:54) illustrate this with the following example: "...consider...the phenomenon of 'overbought' and 'oversold' in the stock market. As share prices rise, effects such as profit-taking conspire eventually to put downward pressure on prices. However, increases in the share price do not cause profit-taking inclinations to rise by the same amount every time. The greater the rise in the shares price, the more vulnerable it is to correction. In other words, the equation is exponential rather than linear."

A time series that reflects a biased random walk or contains evidence of (anti)persistent trends within short-time horizons may be considered a nonlinear system. A nonlinear system exhibits more complex behavior than a linear system, as small changes in the input may result in disproportional changes in the output. However, a nonlinear system may display apparent random behavior even thought it is not random, and it may contain structure when viewed with the proper tools. An important reason for the interest in chaotic behavior is that it can potentially explain fluctuations in the economy and financial markets that appear to be random (Hsieh, 1991:1845).

3.6.3 Identifying chaos in a time series

Chaotic regimes have several generic properties, the identification of which is important in determining whether or not a time series exhibits chaotic behavior. Traditional linear forecasting methods may not work. Therefore, nonlinear models should be considered. The following nonlinear, generic property testing models will also be employed in this study:

- Rescaled range analysis;
- correlation dimension analysis;
- BDS test; and
- Lyapunov exponents.

Each of these tests will be discussed in subsequent subsections.

In summary, Savit (1988:271-289) lists three features necessary for a deterministic sequence to be chaotic:

- It should sample all regions of its domain;
- it should be practically unpredictable in the long-term; and
- there are many initial prices, and the sequence of prices generated by a chaotic map should be periodic, i.e., over a time sequence of the initial prices, it should eventually repeat itself.

3.6.3.1 Rescaled range analysis

Rescaled analysis is a statistical method which was introduced by Harold E Hurst in the 1940s for reservoir control, with the assumption that the uncontrollable part of the system, the influx of water from rainfall, follows a random walk.

Rescaled range analysis measures the bias or trend in a time series. The strength of the trend and the level of noise can be measured by how the rescaled range scales with time. Hurst (1951:770-779) found that most natural phenomena, including river discharges, temperatures, rainfalls, and sunspots, all follow a "biased random walk"[54]. Refer to equation 3-17, in order to determine the Hurst (H) coefficient.

---

[54] A biased random walk is a trend with noise.

$$\frac{R_N}{S} = \left(\frac{N}{2}\right)^N \qquad ...(3\text{-}17)$$

Where: N = Number of observations.

$\frac{R_N}{S}$ = Dimensionless ratio of the average range divided by the standard deviation of the daily fluctuations.

R_N = The difference between the maximum and minimum of the cumulative deviations from the average for a particular N.

Therefore, the slope of the log $\left(\frac{R_N}{S}\right)$ versus the log of N provides an estimate of the Hurst coefficient[55]. According to statistical mechanics, the Hurst coefficient should be equal to 0.5 if the series is a random walk. This is also referred to as the independent Gaussian model. A Hurst coefficient different from 0.5 can be interpreted as a bias or memory effect caused by the fact that the observations were not independent. Since each observation carries a "memory"[56] of all the events that precede it, theoretically, at least, this memory lasts forever (Peters, 1991:64). Boshoff (1983:78) states: "By such infinite memory, it is meant that the span of interdependence is longer than the longest data record examined and that is different from the mathematical concept of infinity."

A Hurst coefficient greater than 0.5 indicates a memory effect that is biased towards the reinforcement of a trend. A Hurst coefficient less than 0.5 indicates a negative bias or a tendency

---

55 The estimate of H makes no assumptions about the shape of the underlying distribution.

56 It must be noted that the memory discussed is not a short-term memory, which is referred to as a Markovian chain. A Markov chain describes the relationship between outcomes (states) in one time period and the outcomes (states) in the next period. The validity of Markov chains with reference to the securities market is questionable, since the procedure assumes that the underlying probability distribution of the data is Gaussian over time. According to Greene (1975:12), Markovian dependence vanishes quickly as the distance between the values increase, but long-term dependence has an infinite memory and the dependence never completely vanishes.

to reverse the ongoing trend, which is referred to as anti-persistence. There are three distinct classifications for the Hurst coefficient:

- **H = 0.50** - Denotes random series. Events are random and uncorrelatated.

- **H = 0 < H < 0.5** - Refers to an anti-persistent, or ergodic series. For example, if a system has been up in the previous period, it is more likely to be down in the next period. Conversely, if the period was down before, it is more likely to be up in the next period (Peters, 1991:64).

- **H = 0.5 < H < 1** - Refers to a persistent time series, which can also be described as a 'fractal', which derives from the fractal Brownian motion[57]. Peters (1991:67) asserts that, because each point is not likely, as in a random walk, the fractal dimension of the probability distribution is not 2 but, rather, it is a number between 1 and 2.

  Mandelbrot (1972:259-289), showed that the inverse of the H coefficient represents a fractal dimension. He explains this by using the following example: a random walk, with H = 0.5, would have a fractal dimension of 2. If H = 0.7, the fractal dimension would be 1/0.7 or 1.43. A fractal time series separates a pure random series from a deterministic system perturbed by random events.

The Hurst coefficient, therefore, describes the likelihood that two consecutive events will occur. For example, a Hurst coefficient of 0.6 indicates a probability of 60 percent that the current trend will continue in the current time horizon, a Hurst coefficient of 0.4 indicates that there is a 60 percent chance that the current signal will be reversed. According to Mandelbrot (1972:284), an H coefficient close to 1 could mean either a very strong long-term dependence or a non-stationary random function. He states: "...when the observed H differs from 1 by a small amount, it may be due solely to sample variation. This finding means that either the time series is stationary with a very strong long run dependence or that it is non-stationary with alternative dependencies. To distinguish between those possibilities, one must analyze both the time series and the sequence of differences of the time series." This can be achieved by scrambling the data series by a

---

57 In fractional Brownian motion, there is no correlation between events across times scales. Because of this relationship, the probability of two events following one another is not a fifty-fifty relationship.

predetermined random number. Hsieh (1991:1842) suggests that the scrambled data be obtained by applying a tent map, using the following rule: (refer to equation 3-18a and 3-18b).

$$Z_t = A_{T\text{-}1}(P) \qquad \text{...(3-18a)}$$

$$x_t = \frac{z_t}{P} \qquad \text{...(3-18b)}$$

Where: A = Any arbitrary number.

P = Large prime number.

Z_t = Integer, called a 'seed', between 0 and P. To generate new seeds, use equation 3-18a.

X_t = Uniformly distributed on the interval [0,1], in the same way as a tent map.

The Hurst coefficient can possibly be trapped by assigning an exponential type weight to past prices in a manner that approximates the nature of the fractal dimension (Boshoff, 1983:109). The Hurst coefficient can be biased at times and can indicate nonperiodic cycles where none may exist (Ambrose, Ancel and Griffiths, 1993:73). The difficulty in interpreting the H coefficient is related to the estimation procedure itself and to pre-asymptotic behavior. Some of the biases created by these problems offset each other or are mitigated by the use of a large data set. Analysis performed on a relatively short data set, without the recognition of the possibility of short-term dependence, may lead to an incorrect conclusion. These discrepancies could be overcome by employing the F-Hurst[58]and the G-Hurst[59].

---

58 For F-Hurst, all values N ≥ 3 are subperiod lengths with all possible starting points. In other words the F-Hurst uses every possible subseries size with all starting points.

59 In G-Hurst computations, a sample of evenly distributed values of N are generated and, for each value of N, a selection of starting points is used to estimate an average R/S value for each subperiod length. Therefore, the G-Hurst reduces the number of observation by selecting uniformly spaced subseries sizes and starting values.

3.6.3.2 Correlation dimension analysis

The second nonlinearity test which can be employed to determine if chaos exists in a time series involves the correlation dimension. For the purposes of this study, the concept of correlation will suffice. The idea behind correlation dimension analysis is to develop a non-parametric statistical test of the null hypothesis that a scalar time series {x(t)} is or is not independently and identically distributed **IID** (Brock, Dechert, Scheinkman and LeBaron, 1988:1).

According to Ramsey, Sayers, and Rothman (1983:3), correlation dimension is "a measure of the rate of scaling the density of points within a given space..." It should be noted that the Hurst coefficient deals with fractal dimensions based on time-based data, whereby a time series will have a dimension between one and two, mainly because it involves only a single variable. However, correlation dimension analysis involves fractal dimensions in phase space, whereby all the variables are included in a system, and according to Peters (1991:155), its dimensionality is dependent on the complexity of the system being studied.

Correlation dimension is, therefore, an estimation of the fractal dimension that measures the probability that two points chosen at random will be within a certain distance of each other and furthermore examines how this probability changes as the distance is increased. According to Peters (1991:232), "White noise will fill its space because its components are uncorrelated and its correlation dimension is equal to whatever dimension it is placed in. A dependent system will be held together by its correlations and will retain its dimension in whatever embedding dimension[60] it is placed, as long as the embedding dimension is greater than the fractal dimension."

The correlation dimension method that was first proposed by Grassberger and Procaccia (1983:189-208) is performed in the following four steps:

- Step 1: Remove autocorrelation, if present. The purpose of this is to remove long-term linear dependency due to share price appreciation (Mulieri, 1991:31). The data can be detrended using ordinary least squares and autoregressive methods, and deseasonalized and transformed as described by Baumol and Benhabib (1989:77-79). After the completion of this process, each residual series satisfies the **IID** assumptions of the random walk hypothesis.

---

60 The space the object is embedded in.

- Step 2: Calculation of the correlation integral $C_m(R)$ for this distance is made using equation 3-19:

$$C_M(R) = \left(\frac{1}{N^2}\right) \times \sum_{i,j=1}^{N} Z(R - |X_i - X_j|) \qquad \text{...(3-19)}$$

Where: $Z(x)$[61] = 1 if $R - |X_i - X_j| > 0$; 0 otherwise.

N = Number of observations.

R = Distance or scale lengths.

C_m = Correlation integral for dimension m.

X_i = Vector-valued observation in a time series.

X_j = Vector-valued observation in a time series.

- Step 3: Calculation of the correlation dimension. If the values of R, C_m should increase at a rate of R to the power of the fractal dimension (Hsieh, 1991:1846), the following relations exists (refer to equation 3-20).

  $$LOG\ (C_M) = D \times LOG\ (R) + CONSTANT \qquad \text{...(3-20)}$$

  By finding the slope of a graph of the log (C_m) with the log (R) through a linear regression, the correlation dimension (D) can be estimated for the embedding dimension (m).

- Step 4: Interpretation of the correlation dimension. Three independent, but similar measures of nonlinear dependence, using dimension estimates apply:

  - If the correlation dimension continues to grow with a corresponding embedding dimension, this indicates that nonlinear dependence exists;

---

61 Z(x) is called a Heaviside function, because it is valued at 0 if the distance between points X_i and X_j is less than R, and at 1 if two points chosen at random are less than R units apart (Peters, 1991:156). The correlation integral is the probability that two points chosen at random are less than R units apart.

- if the correlation dimension estimates are small relative to the associated embedding dimension, this implies the presence of nonlinear dependence in the data; and
- a third test, called the shuffle diagnostic, which was developed by Scheinkman and LeBaron (1989:317). This procedure consists of forming a "scrambled" residual data set by sampling from the residual time series randomly with replacement, and comparing the relative correlation dimension estimates of the original and "scrambled" residual series. If the correlation estimates for the original series are significantly smaller than those for the "scrambled" series, then it can be concluded that the original series contains nonlinear dependencies.

In conclusion, it should be noted that the graphical method associated with correlation dimensions does exhibit the following flaws:

- Scheinkman and LeBaron (1989:314) point out that there is no way to verify that a process has an infinite correlation dimension, using a finite amount of data.

- Ramsey and Yaun (1991:287-297) show that the slope of the graph of $\log(C_m)$ versus $\log(R)$ is biased downward in small data sets. This biases the results in favor of finding chaos, even if there is none.

- Hsieh (1991:1847) comments on the graphical procedure test: "Ideally, we want a way to quantify the accuracy of the correlation dimension. This is not readily available for the correlation dimension plots."

To overcome a few of the shortcomings of correlation dimension analysis, Brock, Dechert, and Scheinkman proposed the so-called BDS test, discussed in section 3.6.3.3.

3.6.3.3 The Brock, Dechert, and Scheinkman (BDS) test

The BDS test is a statistical test based on the correlation integral, devised to overcome problems associated with using Grassberger-Procaccia plots. The test relies on two components of dynamical systems:

- Attractors; and
- correlation dimension (refer to 3.6.3.2).

- An attractor is a set of points towards which the dynamical path of a system converges. A formal definition of an attractor is found in Ramsey (1990:125): "An attractor is a concept set A, such that the set of the orbit $\{X_n\}$, as $n \to \infty$, is A, for almost all initial conditions within the neighborhood of A."

$$W_m(R,N) = \sqrt{N}\left(\frac{D_m(R,N)}{b_m(R,N)}\right) \qquad \textbf{...(3-21)}$$

Where: W_m = BDS statistic.
R = Distance (different scale lengths).
N = Number of observations.
m = Embedding dimension.
b_m = Estimate of the standard deviation[62].
D_m = $C_m - (C_m)^m$.
C_m = Correlation integral for dimension m.

Refer to equation 3-21. According to Brock and Dechert (1991:123), the BDS test detects misspecification caused by the linear mode (being made to fit to nonlinear data), as indicated by a nonzero value. The BDS results are interpreted as follows:

- $W = 0$ - This indicates a stochastic process.

- $W =$ very large - This indicates evidence of a misspecified nonlinear model.

- $W > 1.96$ - Statistically nonlinear mode appears to exist at the 5 percent level.

---

62 Where $b_m = (1, - mC_{m-1})' \sum (1, - mC_{m-1})$.

The BDS test can distinguish between a linear and a nonlinear generating process. However, it cannot detect whether that process is stochastic or deterministic. Therefore, additional evidence, such as that which may be provided by the Lyapunov exponents (discussed in the subsequent section), is needed to make this distinction.

3.6.3.4 Lyapunov exponents

Once the fractal dimension of a nonlinear signal is known and it is has been established that there is evidence of chaos (through the presence of strange attractors in phase space), then it is possible to estimate the predictability of the signal. This process is based on Takens theorem, which states that, if chaotic attributes are found in a time series, then, from a single dimension of that time series, it is possible to extrapolate the dynamics of the series within a range specified by the Lyapunov exponents. It is generally understood that Lyapunov exponents can be used to estimate the ability to predict nonlinear signals.

To compute the largest Lyapunov exponent, a method was developed by Wolf, Swift, Swinney and Vastano (1985:285-317). The method suggested by the authors measures the divergence of nearby points in the reconstructed phase space, and indicates how the rate of divergence scales over fixed intervals of time. Refer to equation 3-22, for the formal equation of the algorithm.

$$L_1 = \left(\frac{1}{t}\right) \times \sum_{j=1}^{m} LOG_2 \left(\frac{L'(t_{j+1})}{L'(t_j)}\right) \qquad \text{...(3-22)}$$

Where: $L'(t_{j+1})$ = Provides the average rate of convergence and divergence.
$L'(t_j)$ = Calculates the varied sample of points on a trajectory in phase space.

As expressed previously the purpose of the Lyapunov exponent is to determine whether a turbulent time series, such as a share price time series, is truly chaotic with a strange attractor, or merely random. Any system which contains at least one positive Lyapunov exponent is usually defined as chaotic, with the magnitude of the exponent reflecting the time scale on which the system dynamics become unpredictable.

3.6.3.5 Conclusion

It must be reiterated that the purpose of discussing chaos theory is to provide an alternative school of thought in the forecasting of share prices. Chaos theory has been gaining quite a lot of popularity in the United States of America as an alternative theory to the efficient market hypothesis.

The primary objectives of research in financial markets are to:

- To understand the nature of the market; and
- to predict the market.

According to Nichols (1993:50), modern finance, especially the efficient market hypothesis, is under attack from both the pragmatic and philosophical schools. This is based on two phenomena:

- Globalization of the financial markets; and
- the technological firepower of their participants.

However, one of the staunchest attacks on modern finance has come from Fama and French (1992:152), who launched an attack on the Capital Asset Pricing Model, and conclude that the model does not describe the last 50 years of average stock returns. This implies that β is not an appropriate predicator of risk, suggesting either that the Capital Asset Pricing Model is wrong, or markets are not efficient, or both. However, Shirreff (1993:61) states, referring to an interview with Fama: "...he insists a [share] price does adjust efficiently to information specific to one company...rejects beta and weakens his views on the EMH."

It should be noted that, at this time and due to the lack of research on the application of chaos theory to the financial markets, this study only provides exploratory research on the subject.

In summary, it can be stated that supporters of chaos theory insist that the notion of 'efficient markets' is a myth, the reason being that investors interpret information haphazardly and irrationally.

3.7 CONCLUSION

The purpose of this chapter was to provide a background on the schools of thought in the forecasting of share prices. The sections on technical and fundamental analysis provided background on technical indicators and fundamental factors which may be considered as inputs for a neural network model. The sections on statistical methods of forecasting provided a benchmark for comparing neural networks with existing statistical methods. The efficient market hypothesis and chaos theory indicated two schools of thought regarding whether or not share prices can be predicted.

Chapter 4 will provide an overview of the research methodology employed in this study.

CHAPTER 4

RESEARCH DESIGN

Man's greatest limitation is the one created in his own mind.
-- Charles-Albert Poissant

4.1 INTRODUCTION

The main thrust of this study is to determine whether neural networks can be utilized in the forecasting of share prices. The theoretical crux of neural networks and the various schools of thought in the forecasting of share prices have been presented in Chapters 2 and 3. This chapter describes the method whereby the effectiveness of neural networks in forecasting may be empirically explored.

The objectives of this study were identified in Chapter 1, but will be repeated here for convenience (refer to Table 4.1).

Table 4.1 - The research objectives of the study

	Objective
1	To develop and implement a neural network model for the forecasting of share prices
2	To identify and investigate the factors that affect the performance of the neural network forecasting model
3	To determine the applicability of a neural network as a forecasting model in comparison with the Box-Jenkins model
4	To determine whether or not the Johannesburg Stock Exchange exhibits chaos

The research design will be carried out via three phases of an experiment. The first phase of the experiment will deal with the development process and the forecasting abilities of neural network models, according to objectives 1 and 2 as listed in the table. The second phase of the experiment will include the construction of a Box-Jenkins model for forecasting the share price time series in connection with objective 3, whereby a comparison between the two methodologies will be performed. The third phase will include a preliminary analysis of the data to determine whether the time series exhibits chaos (nonlinear dependencies). Upon completion of all three phases of the experiment, the results will be reviewed. Final conclusions will be provided in Chapter 5.

4.2 NEURAL NETWORK RESEARCH DESIGN

The crux of this research is to conduct an experimental study to evaluate the effectiveness of neural network implementation, by developing a neural network model for the forecasting of share prices. The specific research hypothesis that this phase seeks to address is the second hypothesis of the study, which states that *the forecasting accuracy of a neural network model is related to the architecture of the network model.* Therefore, the goal is to identify the simplest network, composed of the fewest possible processing elements and connections, which is able to predict with a high level of accuracy. The research methodology and approach employed in phase one areas are summarized in Figure 4.1. The purpose of the proposed methodology and procedures are described as:

- To provide a consistent, disciplined research approach to developing neural network models.

- To maximize the performance of the models developed.

4.2.1 Collection of the data

As stated in Chapter 3, in order for a neural network to make a forecast, historical data has to be presented to the neural network in the form of inputs. The multiplicity of factors complicates the choice and it is almost impossible to be aware of all the possibilities.

Figure 4.1 - Neural network methodology

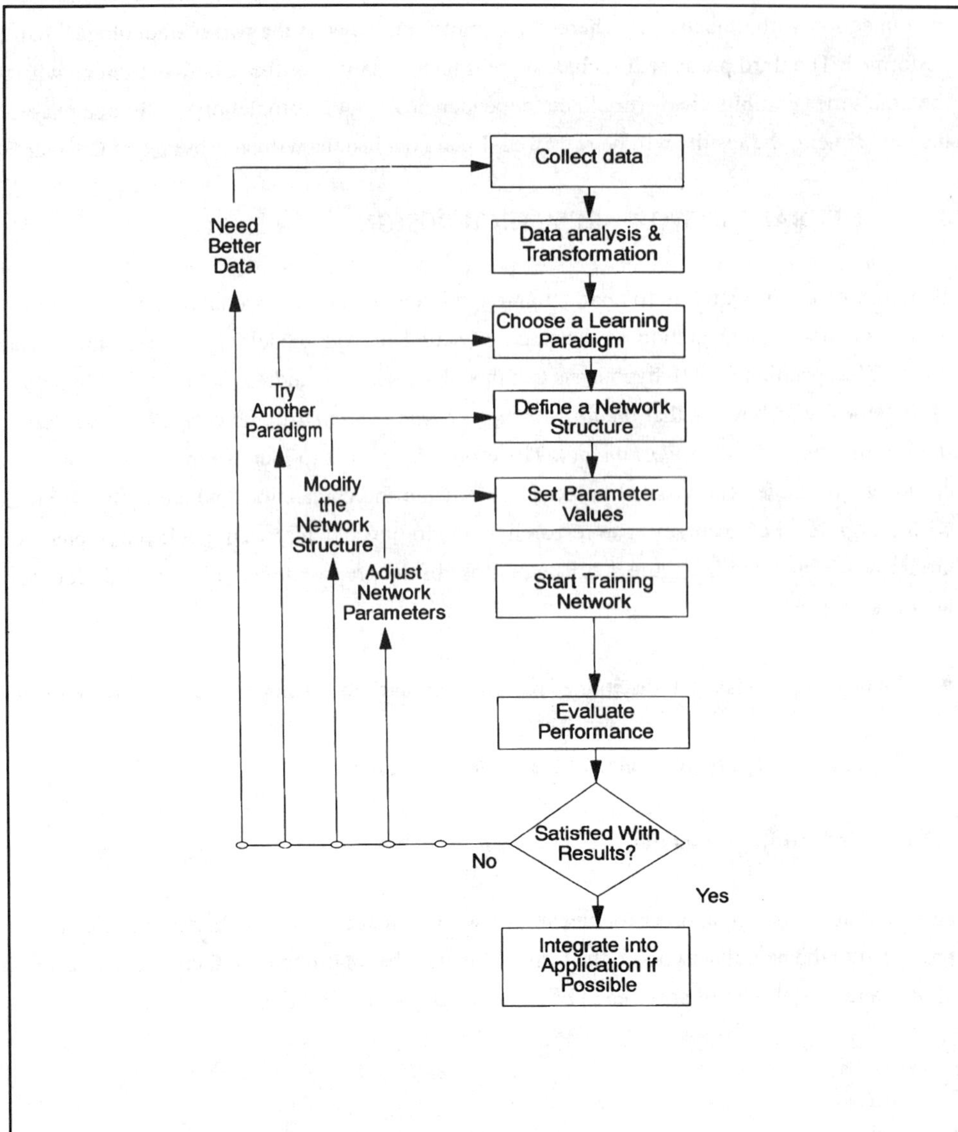

This study has been guided in part by the practicality of performing a large number of calculations. The choice of input is critical in the construction of a neural network, as poor selection can result in an inferior input-output mapping and reduced network performance (References, Zapranis and Bentz, 1993:6). Neural networks are good at picking up underlying relationships implied by the data, but they can do so only as long as these relationships exist. Though neural networks may be able to identify relationships which are not identifiable by conventional non-parametric methods, they should not be blurred by contradictory mappings and, generally, should not be asymmetrically amplified by strong inter-correlations.

The selection of possible influential factors of a share is no trivial task. A lot of influential factors exist, which are neither clearly explained in theory nor clearly identifiable in empirical work. Additionally, factors can develop quite dynamically over time, whereby their degree of influence on the closing price can vary. Possible instability between structural relationships in the data can occur over time and, thus, should be considered. The selection of influential factors should be as representative as possible of the underlying process. They embody an environment within which the neural network fulfills structural analysis. Therefore, it may be necessary to implement a large number of factors into the model in order to increase the probability that the task-oriented environment will be adequately described. According to Gerke and Baun (1993:5), a large number of factors simultaneously enlarges the degrees of freedom in the form of network interconnection weights.

The selection of the inputs was achieved by employing the following approaches:

- Empirical inductive approach - This approach lends itself to the identification of attributes regarding early warning behavior such as the time-lagged structure of the factors, and the calculation of correlations between time-lagged input time series and their corresponding target values.

- Logical deductive approach - This approach supports expert queries concerning the following:

  - Are there any technical indicators which have proved their significance in the field of technical analysis?;
  - which alternating effects of the variables can be described in a mathematical form?;
  - does a common theory exist for the specific forecasting task?; and
  - a thorough review of existing share price forecasting literature for factors which could possibly affect share prices.

When selecting input data, the implications of following a market theory should be kept in mind. Existing market inefficiencies can be detected quantitatively through the use of neural networks. Individual perspectives on the markets also influence the choice of data. Technical analysis may suggest the use of only single-market price data as inputs. However, with neural networks, a synergistic approach can be followed which combines multiple approaches to share price forecasting, because neural networks do not subscribe to any particular form of analysis. That is, they attempt to use all of the input information provided.

The inputs which were identified (and are discussed subsequently) are based on domain knowledge coupled with various statistical analysis tools to determine the correlation between the data and the target market price data. The inputs can be grouped into the following:

- Fundamental inputs;
- technical inputs;
- Johannesburg Stock Exchange indices;
- international indices;
- gold price and foreign exchange rates;
- interest rates; and
- economic statistics.

It should be noted that the data used for the neural network model is not subject to the following statistically related problems:

- Measurement errors;
- misspecification of the model form;
- autocorrelation in the residuals; and
- multicollinearity[63].

---

63 Collinearity occurs when two variables have a correlation greater than 0.70 or less than -0.70 in a regression model, the final result being that the two variables explain the same proportion of variation, where either variable would be sufficient.

The inputs employed in the neural network model are summarized in Table 4.2. Each input has been given an appropriate input number, as well as a brief description in Table 4.2. All later discussions will be conducted by referring to the input number only (applicable to Chapter 5).

Table 4.2 - Inputs used in the construction of the neural network model(s)

Grouping	Input number	Input description
Fundamental inputs	Input 1	Volume
	Input 2	Dividend yield
	Input 3	Price-earnings ratio
Technical inputs	Input 4	Exponential moving average (Price)
	Input 5	Exponential moving average (Volume)
	Input 6	Moving average oscillator (Price)
	Input 7	Moving average oscillator (Volume)
	Input 8	Stochastic indicator (%D)
	Input 9	Stochastic indicator (%K)
	Input 10	Relative strength index
	Input 11	Moving average convergence-divergence (Fast exponential average)
	Input 12	Moving average convergence-divergence (Slow exponential average)
	Input 13	Moving average convergence-divergence (Close)
	Input 14	Log-Delta
	Input 15	Momentum (Price)
	Input 16	Momentum (Volume)
	Input 17	Rate of change
	Input 18	On-balance volume

Grouping	Input number	Input description
	Input 19	Volatility (true range)
	Input 20	Volatility (moving average)
Johannesburg Stock Exchange indices	Input 21	JSE - Industrial holdings index
	Input 22	JSE - Beverages, Hotels and Leisure index
	Input 23	JSE - Building and Construction index
	Input 24	JSE - Chemicals and oils index
	Input 25	JSE - Clothing, Footwear and Textiles index
	Input 26	JSE - Electronics index
	Input 27	JSE - Engineering index
	Input 28	JSE - Fishing index
	Input 29	JSE - Food index
	Input 30	JSE - Motor index
	Input 31	JSE - Paper and Packaging index
	Input 32	JSE - Pharmaceutical and Medical index
	Input 33	JSE - Printing and Publishing index
	Input 34	JSE - Steel index
	Input 35	JSE - Sugar index
	Input 36	JSE - Retailers and Wholesalers index
	Input 37	JSE - Transportation index
	Input 38	JSE - Industrial index
	Input 39	JSE - Overall index
	Input 40	JSE - Gold index
International indices	Input 41	Standard and Poor 500 index
	Input 42	ASA investment corporation index
	Input 43	Brent oil index

Grouping	Input number	Input description
	Input 44	Dow Jones industrial index
	Input 45	Dow Jones transport index
	Input 46	Dow Jones utilities index
	Input 47	Financial Times 30 index
	Input 48	Financial Times gold index
	Input 49	Toronto-Gold index
Gold price and foreign exchange rates	Input 50	Gold-Pm closing price
	Input 51	Dollar-Rand exchange rate
	Input 52	Financial-Rand exchange rate
Interest rates	Input 53	Bank acceptance rate
	Input 54	Eskom 168 rate
	Input 55	Eskom 166 rate
	Input 56	Prime rate
Economic statistics	Input 57	Inflation rate
	Input 58	Export: Total, including bullion
	Input 59	Imports: Total
	Input 60	Liquidations - companies
	Input 61	Insolvencies
	Input 62	Wholesale trade - Total (Real)
	Input 63	Total manufacturing producers index

The output value for the neural network was selected from daily share prices of 45 industrial listed shares over the period 1/2/1991 - 12/31/1992. Data over the period 1/2/1986 - 12/31/1992 is available for testing for nonlinearities in daily share prices should the need be established. Refer to Table 4.3 for shares selected for the output value. Selection criteria will be discussed.

Table 4.3 - Selection of industrial shares used in the summation of the output value

Sector	Share name	Forms part of an index
Retailers & Wholesalers	Edgars stores (Ltd)	X
	Hi-Score holdings (Ltd)	
	OK Bazaars (1929) (Ltd)	
	CNA Gallo (Ltd)	X
	Walton stationary (Ltd)	
	Wooltru (Ltd)	X
Chemicals & Oils	AECI (Ltd)	
	OMNIA (Ltd)	
Clothing, Footwear & Textiles	Da Gama textile company (Ltd)	X
	Seardel investment corporation (Ltd)	X
Electronics	African cables (Ltd)	
	Allied technologies (Ltd)	X
	Ventron corporation (Ltd)	
	Powtech (Ltd)	X
Paper & Packaging	Canadian overseas package industries (Ltd)	
	Holdain (Ltd)	
	Sappi (Ltd)	X
Building & Construction	Anglo Alpha (Ltd)	X
	LTA	X
	Pretoria Portland Cement company (Ltd)	X
	York Timber Organization (Ltd)	

Sector	Share name	Forms part of an index
Engineering	Cementation company (Africa) (Ltd)	
	Fralex (Ltd)	
	Haggie (Ltd)	X
	Edward L Batemann (Ltd)	
	INMINS (Ltd)	
	Unihold (Ltd)	
Fishing	Namibian Sea products (Ltd)	X
	Oceana fishing group (Ltd)	
Food	C G Smith Foods (Ltd)	
	Irvin & Johnson (Ltd)	
Motor	Gentyre industries 'A' (Ltd)	X
	Toyota South Africa (Ltd)	X
Beverages & Hotels	SA Breweries (Ltd)	X
	Suncrush (Ltd)	
Industrial holdings	Anglo American Industrial Corporation (Ltd)	X
	Barlow Rand (Ltd)	X
	Farm-Ag (Ltd)	
	Safmarine & Rennies holdings (Ltd)	X
	W & A Investment corporation (Ltd)	
	UTICO holdings (Ltd)	
Pharmaceutical & Medical	Medi-Clinic corporation (Ltd)	

Sector	Share name	Forms part of an index
Steel & Allied	Highveld steel & vanadium corporation (Ltd)	X
Printing & Publishing	Times Media (Ltd)	X
Transportation	Laser transport holding (Ltd)	

4.2.2 Selection of output values

4.2.2.1 The population size

The share population size comprised 128 eligible industrial shares listed on the Johannesburg Stock Exchange as of December 31, 1986. Refer to Table 4.4 which describes the population from which the sample was drawn in terms of the various sub-sectors that make up the industrial sector.

Table 4.4 - The sample size

Sector	Number of eligible shares	Percentage of total population	Sample size
Beverages & Hotels	3	2	1[64]
Building & Construction	12	1	4
Chemical & Oils	6	5	2
Clothing, Footwear & Textiles	9	7	2
Electronics	11	9	4
Engineering	18	14	6
Fishing	3	2	2

---

64 The sample size was calculated by multiplying the number of eligible shares by the sample size percentage (35%); therefore, the Beverages & Hotels sample size is calculated as follows: $3 \times 0.35 = 1$.

Sector	Number of eligible shares	Percentage of total population	Sample size
Food	6	5	2
Furniture & Household	0	0	0
Industrial Holdings	21	17	7
Motor	5	4	2
Paper & packaging	8	6	3
Pharmaceutical & Medical	2	2	1
Printing & Publishing	3	2	1
Retailers & Wholesalers	17	13	6
Steel & Allied	2	2	1
Tobacco & Match	0	0	0
Transportation	2	2	1
TOTAL	128	100	45

For the purposes of this study, the findings of Klerck's cluster analysis research (1980:152), which grouped the JSE into two homogenous groups, were assumed. Klerck refers to:

- the gold group; and
- the non-gold group.

This study has been confirmed by Carter (1983:4.53), who used multi-dimensional scaling and clustering techniques. This study will focus on the non-gold group (namely, the industrial sector[65]), since the Klerck study indicates that gold share prices are affected by a different set of factors compared to non-gold shares.

---

65 Carter (1983:4.52) indicates that sectors within the industrial and financial index exhibit no tendencies to be grouped together in any rational or consistent manner.

4.2.2.2 Selection criteria

The overall industrial sector consisted of more than the 128 eligible shares. However, for the purposes of this study, a share was found to be eligible if the following data could be obtained for the period 2/18/1986 - 12/31/1992, since this was the extent of data available for the study:

- Daily closing share price of a share;
- daily volume figures; and
- daily dividend and price-earnings yield.

The principal data requirement was that the data had to be obtained at minimal cost and on a daily basis so that the model could be employed by private as well as institutional investors. Examples of data sources are:

- Daily newspapers;
- financial magazines; and
- share data vendors.

One might ask, why the study only focused on a group of shares to the exclusion of a single share. According to Fishman (1993:interview), neural networks are far more powerful than traditional statistical methods in that they can be predictive, even in dynamic systems in which the relationships to be elicited are nonlinear and complex. Nevertheless, they are prone to the same vulnerabilities as classical statistics when there is excessive noise or randomness. This is also the case when there are too many nongeneral and idiosyncratic sources of variance in the training cases used. As with other data, share market time series are more predictable in the aggregate where individual sources of idiosyncratic variance or randomness have a chance to cancel each other out.

4.2.2.3 Sampling

Stratified random proportional sampling was employed, whereby the population was divided into subgroups (provided by the sectorial division of the Johannesburg Stock Exchange, as per the Actuarial Society of South Africa in *The JSE Actuaries Equity Indices 1992*). However, it should be noted that since a proportional sampling was performed, there is a possibility that shares representing an entire sector may not be included. Furthermore, the Furniture and Household and the Tobacco and Match sectors were not sampled, as data was unavailable for these sectors.

For the purposes of comparison with Klerck's study (1980:289-306), which used a population of 71 shares that was eventually reduced to 21 eligible shares (30 percent), it was decided to sample only 35 percent of the population, with a 95 percent confidence interval. The objective here was to obtain a representative selection and thereby increase the probability of realizing a set of significant parameters. This resulted in the selection of 45 listed shares (refer to Table 4.4).

4.2.2.4 Selection of input values

The forecasting of future share prices can follow two distinct approaches. The first, and most powerful approach, depends on the exact knowledge of the laws underlying share price movements. When this knowledge is expressed in terms of precise equations, which, in principle, can be solved, it is possible to predict a future share price once the initial conditions have been completely specified. Azem-Barac, Chen and Karoussos (1993:46) comprehend that the main problem with this approach is that knowledge of the rules governing the behavior of share prices is not always readily available. One possible source of this problem may be the instability of the parameters. However, it is more likely that these problems are caused by the lack of nonlinearities in dividends.

A second, less powerful method for predicting share prices relies on the discovery of strong empirical regularities in the observed system. This represents the approach followed in this study. Several researchers (Kimito and Asakawa, 1990:10) have attempted to use neural networks to predict future share prices by extracting knowledge from the past. This approach, which proposes the use of time-space patterns of factors which could possibly influence share prices, assumes that the share closing price is related to changes in a single time series.

As stated earlier, neural network technology can be applied for the purpose of capturing nonlinear relationships between variables. This study will examine whether or not neural networks can uncover nonlinear and complex relationships between share prices, economic variables, and company characteristics. It should be noted that there are hundreds of possible variables which could possibly affect a share's price, each having infinite possible relationships that could link the variables to share prices. The multiplicity of factors complicates the choice of variables and it is almost impossible to be aware of all the possibilities.

4.2.3 Fundamental Factors (Inputs 1-3)

The criteria employed in the selection of the fundamental factors were:

- Daily back-data for the period February 18, 1986 to December 31, 1992 had to be obtainable; and
- fundamental measurements had to be obtained on a daily basis.

The only three fundamental factors that fulfilled these requirements were:

- Volume;
- dividend yield; and
- price-earnings ratio.

It should be kept in mind throughout the selection of the inputs that neural networks provide a means of capturing nonlinear relationships between variables.

4.2.3.1 Volume (Input 1)

In the language of the stock market, volume refers to the number of shares that have changed hands on a given day. It might be argued that volume is more a technical factor rather than a fundamental factor. However, some find that volume is more of a fundamental factor which represents a measurement of supply and demand based on the perception of a firm's specific characteristics. Arnold (1993:33-34), suggests the following basic rules for volume analysis:

- When prices are rising and volume is increasing, the price will continue to rise;
- when prices are rising and volume is decreasing, the price will decelerate and then turn downward;
- when prices are falling and volume is increasing, the present trend will continue; and
- when volume is not rising or falling, the effect on the price is neutral.

There is an analogy on the stock exchange which states that "volume precedes price". Numerous studies have been done to research this, however, results have been inconclusive. It would be interesting to consider whether this analogy would be valid for a neural network model. However,

Saloner (1977:76), in his study of trading volume on the Johannesburg Stock Exchange, concludes that no relationship exists between the price level of a share and its annual trading volume.

4.2.3.2 Dividend yield (Input 2)

The future value of a share price is the present value of future cash flows. The cash flow of a share has two components: periodic payments of such things as dividends and interest and the value at the time the share is sold. On the basis of the cash flow component, two share price valuation hypotheses have been developed:

- the dividend hypothesis; and
- the earnings hypothesis.

It seems plausible that dividends and changes in market value should determine the value of shares. Also plausible is the belief that earnings matter. A choice between plausible and superficially inconsistent beliefs is unnecessary because, as Miller and Modigliani (1961:411-433) state, "...once the underlying assumptions are made explicit and understood, the two hypotheses are equivalent in a world of uncertainty without taxes and transaction costs." Lorie, Dodd and Kimpton (1985:33-34) feel that the reconciliation of the two hypotheses lies in making explicit the capital expenditure program of a company whose stock is being valued. Once this has been established, the values of shares are solely determined by real considerations and, in each case, the earning power of a company's asset investment policy.

Dividend yields have long been used to evaluate the expected returns from investment in common shares (Goetzmann and Jorion, 1993:664-665). Therefore, the dividend yield is the return accruing to an investor on a share based on the current dividend rate and current price, and provides a market measure of return (refer to equation 4-1).

$$Dividend\ yield = \frac{Dividend\ per\ share}{Market\ price\ per\ share} \times \frac{100}{1} \qquad \textbf{...(4-1)}$$

It is sometimes assumed that there is a substantial positive correlation between the dividend yield and the closing price, as the denominator of the dividend yield formula is the closing price. In research done by Goetzmann and Jorion (1993:663-679), who tested the predictive power of dividend yields using bootstrap methodology and simulations to examine the distribution of test statistics under the null hypothesis of no forecasting ability, it was found that no strong evidence existed to indicate that dividend yields can be used to forecast share prices.

4.2.3.3 Price-earnings ratio (P/E ratio) (Input 3)

The second daily market measure available is the price-earnings ratio, which measures the multiple by which the market capitalizes the earnings-per-share of a company at a given time. According to Du Plessis and Mostert (1990:156), the "...price-earnings ratio is one of the yardsticks most often used to measure the relative status of a share...it serves as a good basis for comparing the relative status of a share." It should be noted that the P/E ratio is influenced by the following factors (Peavy III and Goodman, 1985:64):

- Inflation;
- company debt ratios; and
- company profit margins.

A vast amount of research has been done on the predictive power of earnings and price-earnings in the formulation of a future share price. These studies have concluded that the P/E ratio can be employed as a predictive indicator because the price-earnings ratio is a yardstick often used to measure the relative status of share. Based on this status, the investor will make a decision to purchase or sell a share which, in turn, affects a share price by the normal forces of supply and demand (refer to equation 4-2).

$$Price-earnings\ ratio\ (P/E) = \frac{Market\ price\ per\ share}{Earnings\ per\ share} \quad \text{...(4-2)}$$

As with the dividend yield, it is sometimes assumed that there is a substantially large positive correlation between the P/E ratio and the closing price of share, largely because of the fact that the numerator of the yield is the closing price. Du Plessis and Mostert (1990:156) state that "if a realistic P/E can be determined, it is possible to predict the future market price."

4.2.4 Technical indicators (Inputs 4-20)

From a technical point-of-view of the stock market, it is sometimes assumed that the past price behavior of share prices and correlated information can aid in the prediction of future short-term trends. Neural networks, with their unique self-adaptive capabilities, are able to perform pattern recognition in very noisy time series (White, 1988:23), and are ideally suited for learning patterns in the market and reorganizing them with a high degree of accuracy. For this reason a neural network will be employed where the relationships between a set of past technical indicators and the closing price will indicate when to buy or sell. According to Neftci and Policano (1984:466) "[Technical analysis] may be a crude way of taking nonlinearities into account." Therefore, an abstract synthetic indicator will be used for comparison purposes. The neural network implementation will use data transformed using a set of various technical indicators and volume data, which are claimed to have some forecasting validity[66]. The underlying assumption for using technical indicators for preprocessing financial data is that traders believe these transformations provide useful insights into how the markets will perform in the future regarding trends and turning points. If technical indicators do actually enhance the usefulnessness of the data, they should improve the ability of a neural network to predict market trends and turning points, since neural networks provide the ability to fuse data across multiple markets.

The choice of technical analysis indicators employed in this study was based on the findings of Van Eyden (1991:119) which included an analysis of fifteen different technical analysis techniques in the forecasting of share prices based on:

- Return;
- primary indicator;
- accuracy;
- rating; and
- term.

---

66 The neural network employed in this study assumes that share prices are predictable from temporal and spatial patterns in a set of technical indicators. The neural network will only take a limited set of quantitative technical indicators, selected from those used most often in technical analysis, into account.

The findings indicate that technical analysis is primarily a short-term forecasting instrument[67]. The selection of technical indicators was based on the work of Van Eyden and the work of Lukac, Brorsen and Irwin (1990:14-27). Twelve indicators were selected. Background discussion of each of the indicators selected was provided in Chapter 3 with the exception of the moving average oscillator and volatility (which will be subsequently discussed). For the purposes of convenience, each of the selected indicators will be briefly discussed[68].

The technical indicators used as inputs are:

- The exponential moving average - this moving average calculates an exponential moving average of the closing price or volume. A decay factor was chosen that corresponds to the fractional value which approximates the smoothing characteristics of a moving average parameter value for n = 18, for both the closing price (Input 4) and volume (Input 5).

- The moving average oscillator - (not discussed in Chapter 3) this belongs to the technical analysis group of moving averages. The moving average oscillator calculates the difference between two moving averages. The moving average oscillator measures the rate of change between two moving averages. A moving average oscillator using a parameter value for n = 9 days was employed on the closing price (Input 6) and on volume (Input 7).

- The stochastic indicator - this is an overbought/oversold indicator which compares today's price to the previous highest and lowest prices. This data is then transformed into a range between 0 and 100 and smoothed. The stochastic indicator calculates two values:

---

67 Confirmed by research done by McAdam (1991:74) on the use of technical analysis in the commodity currency and share markets, based on the Johannesburg Stock Exchange.

68 The choice of the **n** (how many days in the past a comparison has to be made) and **m** (the size of the block for on average of the historical values) used with the various indicators was determined by a software optimization program. The value generated by the optimization program was the most optimized value which took the highest return over a five year period into account.

- %K - is computed by taking the difference between the most recent close and the lowest low of the last m days divided by the difference between the highest high and the lowest low of the last m days. The m value applied to the closing price was 21 (Input 9).

- %D - is the n-day moving average of %K. The n value applied to the closing price was 13 (Input 8).

- The relative strength index - this index measures the relative strength of upward movements in price compared to downward movements. Generally, earlier trend-detection techniques tried to eliminate noise, or small changes in prices, to reveal the underlying trend. However, the relative strength index actually uses the characteristics of this noise to follow the trend, and even to warn of imminent changes in the trend. Therefore, the relative strength index is an oscillator which indicates the relationship between an up movement and a down movement, where a stated time period is used to define the extent of this set. A relative strength index value of n = 21 was applied to the closing price (Input 10).

- The moving average convergence-divergence (MACD) - the MACD attempts to determine when a share price is going to change direction by calculating the exponential moving average of the difference between a fast and a slow moving average. A fast exponential moving average was applied to the closing price with a value of n = 12 (Input 11). A slow exponential was then applied to the closing price with a value of n = 26 (Input 12). Finally, a smoothed exponential moving average was calculated with a value of n = 9 (Input 13).

- Log-Delta (Input 14) - it calculates the logarithm of the difference between the current and previous closing prices.

- The momentum - this indicator utilizes price and volume statistics for determining the strength or weakness of a given market and identifying turning points within that market. A momentum value of 10 was applied to both the closing price (Input 15) and volume (Input 16).

- Rate of change - it divides the current closing price by the previous closing price. An n value of 9 was used to calculate the rate of change indicator using closing prices (Input 17).

- On-balance volume - it helps the analyst identify internal strengths and weaknesses of a specific share by providing quantitative information relating volume data to price movement (Input 18).

- Volatility - (not discussed in Chapter 3) The incorporation of the volatility indicator was suggested by Fishman (1993:interview). Volatility is an index computed from an exponential moving average of the true range[69] (Input 19) over a certain n period. An n value of 12 was applied to closing prices (Input 20).

4.2.5 The Johannesburg Stock Exchange indices (Inputs 21- 40)

Since macro-economic time series exhibit smoothing and averaging characteristics, they do not capture all the information available to a market during a certain time period. The effect of this is that market returns and share prices are, at best, weakly related to data that is very noisy relative to macro-economic factors. This bias should be more helpful to establishing a linkage between the time series of market indices and share prices than between share prices and macro variables. To examine the relationship between traditional market indices and the market, all the industrial sector indices as well as broad general indices were included as inputs. As current share prices may reflect the expectations of future earnings, so may the movements in sectorial indices. Research done by Shave (1976:5) on the predictable power of sectoral indices confirms this postulation. From this, it can be inferred that expected future profit performance will be reflected in current sectoral indices with differing lead periods. Furthermore, Barr[70](1990:22) indicates that the Gold index, Industrial index, and the Overall index are positively correlated with both the industrial indices and financial indices and that they represent broad movements in the market.

---

69 The true range is defined as the greatest of the differences between the high and low of the day, the high of the day and the close of the previous day, and the low of the day and the close of the previous day.

70 Barr studied the correlation of 15 macro-economic variables with two factors, namely; industrial orientated indices (factor 1) and predominately financial-orientated indices (factor 2).

A share price index is a generally accepted standard measurement of the movement of share prices as a whole for an entire market or a specific sector of the market. The basic uses for indices according to Du Plessis (1990:167) are:

- The timing of purchase sales;
- the determination of speculative activities;
- the evaluation of the performance of a portfolio; and
- the quantification of risk.

Furthermore, the Actuarial Society of South Africa (1992:3) states the following reasons for the use of indices:

- To provide a description of the market at a point in time in terms of price levels, dividend yields and earnings yields;
- to facilitate equity research; and
- to enable an approximation of the valuation of a portfolio.

However, the strongest argument for including indices in the model can be inferred from the following statement by Boshoff (1983:21): "...the fact that virtually all stocks have a very strong relationship with a market surrogate like an index ... all stocks have [a] common denominator that will be accentuated and isolated in the index compilation process."

4.2.6 International indices (Inputs 41-49)

It is generally accepted that the Johannesburg Stock Exchange is influenced by developing trends in overseas markets (Naidoo, 1990:24). In order to determine the influence of overseas indices on the Johannesburg Stock Exchange, statistical tests were done to determine the significance of the correlation coefficient between changes on the Johannesburg Stock Exchange and international stock markets[71] as measured by their respective broad market indices. Month by month changes on the various stock exchanges were calculated to ensure that there was no

---

[71] Only the full members of the International Federation of Stock Exchanges (FIBV), which at time of writing included 32 members, were used in this study. The I-Net database was used for the comparative study.

overlapping of monthly values and minimal autocorrelation values. Table 4.5 presents the indices which had significant positive correlation with the Johannesburg Stock Exchange.

Table 4.5 - Significant correlations between the Johannesburg Stock Exchange and selected international market indices for the period 1/1/1986 - 12/31/1993

Indices	Correlation	Input number
Standard and Poor 500 index	97.15	Input 41
ASA investment corporation index	93.22	Input 42
Brent oil index	93.12	Input 43
Dow Jones industrial index	92	Input 44
Dow Jones transport index	92.5	Input 45
Dow Jones utilities index	92.14	Input 46
Financial Times 30 index	91.03	Input 47
Financial Times gold index	74	Input 48
Toronto-Gold index	69.24	Input 49

A comment is in order regarding the reason for including the Brent oil index in the table. First, the Brent oil index *per se* does not measure the performance of a certain stock market but is, rather, an indicator of oil prices. According to Chen, Roll and Ross (1986:391), oil prices should be included in any list of systematic factors which influence stock market returns. However, Cochran and Defina (1993:263) indicate that permanent shocks to real oil prices cause permanent shocks to stock prices, and that neither the transitory movements in real oil prices nor uncertainty about real oil prices significantly affect real share prices. To test this proposition and to examine the influence of oil prices on the output the Brent oil index was selected as an input.

4.2.7 Gold price and foreign exchange rates (Inputs 50-52)

4.2.7.1 Gold-Pm closing price (Input 50)

The export of gold accounts for a substantial amount of the Republic of South Africa's mineral exports, as well as the total export of goods and services. According to Ariovich (1983:3), "many believe that local business cycles are largely influenced by cycles in the gold price and that gold exports form a leading generator of economic growth in South Africa; this is discounted in especially listed gold shares on the Johannesburg Stock Exchange." An investigation of the influence of gold on the economy and on share prices is no simple task, since gold influences economic activity via many complicated and interrelated channels, making it difficult to isolate the effect of gold price from a multitude of other factors acting simultaneously. Furthermore, any direct effects of gold prices are followed by secondary and indirect effects on other channels. Myers (1983:76) comments that gold prices do not have a marked influence on the various indices or share prices in the long-term. However, the effect is strongest, not immediately, but after one month on industrial indices and shares. In a more recent study, Barr[72] (1990:32) reports a high level of correlation between gold and industrially-oriented indices, or industrial shares, of 0.733.

4.2.7.2 Dollar-Rand exchange rate (Input 51)

It can be postulated that the Rand/Dollar exchange rate has become increasingly important to investment decision processes since 1985. A decline in the exchange rate has both positive and negative impact on the economy: negative on importers and positive on exporters. However, from an investment point-of-view, a decreasing exchange rate will make investments in South African securities attractive to foreign investors, which will substantially influence future share prices.

A study done by Jordan (1986:9-65) investigated the proposition that share prices are significantly correlated with the Rand/Dollar exchange rate. He concluded that no statistically significant relationship exists between share prices and exchange rate prices. Furthermore, he feels that share prices are vectors by nature, which consist of both a magnitude and a direction, which means that correlations exist only when both of these entities are correlated. Jordan (1986:3) concluded "...that the forecasting accuracy of the Capital Asset Pricing Model could not be improved by adding the Rand/Dollar exchange rate as an additional independent variable to the

---

[72] Refer to footnote 70.

conventional Capital Asset Pricing Model." In a another study done by Miller[73] (1986:62), it was found that the Rand/Dollar exchange rate was tenth on a list of factors which most influence share prices.

It can be argued that the depreciation of the Rand/Dollar exchange rate improves the competitive position of the domestic industry. However, exchange rates do not change in a vacuum: underlying economic factors causing exchange rate changes may also effect share prices. Asprem (1989:596-597) indicates that a vast amount of studies have shown that interest rate changes are negatively correlated with share prices, which he feels would also apply to the relationship between exchange rates and share returns.

4.2.7.3 Financial-Rand exchange (Input 52)

Foreign stock exchanges associate their prices of South African shares to financial rand prices. Hamblin (1987:34) defines the financial rand as "Financial rand account balances plus the rand market value of all script endorsed 'non-resident' and eligible for sale through the financial rand."

It can be postulated that the immediate effect of a higher financial rand price would be an increase in foreign outlay (assuming that perceptions are not amended by a risk adjustment factor associated with cash flow returns and sale proceeds) for a given investment, along with a corresponding decline in discounted returns. This would tend to drive prices downwards. However, should the financial rand price edge downward, buying power would revive as discounted cash flow improves. This would tend to drive prices upwards. Therefore, in the short-term, there is an opposing price relationship between the financial rand and the prices on the Johannesburg Stock Exchange (Hamblin, 1987:37).

4.2.8 Interest rates (Inputs 53-56)

Bethlehem (1980:40) explains that the return on an ordinary share should not be measured by its dividend yield. However, the true return on an ordinary share can only be measured by comparing all expected future dividends and market prices with the rate of interest. According to Graham, Dodd and Cottle (1962:510), "Theoretical analysis suggests that both the dividend yield on

---

73 Miller investigated the influence of 23 macro-economic and business-specific factors on a sample of industrial share prices listed on the Johannesburg Stock Exchange.

common stocks should be strongly affected by changes in interest rates. It is assumed that many investors are constantly making a choice between stock and bond purchases. As the yield on bonds advances, they would be expected to demand correspondingly higher returns on stocks, and conversely as bond yields decline." It is generally assumed that investments in the South African context in gilts and semi-gilts are risk free. Whenever investors feel that dividend yields are out of line with interest rates, shares will either be bought or sold, resulting in structural changes in demand and supply. The resulting change in share prices adjusts the dividend yield to the desired level. Furthermore, it can generally be assumed that interest rates are indicators of whether money is freely available or scarce, providing a link between the state of the economy and share prices. It could be postulated that, when the money supply is large, the following are likely to occur:

- A surplus of funds in search of investment opportunities, leading to an undersupply or scarcity of investment opportunities, causes an upward adjustment in share price (Van Wyk, 1990:84);
- a reduction in interest rates, making it attractive for investors to invest in securities yielding a higher rate of return than interest-bearing instruments, increases demand for shares and results in higher prices; and
- a fear of inflation, whereby investments would be made in shares which may respond favorably to inflationary pressures.

The interest rates included as inputs are:

- The banks acceptance rate (BA)(Input 53) - this is the rate at which discount houses are willing to discount the 3-month bankers acceptances. The BA rate is regarded as a short-term interest rate and an indicator of short-term interest rate movements.

- Eskom 168 (Input 54) and Eskom 166 (Input 55) rates - it refers to stocks (gilts) issued by Eskom. The Eskom rates are generally regarded as indicators of long-term interest rates.

- The prime rate (Input 60) - this is the lowest rate at which a clearing bank will lend money on overdraft.

4.2.8.1 The relationship between interest rates and share prices - South African context

Chute (1983:114-131) studied the relationship between economic data and weekly share price data for the period 1960-1982, and concludes that share prices and indices are at best correlated with long-term interest rates with a leading factor of one month.

McDonald[74] (1986:129-131), by applying correlation analysis, indicates that interest rates do not influence a sample of share prices.

Miller's[75] (1986:74) research findings indicate that the BA rate and the Eskom 168 rate appear as numbers 11 and 23, respectively, out of 23 factors affecting a share price. The findings correlate with a study done by Abdullah and Hayworth (1993:63), which indicated that long-term interest rates are more closely related to share price movements than are short-term interest rates.

Barr 1990[76] (1990:21) indicates that the prime rate and the three-month bank acceptance rate are inversely correlated with industrial indices, concluding that "...thus rising interest rates, which choke off consumer confidence and expenditure, are generally associated with the weakening first factor [industrial indices], and thus a weak industrial market."

Bhana (1993:31-41) studied the relationship between growth in money supply and share prices for the period 1980 to 1989. He concludes:"...changes in current prices are significantly related to lagged values of both unanticipated and anticipated money growth [money supply as measured by an interest rate]."

It is quite evident from these studies that interest rates are not positively correlated with share price movements. This confirms the results of research performed in the U.S.

4.2.9 Economic statistics (Inputs 57-63)

No satisfactory theory would argue that the relationship between the financial markets and the macro-economy is entirely unilateral. A large amount of contradiction exists in the literature reviewed as to which influences the other first. Chen, Roll and Ross (1986:384) feel that share prices are usually considered as responding to external forces even though they may have

---

74 McDonald studied the influence of dividends, earnings per share, inflation and interest rates on 27 share prices for the period September 1981 to December 1984.

75 Refer to footnote 73.

76 Refer to footnote 70.

feedback on the other variables, since all economic variables are endogenous in some way. Nelson (1987:106) feels that the stock market is a powerful leading indicator of the real economy, and that it has been proven that major moves in the economy have almost invariably been proceeded by major moves in the stock market. This view is confirmed in the South African context by Van Coller (1980:41-73), who found that share prices are leading indicators of the economy as a whole and the industrial share index was found to be the most consistent early warning indicator of pending changes in the economy. Van Der Mescht and Smit (1993:45-46) indicate that the Johannesburg Stock Exchange's industrial index is an appropriate indicator of the real economy. Contrary to the previous views, Van Wyk (1990:83) feels that an increase in the level of economic (real factors and monetary factors) activity is associated with an increase in share prices. He deduced that changes in the economy influence share prices rather than market perceptions by investors. For the purposes of this research, only economic variables which could be obtained on a daily basis were included in the model. These will be subsequently discussed.

4.2.9.1 Inflation rate (Input 57)

Specific research on the correlation between the rate of inflation and share prices has generally indicated a negative correlation: Bodie (1976:259-270); Fama and Schwert (1977:115-146) and Nelson (1976:471-483). This phenomenon may be explained by the variability hypothesis (Malkiel, 1979:291-306), which postulates that the negative correlation between share prices and the rate of inflation is caused by a combination of a positive relationship between the rate of inflation and the variability of inflation, and a negative relationship between the variability of inflation and share prices.

Friedman (1977:451-472) contends that the variability of inflation may have an adverse effect on share prices. He explains "...that the variability of inflation influences share prices throughout the effect of the real economic activity. Given that the economic activity and stock returns are positively related, the equity rate is negatively related to the variability of inflation because the variability of inflation is inversely related to economic activity...economic activity and the variability of inflation will be negatively correlated if an increase in the variability of inflation reduces economic efficiency and if that reduction causes a decline in economic activity." An alternative argument to substantiate the variability hypothesis is that asset demands depend on the riskiness of competing assets (Torbin, 1958:65-86). A rise in the variability of inflation increases the risk of all financial assets because there is less certainty about the purchasing power of future cash flows that accrue. An increase in riskiness has the result that a risk premium must be added to the future discounted nominal cash flow rate. This increase in the discount rate may adversely affect share prices in two ways:

- An increase in the discounted rate will cause a decrease in the discounted value of cash flow, and a decrease in the discounted value will result in a decrease in share prices (Malkiel, 1979:291-306).

- An increase in the discounted rate may induce investors to move away from long-term assets to short-term assets, as a change in the discount rate has a much greater relative effect on the value of the former. It can be postulated that a movement away from long-term assets, for example a movement away from equity, will cause share prices to decline.

Little research has been performed on this topic as it applies to the Republic of South Africa. One reference includes the following:

- McDonald[77] (1986:113) indicates that inflation does not have an effect on sampled share prices.

4.2.9.2 Additional diverse economic indicators selected as inputs (Inputs 58 - 63)

- Export: Total, including bullion (Input 58);
- imports: total (Input 59);
- liquidations - companies (Input 60);
- insolvencies (Input 61);
- wholesale trade - total (real) (Input 62); and
- total manufacturing producers index (Input 63).

The selection of inputs was done in accordance with the literature reviewed. The selection is by no means exhaustive, since hundreds of possible variables exist which could possibly affect a share's price. Instead, the above selection represents only a few factors which have been found to affect share prices.

---

77 Refer to footnote 74.

4.3 DATA ANALYSIS AND TRANSFORMATION

Once the appropriate raw input data has been selected, it must be processed and analyzed. However, it is important to feed the neural network as much pertinent information as possible, within the constraints of the problem, since neural networks can often find associations between variables that previously were not noticed (Lawrence, 1993:182). From the literature, the following preprocessing methods are available:

- Statistical outlier detection;
- correlation analysis between an input and an output;
- transformation; and
- normalization.

Each will be subsequently discussed and analyzed.

4.3.1 Statistical outlier[78] detection

The detection of outliers in the data is not a statistical method *per se* but, rather, a prerequisite for any form of data analysis. Statistical outliers are extreme observations in the input/output variables. Since they cause squashing of the normalized variable into a very small range, their existence means that extreme numerical accuracy is required during training (References, Zapranis and Bentz, 1993:7). They may be detected by examining the frequency distribution or by using some more sophisticated multivariate methods, for example, the Mahalanobis distance of a single multivariate observation from the center of the population. In this research, frequency distributions were examined for the purpose of detecting outliers. Outliers were removed by casewise deletion and replaced by mean values.

4.3.2 Correlation analysis

The purpose of correlation analysis is to determine if any correlation exists between the input and output values. In certain literature, the rationale behind the use of correlation is to determine when

---

78 An outlier is a value removed from the other values to such an extreme that its presence cannot be attributed to the random combination of chance causes.

two variables, say X and Y, tend to vary together. It is calculated as the ratio of the covariance of the X value and the square root of the product of the variance of X and the variance of Y. Given this, an input with a significantly positively or negatively correlated value to the output, would be regarded as a reliable input. Therefore, any input which is not significantly correlated would be rejected. Refer to Table 4.6 for the Pearson correlation between the input values and the output value.

Table 4.6 - Pearson correlation analysis between the input values and the output value. Marked correlations are significant at $p < 0.05$ (Casewise deletion of missing values)

	r (X,Y)	R^2	t	P
INPUT 1	-0.1414	**0.0200**	-2.9505	0.003347
INPUT 2	0.8731	**0.7622**	36.9978	0.000000
INPUT 3	0.8987	**0.8077**	42.3552	0.000000
INPUT 4	0.9879	**0.9760**	131.8801	0.000000
INPUT 5	-0.2986	**0.0892**	-6.4660	0.000034
INPUT 6	-0.1735	**0.0301**	-3.6400	0.000306
INPUT 7	-0.0180	0.0003	-0.3729	0.709414
INPUT 8	-0.0795	0.0063	-1.6486	0.099971
INPUT 9	-0.0628	0.0039	-1.2996	0.194429
INPUT 10	-0.1685	**0.0284**	-3.5318	0.000458
INPUT 11	0.9932	**0.9865**	176.4151	0.000000
INPUT 12	0.9804	**0.9613**	102.9417	0.000000
INPUT 13	-0.1565	**0.0245**	-3.2748	0.001144
INPUT 14	-0.1876	**0.0352**	-3.9457	0.000093
INPUT 15	-0.1874	**0.0351**	-3.9417	0.000095
INPUT 16	-0.0054	0.0004	-0.1117	0.911083
INPUT 17	-0.2447	**0.0599**	-5.2139	0.000039
INPUT 18	-0.7002	**0.4902**	-20.2642	0.000000
INPUT 19	-0.1349	**0.0182**	-2.8127	0.005140
INPUT 20	-0.2437	**0.0594**	-5.1920	0.000000
INPUT 21	0.9645	**0.9302**	75.4292	0.000000

	r (X,Y)	R^2	t	P
INPUT 22	0.9142	**0.8358**	46.6264	0.000000
INPUT 23	0.9526	**0.9074**	64.6753	0.000000
INPUT 24	0.8636	**0.7458**	35.3974	0.000000
INPUT 25	-0.4002	**0.1601**	-9.0228	0.000044
INPUT 26	0.9281	**0.8613**	51.4994	0.000000
INPUT 27	0.9113	**0.8304**	45.7315	0.000000
INPUT 28	0.6332	**0.4010**	16.9062	0.000000
INPUT 29	0.8787	**0.7721**	38.0359	0.000000
INPUT 30	0.6671	**0.4450**	18.5031	0.000000
INPUT 31	0.9228	**0.8516**	49.5028	0.000000
INPUT 32	0.8318	**0.6919**	30.9678	0.000000
INPUT 33	0.9106	**0.8292**	45.5327	0.000000
INPUT 34	-0.2413	**0.0582**	-5.1390	0.000000
INPUT 35	0.5352	**0.2864**	13.0913	0.000000
INPUT 36	0.9406	**0.8847**	57.2321	0.000000
INPUT 37	0.8495	**0.7217**	33.2787	0.000000
INPUT 38	0.9812	**0.9628**	105.0813	0.000000
INPUT 39	0.9534	**0.9089**	65.2664	0.000000
INPUT 40	0.1440	**0.0207**	3.0066	0.002798
INPUT 41	0.7928	**0.6285**	26.8797	0.000000
INPUT 42	-0.0163	0.0003	-0.3365	0.736630
INPUT 43	-0.0163	0.0003	-0.3365	0.736630
INPUT 44	0.7810	**0.6099**	25.8379	0.000000
INPUT 45	0.8258	**0.6819**	30.2581	0.000000
INPUT 46	0.8258	**0.6819**	30.2581	0.000000
INPUT 47	0.4784	**0.2289**	11.2573	0.099566
INPUT 48	-0.6327	**0.4003**	-16.8811	0.000000
INPUT 49	-0.6587	**0.4339**	-18.0917	0.000000
INPUT 50	-0.6587	**0.4339**	-18.0917	0.000000
INPUT 51	0.7373	**0.5437**	22.5544	0.000000

	r (X,Y)	R^2	t	P
INPUT 52	-0.2297	**0.0527**	-4.8763	0.000002
INPUT 53	-0.4948	0.2448	-11.7658	7.109116
INPUT 54	0.2408	**0.0580**	5.1276	0.000000
INPUT 55	-0.1589	**0.0253**	-3.3263	0.000956
INPUT 56	-0.4368	0.1908	-10.0338	2.054111
INPUT 57	-0.5071	0.2571	-12.1577	2.073199
INPUT 58	0.3536	0.1251	7.8122	4.405799
INPUT 59	0.1940	**0.0376**	4.0868	0.000052
INPUT 60	0.4573	0.2091	10.6245	1.490509
INPUT 61	0.5936	**0.3523**	15.2404	0.000000
INPUT 62	0.0926	0.0086	1.9215	0.065328
INPUT 63	0.0405	0.0016	0.8368	0.403171

It is evident from Table 4.6, that the following inputs are not significantly correlated with the output:

- Input 7 - (Moving average oscillator on volume);
- Input 8 - (Stochastic indicator (%D);
- Input 9 - (Stochastic indicator (%K);
- Input 16 - (Momentum indicator on volume);
- Input 42 - (ASA investment corporation index);
- Input 43 - (Brent oil index);
- Input 53 - (Bank acceptance rate);
- Input 56 - (Prime rate);
- Input 57 - (Inflation rate);
- Input 58 - (Export:total, including bullion);
- Input 60 - (Liquidations - companies)
- Input 62 - (Wholesale trade -Total (Real)); and
- Input 63 - (Total manufacturing producers index).

Furthermore, in addition to Pearson correlation statistics, cross correlations were calculated between the output and the inputs, indicating either a strong correlation factor with lead time steps (indicating that the input is useful as a leading indicator), or a strong correlation with lag time steps (the input is not useful for predictive purposes). Refer to Table 4.7 for results of cross correlation calculations.

Table 4.7 - Cross correlation data analysis

	Indicator	Time in days
INPUT 1	Lag time	-25 to -15
INPUT 2	-	-
INPUT 3	Lead time	20 to 25
INPUT 4	-	-
INPUT 5	Lag time	-25 to -15
INPUT 6	Lag time	-25 to -15
INPUT 7	Lag time	-10 to 0
INPUT 8	Lag time	-25 to -20
INPUT 9	Lag time	-25 to -20
INPUT 10	-	-
INPUT 11	-	-
INPUT 12	-	-
INPUT 13	Lag time	-25 to -15
INPUT 14	-	-
INPUT 15	Lag time	-5 to 0
INPUT 16	Lag time	-25 to -10
INPUT 17	-	-
INPUT 18	Lag time	-1
INPUT 19	Lag time	-20 to 15
INPUT 20	-	-
INPUT 21	-	-
INPUT 22	-	-

	Indicator	Time in days
INPUT 23	-	-
INPUT 24	-	-
INPUT 25	-	-
INPUT 26	-	-
INPUT 27	Lag time	-25 to -10
INPUT 28	-	-
INPUT 29	Lead time	0 to 25
INPUT 30	-	-
INPUT 31	-	-
INPUT 32	Lag time	-25 to 0
INPUT 33	Lag time	-25 to 0
INPUT 34	Lead time	0 to 26
INPUT 35	-	-
INPUT 36	-	-
INPUT 37	-	-
INPUT 38	-	-
INPUT 39	-	-
INPUT 40	Lead time	5 to 25
INPUT 41	Lead time	15 to 20
INPUT 42	-	-
INPUT 43	-	-
INPUT 44	Lead time	10 to 15
INPUT 45	Lead time	0 to 25
INPUT 46	Lead time	10 to 15
INPUT 47	-	-
INPUT 48	Lead time	5 to 25
INPUT 49	Lead time	10 to 20
INPUT 50	-	-
INPUT 51	-	-
INPUT 52	Lag time	-25 to 0

	Indicator	Time in days
INPUT 53	-	-
INPUT 54	-	-
INPUT 55	-	-
INPUT 56	-	-
INPUT 57	-	-
INPUT 58	-	-
INPUT 59	-	-
INPUT 60	-	-
INPUT 61	-	-
INPUT 62	-	-
INPUT 63	-	-

Table 4.8 indicates the correlation per group compared with the output value. It is evident from the group correlation done that only fundamental factors, JSE indices and interest rate data would have been used, had a linear prediction model been constructed.

Table 4.8 - Correlation analysis between the groupings and the output value. Marked correlations are significant at $p < 0.05$ (Casewise deletion of missing values)

Grouping	R^2	$p < 0.05$
Fundamental inputs	**0.52998**	0.00112
Technical inputs	0.22379	0.11307
Johannesburg Stock Exchange indices	**0.65527**	0.00014
International indices	0.40732	0.16037
Gold price and foreign exchange rates	0.34344	5.00001
Interest rates	**0.12972**	0.00021
Economic indicators	0.14164	0.06551

Table 4.8 indicates that fundamental inputs, Johannesburg Stock Exchange indices and interest rates are the groups which influence a share price. This is confirmed by Figure 4.2, which

provides a graphical representation of a Scree test using computed factor analysis eigenvalues. The literature suggests finding a place on the graph where the decrease of eigenvalues appears to level off. According to this criterion, 2 or 3 group factors should be retained.

Most share market analysis is aimed at explaining and/or predicting future share prices. According to Mohr, Van Der Merwe, Botha and Inggs (1991:126), a major problem in economic analysis and, therefore, stock market analysis, is the establishment of causation between different variables. However, frequently, such causation is inferred from the observed correlation between variables.

Unfortunately, correlation analysis can never show causation. All it can show is a link between variables. Even if statistical methods show a close correlation between a set of causes and the observed event(s), there will be great difficulty in establishing the existence of a casual link. A problem identified by Mohr *et al* (1991:126) is the existence of nonsense correlations which they define as "...close correlations between sets of data where there could not, by any sane reasoning, be a causal connection...which is quite relevant in economic data." Thus, statistical evidence can never prove or reject a causal link, no matter how close or significant the correlation between the observed variables.

Figure 4.2 - The factor analysis eigenvalues

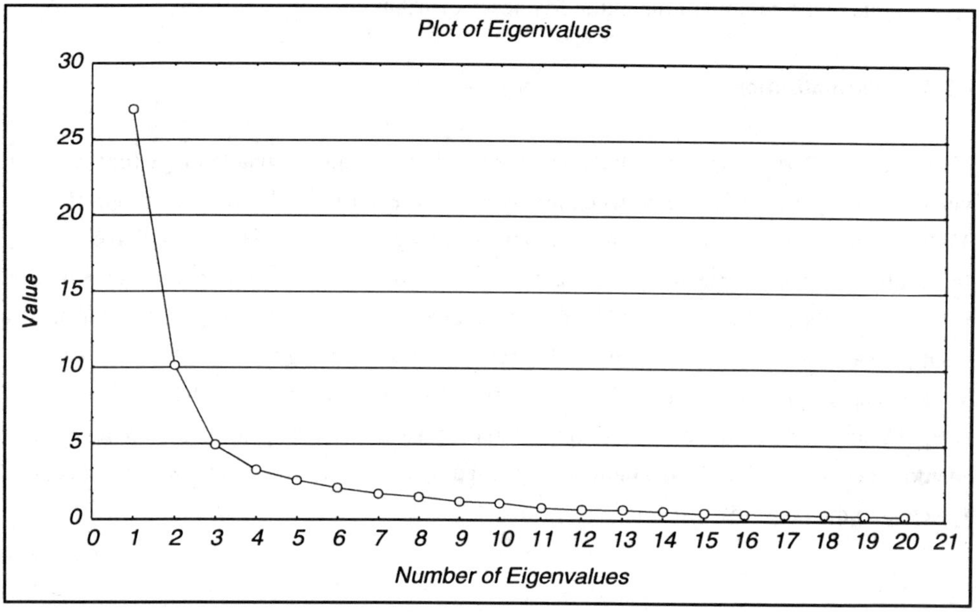

4.3.3 Transformation

Transformation is performed on each data input to distribute the data evenly. The goal is to ensure that the statistical distribution of values for each network input and output is uniform. Several methods are available. Though none were applied to the models developed in this study, two such methods are described below:

- Statistical measurement of central tendency and variance - The statistical measurement of central tendency and variance helps to remove outliers that spread out the distribution of data, which tends to increase uniformity. In this method, the standard deviation and the mean for the input data associated with each input are first determined. The minimum value is then set to the mean minus some factor of standard deviations and, conversely, the maximum value is set to the mean plus some factor of standard deviations. All data less than the minium value is set to the minimum value and all values greater than the maximum value are set to the maximum value.

- Minimizing the standard deviation - This method minimizes the standard deviation of the heights of the column of the initial frequency distribution.

4.3.4 Normalization

Normalization is performed on each data input to scale it into an acceptable range for the neural network. One particular problem when inputs values are not normalized is saturation (Chuah, 1992:33). When large values from the unit in the input layer are multiplied by very large weights, the result may be very large input values at units in the hidden layer. The output values produced at the units in the hidden layer will be included in one of many successive weight updates. As a result, it may take an excessive number of iterations before learning takes place, since the small weight changes move the units in the hidden layer out of saturation very slowly.

The standard method of data normalization applied in this study was linear scaling. This method involves scaling the data into a range used by the input neurons in the neural network, typically in the range of -1 to 1, using equation 4-3

$$x_i = \frac{(X_i - X_{i,min}) \times (h_i - l_i)}{(X_i - X_{i,min})} + l_i \qquad \textbf{...(4-3)}$$

Where: i = The ith neuron in the input or output layer.

x_i = Normalized value.

X_i = Original value.

$X_{i,min}$ = Minimum of all original i^{th} neurons in the input or output layer.

$X_{i,max}$ = Maximum of all original i^{th} neurons in the input or output layer.

h_i = Largest normalized value.

l_i = Smallest normalized value.

4.4 CHOICE OF LEARNING PARADIGM

The most commonly used neural network paradigm for forecasting, especially economic forecasting, is the backpropagation paradigm[79]. To reiterate, backpropagation is a learning algorithm for a multilayered neural network in which the weights are modified via propagation of an error gradient "backward" from the outputs to the inputs.

4.5 DEFINING THE NETWORK STRUCTURE AND SELECTION OF PARAMETER VALUES

As noted earlier, the second objective of this research is to identify and investigate the factors that affect the performance of a neural network forecasting model. These factors include:

- The amount of data required;
- the number of neurons;
- the number of hidden layers; and
- the selection of training, testing and running tolerances.

Background regarding the number of neurons and the number of hidden layers was presented in Chapter 2. Each of the other factors will be discussed subsequently.

4.5.1 The amount of data required

The amount of data required varies according to the application. For example, in applications where classification problems, such as credit scoring or financial distress forecasting, require a substantial amount of historical data, the more data used the better. A problem unique to time series data is deciding on the amount of historical data to use as input to a neural network. Determining the appropriate time period for historical inputs and the future output is one of the biggest challenges in financial forecasting. However, the literature provides the following guidelines:

---

79 Refer to Chapter 2 for the reasons behind the selection of the backpropagation paradigm for this research.

- Guideline 1 - According to the vendor of the neural network product used, the following formula can be used (refer to equation 4-4).

$$\text{Data} = 2 \times (inputs + neurons + ouputs)\ up\ to\ 10 \times (inputs + neurons + ouputs) \quad ...(4\text{-}4$$

Applying this formula to the research problem (64 inputs, 21 neurons[80] and 1 output), the amount of data required could be anything from 172[81] data points to 860[82] data points.

- Guideline 2 - Further reports indicate that an appropriate amount of data might vary between 200 days and 600 days. The intent is to include enough data as required to capture the linear and nonlinear dynamics of the time series. It is generally felt that these dynamics cannot be captured with an extensive amount of data, which would adversely affect the short-term forecasting capabilities of the model. The neural network product vendor confirms this and advises that the only exception to their suggested guideline (refer to guideline 1) is financial data. Because financial data behavior can change frequently, it should be limited to a period during which the market's behavior is stable, in this case, between 2 and 3 years. Accordingly, for daily data, about 500-750 facts should be used.

- Guideline 3 - According to Katz (1992:66), "As a rule, the amount of data should be at least two times the number of interconnections between the neurons."

This research was guided by the recommendations of the software package. Thus, the minimum and maximum data values were added together and the average value was calculated. A total number of 516[83] data points were employed in the neural network model.

---

80 An heuristic for the initial amount of neurons used in the data selection is a third of the inputs (Fishman, 1993:interview).

81 2 x (64 + 21 + 1) = 172.

82 10 x (64 + 21 + 1) = 860.

83 (860 + 172)/2 = 516.

4.5.2 The number of neurons

A good neural network model for forecasting should not only learn the training patterns, but also respond to out-of-sample patterns correctly. In general, the smallest number of neurons consistent with good forecasts is best (Katz, 1992:66). If there are too many neurons, the network may memorize the facts in the training set and provide perfect results yet not generalize well with unseen data. This will result in over-optimization. If, on the other hand, there are too few neurons, the network may generalize well but yield predictions that are insufficiently accurate to be useful. Based on the literature, the following guidelines are available:

- Guideline 1 - One estimate for the best number of hidden neurons, as suggested by the maker of the neural network software used in the study, is to use half the sum of inputs plus outputs. Accordingly, 33 neurons should be employed in the research model.

- Guideline 2 - A second suggestion is that a neural network should be trained using between two and ten times as many facts as neurons.

- Guideline 3 - Katz (1992:66) recommends that the optimal number of neurons is frequently between one-half and three times the number of input layer neurons.

- Guideline 4 - Fishman (1993:interview) advises that the optimal number of neurons is a third of the sum of the inputs and outputs.

- Guideline 5 - Kolmogorov's mapping neural network existence theory states that any continuous function can be implemented with the neural network structure using $2n + 1$ hidden neurons (where n is the number of inputs).

The above guidelines are in general agreement. However, for this study, a genetic algorithm training option was applied to selecting the number of neurons, based on a network's performance with regard to the lowest root mean square error and the highest coefficient of determination.

The foundations of the genetic algorithm date back to the work of Holland in 1975, published as *Adaptation in Natural and Artificial Systems*. His analysis of natural adaptive systems shows that natural evolution embodies a generate-and-test strategy that can rapidly identify and exploit regularities in the environment. His work indicates that even in large and complicated search spaces, given certain conditions in the problem domain, genetic algorithms tend to converge to solutions that are globally optimal or nearly so.

There are four stages in the genetic search process:

- Initialization stage - The population of the genetic structure is randomly distributed in the solution space and is selected as the starting point of each search.

- Selection - On completion of the initialization stage, each structure is evaluated using a fitness function and is assigned a utility value. On the basis of their respective utility values, structures in the current population are selected for reproduction. A stochastic procedure ensures that the expected number of offspring are associated with a given structure. Thus, structures with a high performance may be chosen for replication several times, while poorly performing structures may not be chosen at all. In the absence of other mechanisms,[84] the structures which perform best in the initial population will tend to occupy an increasingly larger proportion of the population over time.

- Crossover - The selected structures from the previous phase are combined using the technique of crossover[85]. The purpose of crossover serves to complement the search function, that is:

  - It provides new points for further testing of schema already presented to the population; and
  - it introduces instances of new schema[86] into the population.

  For generating new solutions for evaluation, the crossover draws on the information present in the solutions of the current population.

---

84 Such as selective pressure (Wong, Tan and Zang, 1992:60).

85 Crossover operates by swapping corresponding segments of string representations of the parents.

86 Schema are defined as subset of strings with similarities in certain positions.

- Mutation - This process provides the means for introducing new information into the population by arbitrarily altering new information. This ensures that the probability of reaching any point in the search space is never zero.

In this study, the purpose of the genetic algorithm is to automate the design of a neural network. The genetic algorithm employed in this research is based on the work of Wong, Tan and Zang, (1992:61-63). The method is based on the principle that the cycles of learning are nestled within cycles of evolution in populations. Each learning cycle represents an individual neural network. The learning algorithm then compares the network's actual outputs to the desired outputs, and modifies the network's connection weights so that it performs the desired input-output mapping task more accurately. On completion of an evolution cycle, one population of network design is processed according to its associated fitness values, which are computed during learning cycles to yield an offspring population of more highly-adapted network designs.

Basically the genetic algorithm performs network optimization of the interconnection weights between neurons, with each network being ranked according to one of several statistical measures available. In the genetic algorithm neural network mutation, as opposed to biological mutation, a random modification of weights occurs. These weights are associated with a single "parent" network and are modified to produce a "child" network according to predefined mutation rates, ranges and distributions for each interconnection. The genetic algorithm employs neural network crossovers, as opposed to biological crossovers, by combining weights associated with two or more parent networks to produce a child network using a mixture of fixed, random, linear, and Gaussian distributions. After mutation and crossover have occurred, each network is ranked according to one of several statistical measures. Therefore, any given child network that produces better results than its parent becomes a parent network itself.

The selection criterion employed for this research was that the genetic algorithm had to determine the optimal number of neurons given selection parameters of between 1 and 64 neurons. (refer to Figure 4.3 for results). Using the coefficient of determination as a measure, the best neural network, with a coefficient of correlation of 0.982, included 21 neurons. Disturbingly evident was that there is no clear-cut pattern in the relationship between the number of neurons, R^2 and RMS, and that the only way to determine the optimal number of neurons in the hidden layer was through a genetic algorithm. However, it should be noted that guideline 4 (section 4.5.2) confirms the results of the genetic algorithm.

According to Wong, Tan and Zhang (1992:64), "The primary drawback of the genetic algorithm arises in its flexibility...In certain problems, it is not clear as to how it can be formulated so that the genetic algorithm can produce optimal solutions efficiently. Another drawback is that genetic algorithms are computational intensive, requiring much processing power. However, it is readily amenable to parallel implementation, which should render it feasible for use in real-time if parallel hardware is adopted."

Figure 4.3 - The optimal number of neurons in the hidden layer according to the genetic algorithm option

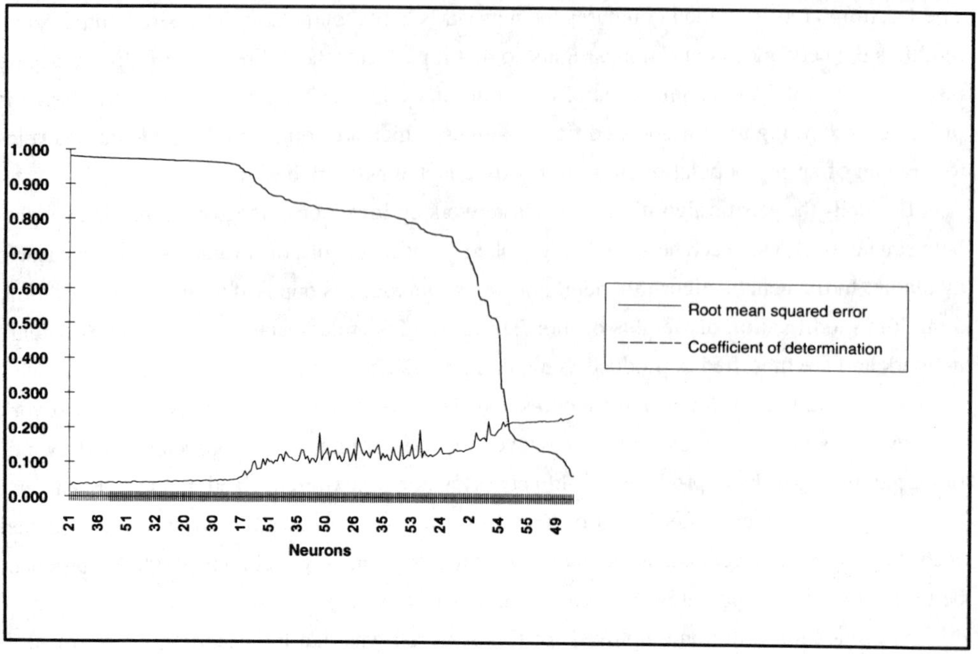

4.5.3 The number of hidden layers

Hidden layer(s) are of obvious importance because of their substantial impact on a neural network's ability to learn. However, the impact of the number of hidden layers to forecasting problems is not so obvious. As part of this work, genetic algorithms were applied to the study of the behavior of two hidden layers with a parameter selection of between 1 and 66 neurons. The results of this analysis are displayed in Figure 4.4. The Figure illustrates that, for a neural network with 2 hidden layers, the highest coefficient of determination is obtained with a hidden layer consisting of 26 neurons (layer one) and a hidden layer consisting of 11 neurons (layer two). The choice between either one or two hidden layers can be difficult and, if empirically derived, a very time-consuming task (refer to Table 4.9). Table 4.9 indicates that, in this case, there was little difference in performance for the one and two hidden-layer networks, except for training time. Based upon this analysis, a neural network with a single hidden layer was chosen.

Figure 4.4 - The optimal number of neurons in the two hidden-layer network according to the genetic algorithm option

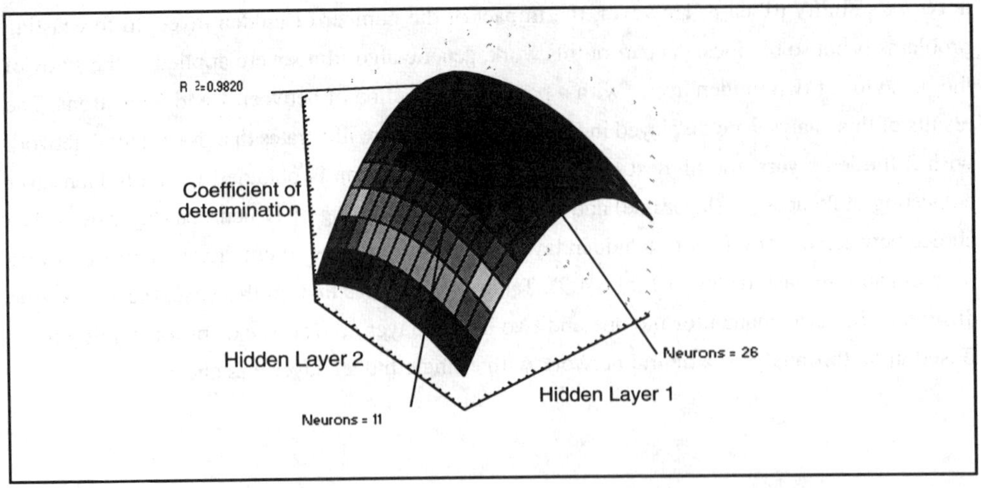

Table 4.9 - Layer comparison

Layer	Average error	Root mean squared error	Coefficient of correlation	Training time
Single	0.027	0.033	0.982	00h45
Multi	0.028	0.034	0.982	01h56

4.6 SETTING OF PARAMETER VALUES, TRAINING AND TESTING

4.6.1 Software used

The subsequent sections will be discussed in accordance with the specifications of the software programs used in this study.

4.6.2 Creation of the data file

The neural network software used in this study comes with a secondary program which facilitates the definition of the training fact, testing fact and running fact files. All data preprocessing was performed using *Excel.* After completion of preprocessing tasks, the data files in *Excel* format were read into the secondary program, where the data was then manipulated as follows:

- Shuffling of rows. The purpose of this is to reorder the data set randomly since neural networks often learn more effectively when the training facts are in random order. This also helps to minimize the possibility of memorization.

On completion of this, the data is saved. By default, the program selects 10% of data (52 data points) to be used in the training phase.

4.6.3 Parameters

The following parameters were selected for both training and testing, namely:

- Learning setup - The purpose of the learning setup is to allow alterations to the learning rate as the accuracy of the network output improves. It also specifies what size of correction the neural network must make to interconnection weights relative to output error. A constant learning rate of 1.0 was applied.

- Training tolerance - The purpose of the training tolerance is to provide a boundary on neural network output error. The training tolerance was set at 0.1. This indicates that the predicted output value must be within 10% of the range of the actual output to be considered correct. The output for the network employed in this research has a minimum of 92519 and a maximum of 149383 for a range of 56864. With a training tolerance of 0.1, any output value within +/– 5686.4 of the training pattern is considered to be a correct answer. Any output with an absolute error greater than +/– 5686.5 is considered incorrect, forcing the neural network to retrain until the output is within the acceptable training tolerance.

4.6.4 Training

Training is the procedure by which the neural network learns. However, knowing whether the network has successfully learned represents a primary issue of interest. Approaches to determining whether the network has learned include the following:

- Analyzing statistical measures,
- analyzing a histogram; and
- analyzing good facts versus bad facts.

4.6.4.1 Analyzing statistical measures

Refer to Figure 4.5 for an interpretation of statistical measures. It can be noted that the coefficient of determination (R^2) value is initially low (0.56) and it steadily increases to a higher value (0.98). This can be attributed to the fact that, in the beginning of the learning phase, the neural network gets more facts incorrect than correct. The R^2 value will increase as the number of training iterations increase until the neural network has learned all the facts correctly. The average error measures the difference between each actual and predicted output. The average error is zero for a perfectly trained network and increases towards one for a less well-trained network. The average error value initially started with a value of 0.1191 and, on completion of training, was reduced to 0.0294. The root mean squared (RMS) error is similar to the average error except that the square of the differences, rather than their actual absolute values, are used, putting a higher weight on larger errors. Therefore, a network with smaller errors on most of the outputs and larger errors on a few will have a smaller average error (closer to 0) and a larger RMS error (closer to 1). The initial RMS error was 0.1931 with a final value of 0.033. Based on the final statistical measures (average error = 0.0294; root mean squared error = 0.033 and coefficient of determination = 0.98), it can be concluded, that the neural network did indeed train.

Figure 4.5 - Training statistics

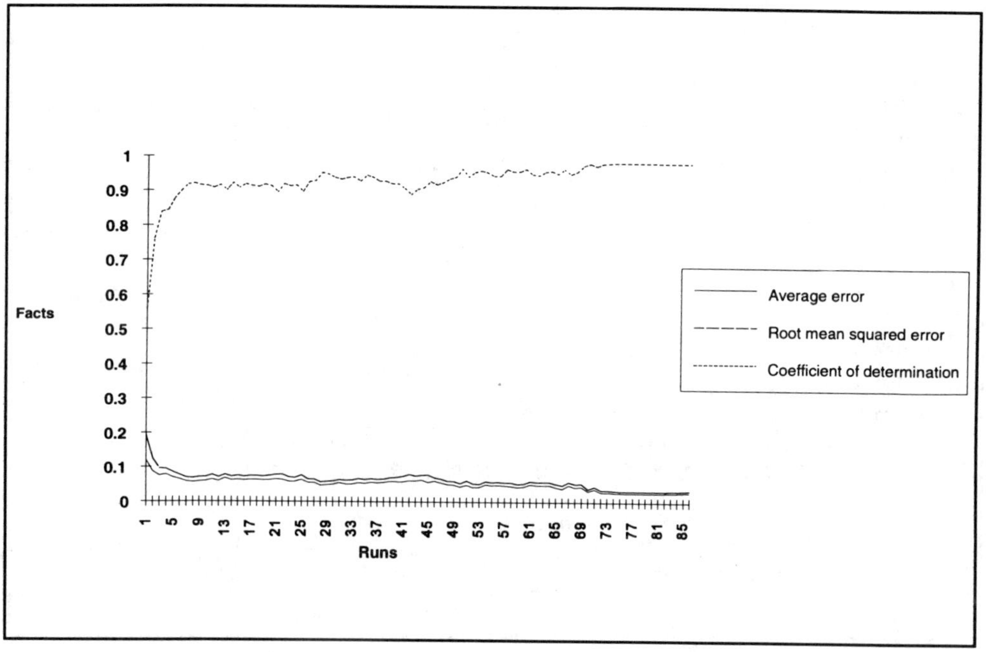

Figure 4.6 - Bad facts versus good facts

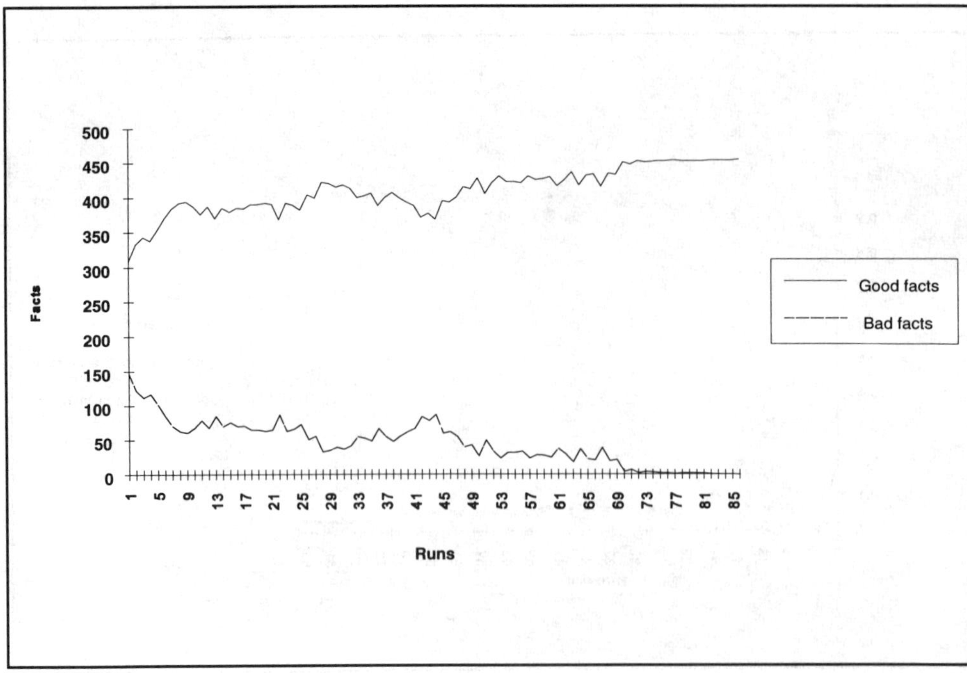

4.6.4.2 Analyzing good facts versus bad facts

A fact is the sequence number of the example fact (output). Bad facts are the facts the neural network predicted incorrectly during a specific run, while the good facts are those that the neural network predicted correctly. Generally, the neural network will get more facts wrong during initial training iterations but improve during the course of the training process. As illustrated in Figure 4.6, the neural network had 146 bad facts and 309 good facts over the initial run. However, during the final run, it had no bad facts and 455 good facts. In other words it learned all the patterns correctly. From this, it can be deduced that the neural network did indeed learn.

4.6.4.3 Analyzing a histogram

Neural network histograms can be thought of as useful indicators of the mental health of a neural network. The first histogram shows the connection between the input and hidden layers (refer to Figure 4.7), while the second histogram shows the connections between the hidden and the output layers (refer to Figure 4.8). The literature indicates that, if the histogram resembles a bell-shaped curve, the neural network is either still learning or has learned correctly. However, if during training, the histogram distribution is heavily biased to the extremes, this may indicate that the neural network has too few neurons or the parameter settings are wrong.

Figure 4.7 - Connection between the input and hidden layers

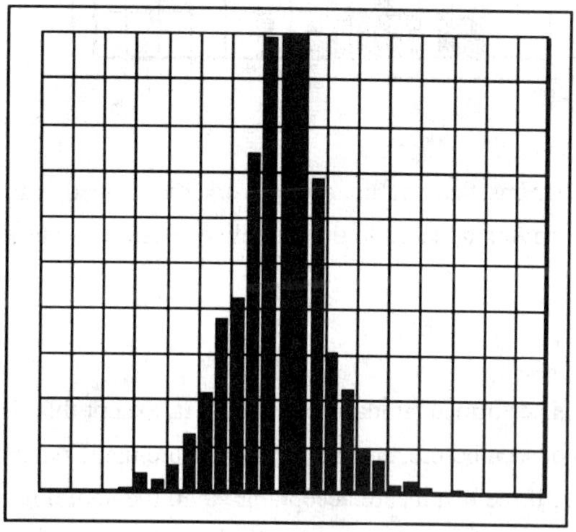

Figure 4.8 - Connections between the hidden and output layer

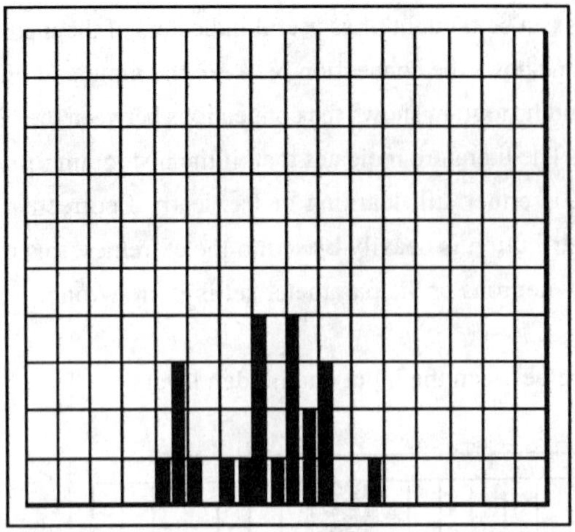

It is evident from the histograms that the neural network did indeed learn. Thus, the neural network did train correctly, having adhered to the guidelines described above.

4.6.5 Testing

Testing the neural network is performed similarly as training it, except that the neural network is presented with facts it has not seen before, and no corrections are made when the neural network makes incorrect predictions. If the results are acceptable, then the neural network model can be fully employed, which entails presenting the neural network with new input data for forecasting purposes. Refer to Table 4.10 for a summary of testing results.

Table 4.10 - Testing statistics

Runs	Good facts	Bad facts	Average error	Root mean squared error	Coefficient of determination
86	50	1	0.0355	0.0411	0.9124

It is evident from the testing results summarized in Table 4.10 that the neural network did indeed train correctly, particularly in regard to the high coefficient of correlation. (refer to Figure 4.9 for actual outputs compared to forecasted outputs).

Figure 4.9 - Actual versus forecasted outputs on the testing set

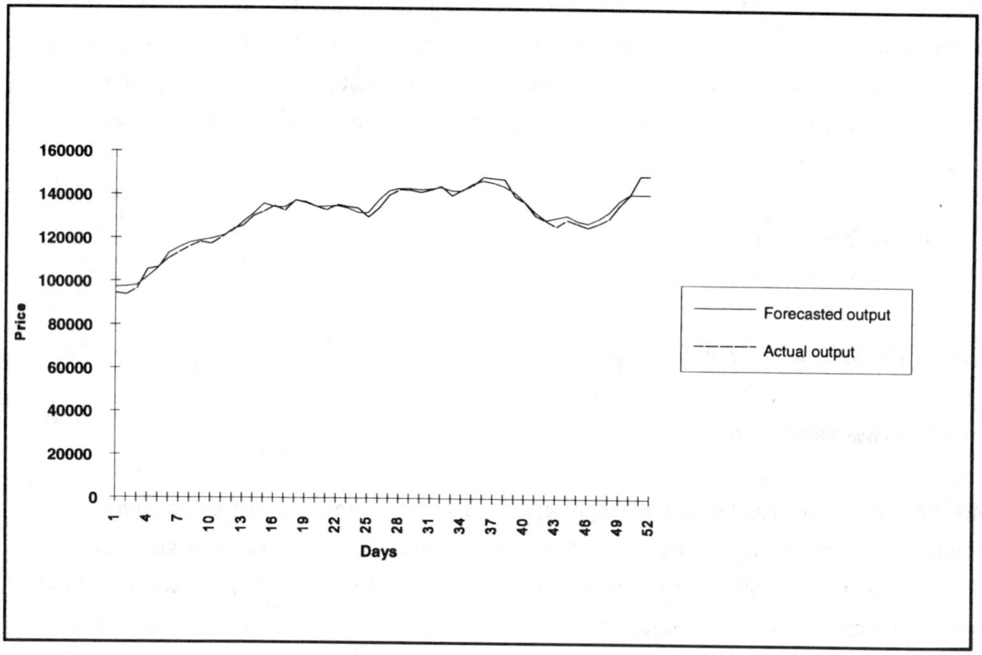

On the basis of the testing and training statistic results, the network parameters were accepted, and there was no need for any further adjustments to the network. In phase 2 of the research experiment, a 7-day prediction based on 50 days of data will be performed using data not utilized as part of the training and testing set. In addition, results using the trained neural network will be compared with the Box-Jenkins methodology.

4.6.6 Application of sensitivity analysis techniques

One of the general criticisms against neural networks is that their complexity makes them difficult to understand, which implies that, in order for one to trust the results of a neural network, the knowledge learned by the networks during the training process should somehow be revealed and confirmed, particularly regarding the correct selection of inputs. However, some inputs will have a larger influence on the output than others. One of the problems with attempting to predict future share prices is that a large number of indicators may be potentially relevant. In order to simultaneously maintain reasonable training times and generate good predictions, it is necessary to develop methodologies for efficiently selecting appropriate inputs. Since a large number of these inputs, as network parameters, may be available, parameter significance analysis can be helpful. Two approaches to input parameter significance analysis are:

- Cross-validation; and
- approximate sensitivity analysis.

Each will be subsequently discussed.

4.6.6.1 Cross-validation

Moody and Utans (1992:683-690) suggest a number of techniques in this category. These techniques are based on the calculation of the cross-validation error. Data is divided into 5 or more subsets (v) with 80% overlapping and 20% original input vectors. Each subset is then used to train a separate network. On completion of training, each network is cross-validated with other subsets of data, and an error figure is established. Based on this v-fold cross-validation error, a three step heuristic algorithm is suggested:

- Optimum network topology through competition - Multiple networks with varying numbers of hidden layers or nodes are trained in parallel on v subsets of data, and the network with the optimum architecture is selected through cross-validation.

- Pruning input variables - Using the v-fold cross-validation approach, one input variable is replaced by its mean value to eliminate its effect on the network. Networks are trained, and the performance of each network is assessed on each subset of data (Moody, 1992:847-848).

- Pruning weights - The assumption is that most networks are too large and contain many redundant weights. If such weights can be identified and eliminated, better prediction performance can be realized. This method involves removing redundant weights, retraining networks, assessing their performance based on a saliency figure, and finally selecting the network with the optimum set of nodes and interconnections.

Neural network parameters such as the learning rate, momentum, and the activation function should all be varied in a systematic way. In this study, approximate sensitivity analysis techniques will be utilized.

4.6.6.2 Approximate sensitivity analysis

Neural networks have often been criticized for their black-box nature, in that it is difficult to examine a trained neural network and infer rules from it. However, neural networks typically implement their mappings through specific interconnection weights between the various layers and nodes. These weight values may serve as useful indicators of the importance of input variables by analyzing their contribution to network operation by means of heuristics. Heuristics available include:

- Sensitivity analysis; and
- weight analysis.

- Sensitivity analysis - this involves noting changes in the output which are caused by a d percent change in the inputs, while keeping all other inputs the same. Therefore, the sensitivity approach measures the variables' impact on the magnitude of the residual for each observation. The procedure works as follows: (refer to equation 4-5)

- All values for one of the input variables (*Var x*) are replaced with the variable's unconditional expectation (arithmetic mean);
- the neural network's output is then recomputed using the new input matrix and the existing weights matrix;
- the absolute residual from the output is compared with the absolute residual of the output generated by the original input matrix; and
- the above steps are then repeated for each input variable.

$$Contribution_{var\ x} = \frac{Target - Prediction_{new}}{Target - Prediction_{orginal}} \qquad \text{...(4-5)}$$

Baestaens, Van Den Bergh and Vaudrey (1993:9) suggest that a ratio below 1 implies that the original residuals exceed the recomputed residual and the variable under test contributed negatively to the solution. Conversely, a ratio above 1 indicates that the variable tends to reduce the original residual and that it contributed positively to the desired solution. A ratio around 1, [0.75, 1.25] range, signals a neutral contribution.

The following sensitivity analyses were done on the inputs: (refer to Table 4.11)

- Absolute minimum sensitivity indicates the smallest number of changes (positive or negative) that an input causes in the output for all the facts. A large number means that the input had no effect on the output.

- Absolute maximum sensitivity indicates the largest number change an input has caused in on the output for all the facts. The larger the number, the larger the effect on the output.

- Mean sensitivity indicates the average number of changes an input causes over all the facts. In general, it indicates whether the effect of the input is positive or negative and provides an approximation of the overall effect.

- Standard deviation indicates the spread of the changes over all the facts. A small number means that, for a specific input, most of the facts had the same amount of change in the output. A large number means that the effect on the output varied greatly from fact to fact.

Table 4.11 - Sensitivity analysis results

	Absolute minimum	Absolute maximum	Mean	Standard deviation	Ranked on mean	Ranked on σ
Input 1	0.0007	0.0112	0.0058	0.0027	20	9
Input 2	0.0007	0.0136	0.0061	0.0034	17	15
Input 3	0.0012	0.0227	0.013	0.0051	5	40
Input 4	0.0017	0.0229	0.0137	0.0058	4	51
Input 5	0	0.0229	-0.0104	0.0066	55	57
Input 6	0	0.0104	-0.0021	0.0021	37	4
Input 7	0	0.01	-0.005	0.0019	42	2
Input 8	0	0.0056	-0.0009	0.002	35	3
Input 9	0.0002	0.0117	0.0057	0.0033	21	14
Input 10	0	0.0041	-0.0008	0.0017	33	1
Input 11	0.0004	0.0283	0.0146	0.0081	3	59
Input 12	0.0017	0.0344	0.0152	0.0086	2	60
Input 13	0.0007	0.0153	0.0059	0.003	19	11
Input 14	0	0.0156	-0.0008	0.005	34	39
Input 15	0.0002	0.0209	-0.0119	0.0057	56	49
Input 16	0.0002	0.0148	-0.0072	0.0052	50	44
Input 17	0	0.0373	-0.0196	0.0118	62	63
Input 18	0.0004	0.0285	-0.0119	0.0111	57	62
Input 19	0	0.0253	0.0031	0.0052	25	42
Input 20	0	0.0092	-0.0029	0.0026	38	8
Input 21	0.0002	0.0249	0.0115	0.0061	6	53
Input 22	0	0.0178	0.0012	0.004	30	22
Input 23	0.0017	0.0209	0.0103	0.0039	7	21
Input 24	0	0.018	0.006	0.005	18	38
Input 25	0	0.009	-4.787	0.0044	63	28
Input 26	0.0017	0.0234	0.0099	0.0045	9	29
Input 27	0.0012	0.0185	0.0088	0.005	10	37
Input 28	0.0002	0.0209	-0.0061	0.0052	44	43
Input 29	0.0004	0.0148	-0.0066	0.0038	47	20
Input 30	0.0026	0.0363	0.0177	0.0079	1	58
Input 31	0.0017	0.0231	0.0073	0.0044	12	27
Input 32	0.0002	0.01	-0.0045	0.0032	39	12
Input 33	0.0012	0.0214	0.0066	0.0048	14	34

	Absolute minimum	Absolute maximum	Mean	Standard deviation	Ranked on mean	Ranked on σ
Input 34	0	0.0168	0.0007	0.004	32	23
Input 35	0.0014	0.0173	0.0065	0.0029	15	10
Input 36	0.0004	0.0195	0.0044	0.0038	24	19
Input 37	0	0.0107	0.002	0.0026	27	7
Input 38	0.0002	0.0161	0.0049	0.0048	23	35
Input 39	0.0009	0.0268	0.0071	0.0053	13	45
Input 40	0	0.0134	0.0026	0.0034	26	16
Input 41	0	0.0212	0.0012	0.0055	31	47
Input 42	0.0009	0.0144	-0.0066	0.0032	48	13
Input 43	0.0007	0.0219	-0.0127	0.0061	58	55
Input 44	0	0.0134	0.0051	0.0046	22	30
Input 45	0.0002	0.0161	-0.0065	0.0051	46	41
Input 46	0.0014	0.0319	-0.0132	0.0062	60	56
Input 47	0.0004	0.0141	0.0063	0.0038	16	18
Input 48	0.0009	0.0249	-0.0049	0.0046	41	31
Input 49	0.0012	0.0229	-0.0131	0.0057	59	50
Input 50	0.0007	0.0119	-0.0047	0.0025	40	6
Input 51	0	0.0073	0.0017	0.0023	28	5
Input 52	0.0017	0.0268	-0.0096	0.0054	54	46
Input 53	0.0002	0.0141	-0.0058	0.0047	43	32
Input 54	0.0002	0.0178	0.0082	0.0043	11	25
Input 55	0	0.0134	0.0015	0.0058	29	52
Input 56	0.0002	0.0178	-0.0089	0.0061	52	54
Input 57	0.0002	0.0136	-0.0063	0.0057	45	48
Input 58	0	0.0151	-0.0009	0.0042	36	24
Input 59	0.0007	0.0185	-0.0082	0.0043	51	26
Input 60	0.0002	0.0141	-0.007	0.0037	49	17
Input 61	0.0017	0.0249	0.01	0.0049	8	36
Input 62	0	0.0349	-0.0184	0.0104	61	61
Input 63	0	0.0185	-0.0092	0.0047	53	33

Based on the criterion of discarding inputs with means closest to 0.0, 20 inputs were discarded. These include the following inputs::

- Input 1 - Volume;
- Input 6 - Moving average oscillator (Price);
- Input 8 - Stochastic indicator (%D);
- Input 9 - Stochastic indicator (%K);
- Input 10 - Relative strength index;

- Input 13 - Moving average convergence-divergence (Close);
- Input 14 - Log-Delta;
- Input 19 - Volatility (True range);
- Input 20 - Volatility (Moving average);
- Input 22 - JSE Beverages, Hotels, and Leisure index;
- Input 32 - JSE Pharmaceutical and Medical index;
- Input 34 - JSE Steel index;
- Input 36 - JSE Retailer and Wholesaler index;
- Input 37 - JSE Transport index;
- Input 38 - JSE Industrial index;
- Input 40 - JSE Gold index;
- Input 41 - Standard and Poor 500 index;
- Input 44 - DJ-Industrial index;
- Input 48 - Financial time Gold Index; and
- Input 50 - Gold-PM.

It is quite evident from the list that the majority of inputs, which were discarded, were either of the type common to technical analysis or gold-related. To determine the validity of the sensitivity analysis, the neural network was retrained and tested using the remaining 40 inputs and initial parameters (refer to section 4.6.3). In addition, the number of neurons in the hidden layer was reduced to 14[87]. The results of the modified neural network are summarized in Table 4.12.

Table 4.12 - Training and testing statistics based on the modified neural network

Sequence	Average error	Root mean squared error	Coefficient of determination
Training	0.0384	0.0456	0.9684
Testing	0.0366	0.0441	0.9702

It is evident from the table that the pruning of inputs did not significantly change the performance of the neural network in terms of the coefficient of determination. However, training time was

87 Based on the heuristic that the number of neurons in the hidden layer should be about a third of the inputs and output.

reduced from 45 to 32 minutes. One potential problem with sensitivity analysis is that, although inputs can be reduced in number, the synergetic relationship between inputs is virtually unknown, being based on a complex nonlinear function. Therefore, the application of sensitivity analysis should be used with extreme caution. It should be noted that, at this time, sensitivity analysis is still in its experimental phase, and that the only justification for sensitivity analysis lies in the argument that, if a model captures the relationships between the input and the output accurately, then the relationships are very likely to exist in the training sample.

- Weight analysis - the method of weight analysis has been suggested by Sen, Oliver and Sen (1992:34) as an approximation of calculating the derivative of the output with respect to the number of input variables. The method is based on the assumption that a neural network is most sensitive to those input variables which are connected with the largest overall network weights (refer to Tables 4.13 and 4.14).

Table 4.13 - Weighted matrix: Weights between the inputs and hidden layers units 1 through 11

	Hidden units										
Inputs	1	2	3	4	5	6	7	8	9	10	11
1	-0.84	0.31	-0.11	-0.69	0.15	0.20	0.03	-1.40	-0.13	0.77	0.22
2	0.18	-0.85	-0.03	-0.29	-0.22	0.07	0.04	-1.50	2.10	0.94	0.01
3	-0.81	-1.96	-1.22	-1.14	-0.76	1.40	-0.39	-0.05	-0.04	0.77	-1.29
4	-2.13	-0.39	-1.36	-2.35	-0.27	1.22	-1.08	-0.84	-2.02	0.67	1.37
5	0.13	-0.42	-0.52	-2.74	-2.42	-0.22	0.29	-0.27	-1.51	-1.35	-0.59
6	-1.72	-1.27	-1.03	-2.69	-2.24	-0.06	0.33	-0.66	1.43	0.07	-0.46
7	0.34	-0.92	-0.47	-1.95	-1.44	-0.45	0.15	-0.66	0.65	-0.30	-0.19
8	-1.10	-1.52	-1.12	-0.88	-1.36	-0.18	0.17	0.52	0.90	0.27	1.06
9	-2.45	-1.63	-0.55	-0.15	-2.15	0.18	-0.66	-0.96	1.40	0.56	-0.54
10	-1.04	-1.25	-1.16	-1.48	-3.06	0.60	0.66	-0.75	0.97	-0.08	-1.13
11	-1.63	-0.83	-1.21	-0.42	-0.62	1.20	-1.04	-1.60	-0.28	1.29	0.71
12	-1.20	-1.20	-1.70	-0.78	-1.02	0.31	-0.28	-1.34	-0.60	2.00	1.11
13	-2.83	-1.40	-0.48	-1.43	-2.32	1.40	-0.11	-0.28	1.66	0.16	-1.09
14	-1.74	0.51	-1.80	-0.56	-1.35	0.56	1.36	-1.92	-4.68	0.86	1.81
15	-0.38	-0.08	-1.78	-1.81	-1.34	-1.38	1.11	-0.10	-0.65	-0.76	-0.01

Inputs	Hidden units 1	2	3	4	5	6	7	8	9	10	11
16	0.33	0.16	-0.20	-0.77	-0.12	-1.08	0.40	0.36	0.65	-0.46	0.06
17	-0.43	0.50	-2.16	-0.95	-1.88	-2.19	1.32	-0.24	-3.38	-1.60	-2.48
18	0.24	-0.26	-1.59	-1.07	-2.56	-1.49	1.41	0.17	-1.27	-0.28	-3.42
19	-0.99	-0.55	-1.28	-1.62	-1.09	0.05	-0.43	-0.02	-3.29	-0.05	0.74
20	-0.33	-0.87	-0.45	-1.11	-0.39	-0.14	0.78	-0.77	-1.95	0.25	-0.64
21	-1.81	-0.37	-1.38	-1.34	-1.28	0.34	-1.06	0.08	-1.56	1.04	-0.45
22	-2.16	-1.55	-1.55	-0.11	-0.79	-0.22	0.35	-1.66	-0.59	0.01	1.01
23	-2.97	-0.60	-2.11	-1.48	-2.09	1.44	0.28	-1.49	-0.24	0.77	1.08
24	-1.31	-0.70	-0.89	-1.43	-0.26	0.46	-1.73	0.12	-0.09	-0.45	-0.95
25	-0.88	-0.91	-0.70	-1.25	-2.45	-0.23	1.05	0.05	1.05	0.88	-2.29
26	-1.08	0.11	0.62	-0.10	-0.56	0.66	0.34	-1.17	2.00	1.13	-0.51
27	-1.16	-0.32	-2.39	-0.34	-1.36	0.80	-1.46	-1.12	-0.71	-0.03	1.46
28	-0.92	-0.69	-2.04	-2.06	-0.25	0.53	0.64	0.47	-1.26	-0.82	-0.21
29	0.00	-0.52	-0.79	-0.06	0.06	-0.18	1.21	-0.47	-0.37	0.04	-0.17
30	-2.31	-1.36	-0.32	-0.93	-1.60	0.09	-1.23	-1.53	1.60	1.54	1.56
31	-0.61	-1.09	-0.81	-0.82	-0.42	0.31	-0.81	-0.81	0.06	0.05	0.50
32	-0.61	0.02	-0.71	-1.07	-0.17	-0.45	0.51	-0.79	-1.70	-0.39	-0.04
33	-0.80	-0.42	-2.03	-0.84	-1.13	-0.84	-0.63	-0.36	-1.25	0.81	-0.09
34	-1.81	-1.32	-1.64	-1.70	-2.45	-0.05	0.46	-1.31	1.15	0.00	-1.21
35	-1.87	-0.95	-1.90	-1.22	-1.95	0.70	0.23	-1.73	2.64	0.60	0.98
36	-1.35	-1.56	-0.97	0.53	-1.61	-0.08	-0.08	-0.12	-0.57	0.04	0.41
37	-0.23	0.00	-0.62	0.20	-1.06	0.44	-0.54	-0.06	-0.93	-0.28	0.80
38	-1.29	-1.37	-1.38	-1.72	-0.13	0.74	-1.17	-0.58	-0.58	-0.27	-0.51
39	-1.10	-2.74	-1.03	-1.62	-1.96	0.19	0.33	-1.53	0.39	0.98	0.78
40	-1.64	-0.50	-1.82	-2.19	-0.50	-0.21	-1.21	0.11	1.24	-0.20	-2.01
41	-1.82	-0.56	-1.48	0.49	-1.83	0.00	-1.16	-0.46	-1.25	-0.65	-0.64
42	1.22	1.30	-0.18	-0.92	1.85	0.24	0.70	0.45	-1.45	-0.55	-2.87
43	1.22	0.86	-0.95	-1.35	0.10	-1.23	1.16	1.12	-0.69	-0.76	-2.07
44	-1.16	-1.44	-0.04	-1.64	-1.68	0.04	-1.05	-0.47	-1.86	0.51	0.46
45	-0.88	0.10	-1.43	-0.93	-1.06	0.18	0.06	-0.29	-1.91	-1.14	-0.84
46	-2.40	-0.71	-2.20	-1.40	-1.24	-0.14	0.23	0.33	-2.91	-1.40	-0.24
47	-1.17	-1.06	0.25	-0.36	-1.02	0.20	-0.53	-0.81	3.04	0.75	-0.87
48	-1.69	-0.74	-1.82	-1.68	-2.66	0.47	0.12	0.29	0.26	-0.44	-1.10

	Hidden units										
Inputs	1	2	3	4	5	6	7	8	9	10	11
49	0.29	0.25	0.45	-1.35	-0.99	-1.13	0.66	-0.20	-0.80	-1.17	-2.67
50	-0.63	-0.09	0.20	-2.41	-0.97	0.42	0.69	0.57	0.39	-0.21	-1.40
51	-1.27	-1.04	0.16	-1.35	-0.57	0.12	-0.80	0.79	-0.18	-0.26	-0.16
52	-1.30	0.65	-1.70	-1.23	-1.34	0.62	1.42	0.99	-3.04	-0.58	-0.01
53	-2.40	-1.98	-1.84	-0.74	-2.40	-1.12	0.07	0.06	1.37	-0.19	-1.96
54	-0.52	-0.42	-0.99	-1.55	-0.82	0.43	-1.22	-1.30	3.02	0.37	-0.15
55	-1.30	-0.16	-2.47	-1.48	-1.79	-0.84	0.84	-0.48	2.82	1.20	-0.46
56	-1.69	0.33	-1.67	-1.51	-1.26	-1.10	0.70	-1.09	1.33	-0.47	-2.53
57	-1.72	-0.33	-0.74	-2.78	-2.56	-0.75	0.53	-0.97	0.36	-0.37	-2.00
58	-1.53	-2.25	-0.33	-1.59	-1.01	-0.45	-0.42	-0.29	-1.44	-0.42	0.67
59	-0.20	0.78	-2.14	-0.56	-1.16	-0.15	-0.05	-0.87	-1.60	-1.10	-0.23
60	-0.22	0.94	-0.70	-0.31	-0.52	-0.42	0.70	0.05	-0.78	-0.64	0.20
61	-1.94	-1.49	-3.05	-0.34	-0.64	0.26	-0.68	-1.24	-2.39	0.85	0.33
62	-0.89	0.51	-1.78	-0.65	-0.43	-1.81	1.01	0.37	-3.07	-1.59	-0.29
63	-1.50	-0.76	-1.26	-0.45	-1.77	-0.33	0.90	-1.08	-0.47	-0.84	-0.45
B1[88]	5.51	4.32	-4.15	-2.17	-1.42	-3.84	4.38	3.72	-4.82	-4.71	-4.56

Table 4.14 - Weighted matrix: Weights between the inputs and hidden layers units 12 through 21

	Hidden units									
Inputs	12	13	14	15	16	17	18	19	20	21
1	-1.23	-0.71	-0.47	-0.42	-0.48	0.31	-0.24	-0.52	0.80	0.33
2	-1.38	0.32	-0.24	-0.78	1.56	0.52	-1.40	-0.81	0.94	0.31
3	-0.13	-0.28	-1.58	-2.05	2.32	-0.34	-1.60	-0.67	0.67	1.07
4	-0.97	-1.59	-1.50	-1.31	3.22	0.51	-2.01	-1.05	-0.38	1.06
5	-0.67	0.17	1.70	-0.24	-2.38	-1.42	-1.01	0.39	1.11	0.00

---

88 B1 = a threshold neuron which is added to each layer of a neural network with the exception of the output layer. The output of the threshold neuron is always the maximum value of the transfer function. Research has found that neural networks work better when they have threshold neurons.

Inputs	Hidden units									
	12	13	14	15	16	17	18	19	20	21
6	-0.28	0.67	0.33	-1.16	0.14	-0.10	-2.22	-0.79	0.37	-0.52
7	-0.91	-0.37	0.61	-1.05	0.31	-0.83	-1.27	-0.80	-1.17	-0.32
8	-0.52	-1.59	1.08	-1.61	1.59	0.10	-2.06	-1.08	1.52	-0.19
9	-1.34	-0.83	0.54	-0.55	2.47	-1.29	-0.35	-1.33	0.09	0.54
10	0.14	-0.97	0.01	-0.86	1.28	0.16	-0.63	-1.65	0.91	-0.16
11	-1.65	-1.97	-0.57	-1.86	4.49	-0.64	-1.06	-1.93	1.61	0.14
12	0.02	-1.22	-0.14	-1.37	3.40	-0.26	-0.50	-0.29	0.24	1.65
13	-1.38	-1.24	0.28	-0.82	1.66	0.02	-1.43	-1.73	1.64	0.43
14	-0.37	-0.06	1.09	-0.24	-3.74	1.09	-0.75	0.19	-3.18	-0.15
15	-1.06	-1.17	-0.42	-1.38	1.37	-1.11	-1.74	-0.46	0.34	-0.74
16	-0.52	-0.64	0.65	0.44	-1.62	-0.39	-1.53	0.28	-1.04	0.30
17	-1.32	-1.32	0.88	0.09	2.70	-2.25	-2.08	0.66	-0.82	0.13
18	-0.72	0.42	2.47	-0.10	-1.15	-1.76	-1.53	-0.48	-1.09	0.87
19	-2.31	-1.49	0.34	-0.52	0.62	-0.18	-1.35	-1.18	0.84	1.24
20	0.29	-0.77	0.46	-0.68	1.41	0.46	-1.21	-0.75	-1.08	-0.29
21	0.02	-0.89	-0.17	-1.57	3.73	-0.99	-0.72	-0.45	-1.12	1.19
22	-1.13	-1.44	-1.04	-0.42	4.67	-0.22	-0.70	-0.35	0.24	0.86
23	-1.05	-0.69	-1.11	-0.87	4.11	0.80	-1.11	-3.08	0.54	1.01
24	-1.11	-0.85	-0.61	-0.50	3.13	-0.31	-0.63	-1.56	0.06	0.57
25	-1.70	-1.96	-0.05	-0.49	0.65	-2.63	-2.15	-0.85	-0.35	-0.39
26	-0.25	-0.35	-0.58	-1.57	1.32	0.09	-0.83	-0.10	2.07	1.14
27	-0.49	-1.41	-0.49	0.06	2.36	0.01	-0.52	-0.25	0.88	0.81
28	-0.88	-0.46	-0.28	-0.09	1.99	-0.19	-1.22	-1.05	0.57	-1.02
29	-0.70	0.22	0.97	-0.88	2.87	0.03	-0.49	-0.22	-0.19	-0.73
30	-0.79	-1.75	-1.95	-2.50	2.38	1.59	-0.93	-1.44	0.72	1.75
31	-0.42	-0.57	-1.46	-1.18	2.17	0.80	-0.28	-0.24	-0.16	1.13
32	-0.67	-0.08	0.03	-0.16	1.78	-0.64	-0.04	-1.10	1.13	0.08
33	-0.48	-1.56	-0.67	-0.20	3.38	-1.43	-0.28	-0.33	0.38	1.03
34	-2.02	-1.82	-0.84	-0.50	1.56	-1.61	-1.82	0.19	-0.61	0.81
35	-0.93	-1.30	-0.44	-1.67	1.65	0.52	-1.47	-1.64	0.71	0.84
36	-0.39	-0.95	-1.71	-1.12	3.44	-0.42	-0.74	-1.89	1.35	0.95
37	-0.46	-0.53	0.29	0.49	1.96	-0.44	-0.71	-0.76	1.69	0.28
38	-0.68	-1.07	-0.94	-0.45	2.82	-1.47	-0.65	-1.07	-0.82	-0.12

Inputs	Hidden units									
	12	13	14	15	16	17	18	19	20	21
39	-1.52	-0.21	-0.04	-0.31	4.11	0.38	-0.18	-1.77	0.87	1.29
40	-1.42	0.02	0.53	-1.89	-0.31	0.07	-0.75	-0.13	0.34	0.66
41	-0.52	0.16	0.52	-0.65	0.84	-1.08	-0.26	-0.63	-0.17	1.04
42	-1.80	0.24	0.33	1.45	-1.80	-2.17	-2.02	1.03	-1.95	-0.70
43	-1.61	-0.54	0.39	1.04	-0.49	-2.17	-2.25	0.29	-1.58	-0.49
44	0.76	-1.39	0.70	-0.10	1.01	-1.54	-1.13	-0.61	0.88	-0.17
45	0.05	-1.33	0.63	0.13	2.89	-1.85	-1.91	-0.92	-1.22	0.17
46	-1.22	-0.61	1.17	-1.67	3.12	-1.97	-1.70	-1.17	-2.19	-1.53
47	-0.61	-0.63	0.11	-2.12	1.43	0.44	-0.67	-0.87	0.54	0.14
48	-1.24	-2.44	0.90	-0.05	-0.94	-1.87	-2.21	-2.02	-0.89	-1.19
49	-2.11	-0.15	-0.14	0.79	-0.18	-0.82	-2.04	-0.04	-1.72	-0.87
50	-1.17	0.39	0.74	0.69	0.75	0.11	-1.98	1.08	-1.85	-0.59
51	-1.13	-0.78	-0.12	-1.40	-0.40	-0.63	-1.28	-0.35	0.41	-0.04
52	-1.45	-0.50	1.00	-0.50	1.11	-3.52	-1.72	-0.53	-0.85	-1.31
53	-1.58	-1.93	1.34	-0.91	1.31	-1.53	-1.41	-1.09	-1.02	0.28
54	-0.65	-1.27	0.15	-0.52	1.91	-0.64	-2.73	-1.66	0.02	0.85
55	-1.47	-0.81	0.44	-1.22	1.04	-1.68	-2.57	-1.42	0.24	0.34
56	-2.01	-0.40	0.99	0.76	1.58	-2.69	-1.35	-0.87	-1.23	0.23
57	-0.97	-1.21	0.98	0.49	0.66	-1.73	-2.01	-0.72	-0.96	0.51
58	0.23	-0.30	0.01	-0.54	-1.74	-0.35	-0.25	-1.50	-0.06	0.76
59	-0.62	0.24	0.14	-0.10	-0.12	-3.23	-1.22	-1.22	-1.43	-0.89
60	0.04	-0.59	-0.34	-1.35	0.90	4.00	-0.86	-0.36	-0.09	-0.36
61	0.01	-0.88	-0.51	-1.83	1.57	-0.54	-0.07	-0.22	0.31	1.20
62	-0.25	1.14	1.46	-0.52	1.96	-1.12	-0.76	0.56	-0.14	-0.01
63	1.12	-0.45	0.14	-0.32	0.96	-1.60	-0.95	-1.25	-0.01	-0.51
B1	-2.33	4.80	4.11	3.34	-3.78	-4.69	-4.55	4.53	-3.77	21

On completion of training, network weights from each input were added together, creating an absolute value. These absolute sums were ranked for all inputs. The idea is that the larger the total, the more significant the corresponding input variable, since it would have a larger effect on the output. According to the literature, for the case studied here, absolute sums between -0.4 and 0.4 should be pruned. Figure 4.10 provides a bar graph of sums of network weights associated with each input.

It was evident from the absolute weight analysis that the following inputs should be pruned:

- Input 2 - Dividend yield;
- Input 29 - JSE-Motor index; and
- Input 37 - JSE-Transportation index.

After pruning inputs using this approach, the neural network was then trained with 60 inputs and 1 output, with 20 neurons in the hidden layer. Refer to Table 4.15, for statistics. It can be noted from the statistics that the R^2 of the modified network for training is comparable to that of the initial neural network model. However, training R^2 decreased by 0.0038, and training time decreased from 45 to 31 minutes. It should be noted that single weight analysis (magnitude and sign) can be misleading in the sense that it excludes the bias (Baestaens, Van den Bergh and Vaudrey, 1993:8).

Table 4.15 - Training and testing statistics

Sequence	Average error	Root mean squared error	Coefficient of determination
Training	0.0308	0.0383	0.9762
Testing	0.0259	0.033	0.93

Figure 4.10 - Weighted analysis scores

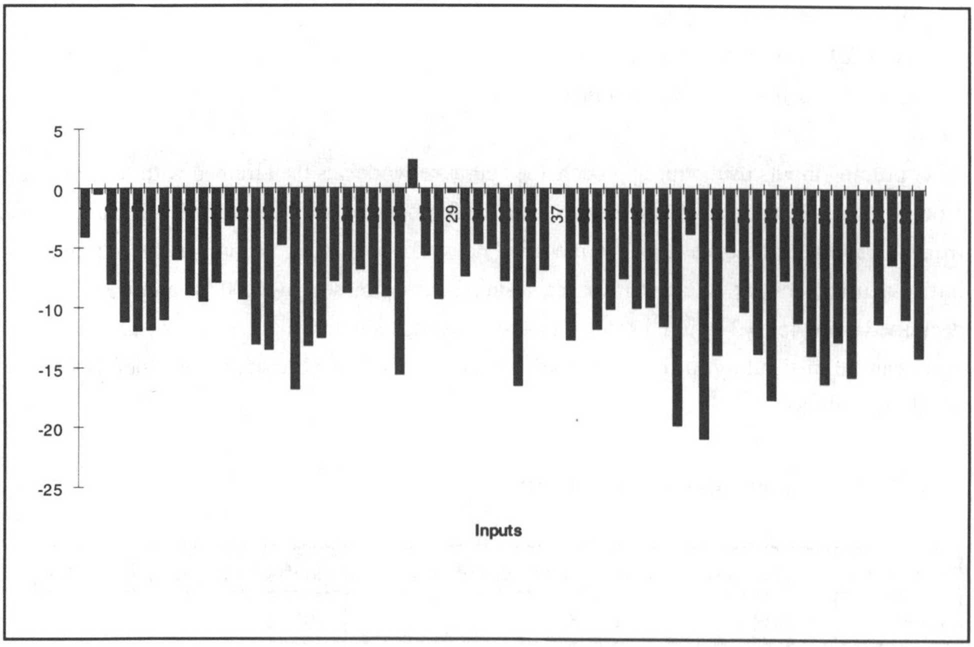

Furthermore, large weights do not necessarily result in sigmoid saturation since they may be associated with very low input values. Interpreting single weights in isolation does not improve one's understanding of a variable's total contribution to the solution: different input values will interact with the weight patterns in different ways, so the input values themselves should be included in the analysis.

Gorman and Sejnowski (1988:75-89) suggest clustering the observations using a weighted matrix that depends on the weights associated with connections between the input and the *i*th hidden unit. The Euclidian distance is computed for each pair of weight-state vectors and is written on a distance matrix. Finally, a hierarchical clustering technique is applied to the matrix whereby each cluster contains a number of observations with similar weight-state vectors. By averaging all of these observations within each cluster, the cluster's centroid is calculated. Based on this, the centroids are ranked according to the output or activation level of the relevant hidden unit. This procedure is repeated for each unit independently. However, the weight-state approach is only suitable for neural networks consisting of just one hidden layer and no direct connections between the input and output layers.

One form of sensitivity analysis involves the perturbation of input variables. Using a test data set, the method involves varying the input of one of the variables in small steps over the range of -0.9 to 0.9 (or across the full input range), while holding the other inputs at their respective mean values. However, it is recommended that such experimental approaches to sensitivity analysis be further refined before considering them appropriate for application.

4.6.7 Comparative studies

Other international studies on the application of neural networks in the securities markets are discussed below.

Kimoto, Asakawa, Yoda and Takeoko (1993:343-350) developed a method to check whether neural networks could produce a successful model for share market prediction. The neural network was trained on data covering the period January 1985 to September 1989. The authors conclude that neural networks, as a prediction system, made excellent profits in the simulation exercise.

White (1993:315-317) used a neural network to analyze 5000 days of return data for IBM. The training sample covered trading days during the period 1974 to 1978. The evaluation periods covered 1972 through 1974 and 1978 up to 1980. The purpose of the study was to provide evidence against the simple efficient market hypothesis. The research concludes that neural networks are not appropriate for forecasting of a share's returns, accepting the efficient market hypothesis.

Yoon and Swales (1993:329-335) compared a multiple discriminate model's share price predictive power to that of a neural network. The data used in this study was gathered from *Fortune 500* and *Business Week*'s top 1000 companies, providing the total return and market valuation data. The companies were classified into two groups according to investors' total returns. The study concludes that the "...comparison of the neural network technique with the multiple discriminate analysis approach indicated that the neural network approach can significantly improve the predictability of stock price performance."

Kamijo and Tanigawa (1993:357-360) constructed a recurrent neural network model for share price pattern recognition in the form of Japanese-style "candlesticks" and developed a method of evaluating the neural network. Data was gathered from the Tokyo Stock Exchange for a period of two years. The results indicate that the neural network accurately recognized the pattern in 15 out of 16 experiments, and that the number of mismatched patterns was 1.06 per name on average over all of the experiments.

4.6.8 Summary

The neural network model developed in this study employed 63 inputs and 1 output. It was trained on 90% of the available data. Training results were found to be acceptable. The neural network was then tested, and these results were also being found to be acceptable. To assess the relative importance of the inputs, sensitivity analysis and absolute weight analysis methods were employed. However, these methods did not produce a clear-cut indication of which inputs were important. The second phase of the experiment will be addressed next.

4.7 BOX-JENKINS

The second phase of the experiment is to construct a Box-Jenkins model for forecasting the share price time series according to objective number three listed earlier, and then to perform a comparison between neural networks and Box-Jenkins.

4.7.1 Introduction

The Box-Jenkins method of forecasting was used to develop an appropriate model for forecasting the time series employed in this study. The approach employed involved an iterative process of identifying a possibly useful model, which was then checked against the historical data set to determine whether it accurately predicted the series. The model was regarded appropriate when the residuals between the forecasts and the historical data points were small, randomly distributed and independent.

With the aid of a statistical computer program, an ARMA model was identified and the coefficient was calculated using a nonlinear least squares method. Forecasts for 50 future periods were made and 95% confidence intervals were constructed for the estimates in order to facilitate the comparison between neural networks and Box-Jenkins methods. The following steps were performed in the identification of the model:

- Determining if the time series is stationary or non-stationary ;
- estimating parameters in the candidate models; and
- diagnostic checking.

4.7.2 Determining if the time series is stationary or non-stationary

The first step in identifying the model was to apply the autocorrelation function to the time series. It is evident from Figure 4.12 that the time series was non-stationary. This is implied because of the failure of the estimated autocorrelation function to decrease toward zero at larger lags, which typically occurs after the second or third lag. The results confirm the work of Du Toit (1986:4.19) who states "...given the total number of shares and the percentage of cases out of the total sample of 180 shares where the null hypotheses of stationary and mean square values had to be rejected, one may assume that the shares examined exhibited non-stationarity."

Figure 4.11 - Autocorrelation of the data

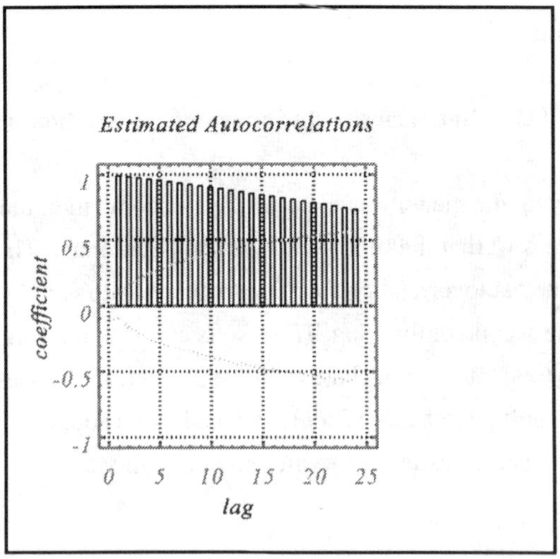

4.7.3 Estimating parameters in the candidate models

By comparing the autocorrelation (Figure 4.11) and the partial-autocorrelation coefficients (Figure 4.12) of the data with the corresponding distributions of various ARMA models, an ARMA (1,1) process was suggested. The behavior of the ACF and PACF for the selected ARMA (1,1) scheme shows that both trail off exponentially and may contain damped oscillations.

4.7.4 Diagnostic checking

The autocorrelation check for white noise indicated that all the probability values were less than 0.05, indicating that the time series contained more than white noise. The t-test values of the estimated coefficients were significant (i.e., t-test value > 2), indicating that the correct model had been fitted. Furthermore, Akaike's information criterion (AIC value) was fitted to the model. The minimum AIC occurred using the ARMA (1,1) model, which suggested that the correct model had been selected. Supplementary to these tests, an autocorrelation check on the residuals was performed. This test indicated that all the probability values were greater than 0.05, and therefore the correct model had been fitted.

Figure 4.12 - Partial-autocorrelation

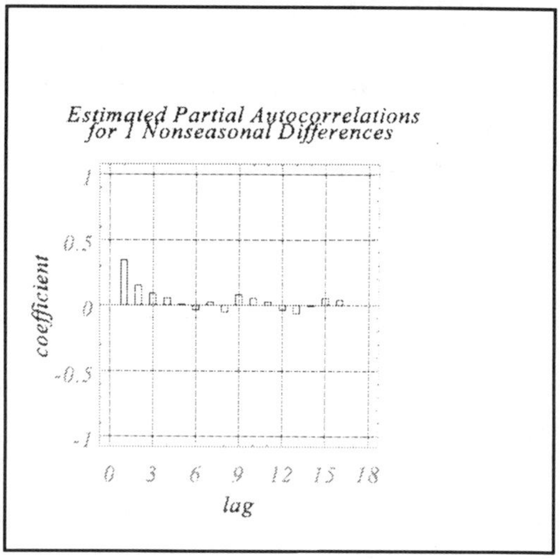

Based on the diagnostic described, the following model was suggested: (refer to equation 4-6)

$$\nabla Z_t - 0.7750\ \nabla Z_{t-1} = a_t - 0.50185 a_{t-1} \qquad \textbf{...(4-6)}$$

4.7.5 Comparison of neural networks and Box-Jenkins

The effectiveness of neural network and Box-Jenkins models for both simulated and actual time-series are now presented. The performance measures used in the study for model selection are related with forecasting accuracy. Measures of forecast accuracy serve several purposes:

- To provide an interpreted measure of a model's usefulness;
- to compare the accuracy of several models; and
- to select an optimal model.

Numerous measures of forecasting accuracy are available to fulfill the above purposes. The effectiveness and accuracy of the two forecasting models developed in this study were measured according to two different error measures:

- Mean squared error (MSE)[89]; and
- Mean absolute percentage error (MAPE)[90].

It should be noted that each of these measures has its advantages and disadvantages, depending on the given forecasting situation. This provides the motivation for utilizing more than a single measure. (refer to equations 4.7 to 4.9).

$$e_t = X_t - F_t \qquad \text{...(4-7)}$$

$$MSE = \sum_{l=1}^{N} \frac{e_i^2}{n} \qquad \text{...(4-8)}$$

$$MAPE = \sum_{n}^{t=1} \frac{|X_t - F_t|}{X_t} \qquad \text{...(4-9)}$$

Where: X_t = The actual observation for time period t.
F_t = The forecast for time period t.

4.7.5.1 Experimental results - simulated time series

The simulated time series represented the period 1/2/1991 - 12/31/1992. This period was used to test the neural network, as well as to formulate the Box-Jenkins model. Table 4.16 provides results based on performance according to the error measures employed as well the coefficients of determination.

---

89 MSE averages the sizes of the forecast errors squared and penalizes more for large errors. Therefore, it is more sensitive to unusually large errors.

90 MAPE averages the percentage of relative error to introduce a unit-free scale of evaluation. MAPE is appropriate for comparing the empirical results of different methods from different series of data.

Table 4.16 - Results for error measures and the coefficient of determination on the simulated time series

	Neural Networks	Box-Jenkins
MSE	100.37	220.56
MAPE	8.12	11.41
R^2	0.98	0.75

As shown in Table 4.16, the neural network yielded a higher coefficient of determination with corresponding lower error measures.

4.7.5.2 Experimental results - actual time series

The purpose of this study was to determine if neural networks could predict a relative share price seven days ahead on a separate data series, and to compare this performance with that of the Box-Jenkins model. In order to determine this, results generated by both neural networks and Box-Jenkins were compared to actual results beyond the period 1/2/1991 - 12/31/1992. A brief sample of the time series, consisting of 50 share closing prices from 1/2/1993 - 2/21/93, was employed for the experiment. Table 4.17 provides the results of this experiment.

Table 4.17 - Results for error measures and the coefficient of determination over the actual time series

	Neural Networks	Box-Jenkins
MSE	7905.70	12006.72
MAPE	10.08	16.79
R^2	0.92	0.60

As shown in Table 4.17, the neural network model produced superior results relative to the Box-Jenkins model on the actual seven-day out-of-sample data set.

4.7.6 Conclusion

Analysis based on simulated data indicates that the neural network forecasting model developed in the study provides a better alternative than the Box-Jenkins model. Analysis based on results over a limited set of actual out-of-sample data confirms this finding. One of the major disadvantages of the Box-Jenkins method is the relatively long period of time required to manually identify an appropriate model. The Box-Jenkins approach requires, on average, more than one hour per series (Kang, 1992:124). In this regard, the neural network method is more cost-effective than the Box-Jenkins method. Another advantage of neural network models, when compared with Box-Jenkins models, is their ease of operation. No human interpretation is necessary. That is, the model's learning and forecasting processes are all performed automatically. However, in terms of storage and computation requirements, the neural network developed here is at a disadvantage relative to the Box-Jenkins model.

4.8 DETERMINING THE NONLINEAR DYNAMICS OF SHARE PRICES ON THE JOHANNESBURG STOCK EXCHANGE

4.8.1 Introduction

Inspired by the strong evidence provided by the high coefficients of determination of both the neural network model and the Box-Jenkins model, the efficient market hypothesis may be tentatively refuted. To further study the efficient market hypothesis, several nonlinear generic-property testing models were employed. The data used for these tests included the data applied to the construction of the neural network and Box-Jenkins models (1/2/1991 - 12/31/1992). However, according to the literature reviewed, it is generally felt that nonlinear dynamics analysis should be done with at least 2000 data points. As the time period just mentioned includes only 516 points, analysis would have been open to criticism. To overcome this, the closing prices of the shares used in the development of the neural network where accumulated from 1/2/1986 - 12/31/1992, providing 2004 total data points. The following nonlinear generic-property testing models where employed (background material on this was presented in Chapter 3, sections 3.6.3.1 - 3.6.3.4):

- Rescaled analysis;
- correlation dimension analysis;

- BDS statistic test; and
- Lyapanov exponent.

4.8.2 Rescaled analysis

This method of statistical analysis is based upon the idea that, if a time series is generated by a completely random process, then the data points which are far removed in time may be considered independent. At this time, two of the studies undertaken in rescaled analysis include:

- Boshoff (1983) - This research indicates that, by demonstrating the existence of any one or more dependencies (short-term serial dependence, long-term dependence and cyclical dependence), it is possible to refute the random walk hypothesis. Boshoff's (1983:108) research on the H coefficient indicates that "... 90% of the time series analyzed, H was found to be significantly greater than 0.5 after allowing for the predicted upward bias. In other words, the null hypothesis must be rejected by the evidence at hand that supports an alternative hypothesis of $H \neq 0.5$ and specifically $H > 0.5$."

- Terespolsky (1991) - The purpose of this research paper was to provide an update to Boshoff's work. However, Terespolsky (1991:20) criticizes Boshoff's methodology, arguing "...Boshoff's argument that refutes the random walk hypothesis...begs a fundamental explanation. Mandelbrot (1969) has stated that in analyzing price time series, the change in price is used instead of the price itself. Boshoff stated that he attempted to disprove the Random Walk Hypothesis by explicitly using the price itself. However, in order to obtain any meaningful results for H, the changes in the price must be calculated." The results of the study indicate that, in general, share prices on the Johannesburg Stock Exchange do exhibit long-term persistence. Furthermore, the results indicate that over 80% of both the weekly and daily H coefficients are significantly different from 0.5 and that these values are generally greater than 0.6.

It is evident from both studies, even though one study employs share prices while the other employs changes in share prices, that a dependency does exist on the Johannesburg Stock Exchange. This is confirmed by the high R^2 readings discussed earlier. The rescaled analysis performed here differs from the studies mentioned above in that it analyzes a group of shares rather than specific shares. The analysis is done in accordance with Boshoff's method of using share prices rather than using returns. Also, the percentage change was not used for rescaled analysis, since the nature of rescaled analysis is to measure the cumulative deviation from the mean for various periods of time and to examine how the range of these deviations scales over time. Percentage changes are thus not appropriate, because the percentage change series does not add up to its cumulative equivalent. This error can profoundly change the results.

The H coefficient of the rescaled analysis for the period 1/2/1991 - 12/31/1992 was 0.67, with a t-statistic of 70.85 and p-value of 4.95. The H coefficient of the rescaled analysis for the period 1/2/1986 - 12/31/1992 was 0.70, with a t-statistic of 73.37 and p value of 9. According to these results, a long-term dependency exists on the Johannesburg Stock Exchange and the time series can be described as persistent.

4.8.3 Correlation dimension analysis and BDS statistic

Empirical methods derived from previous economic studies of chaotic systems (Brock, 1986:168-195 and Deneckere and Pelikan, 1986:13-25) were used here. For the purpose of meeting this study's objectives, a three-step process were followed:

- Calculation of the correlation dimension for various embedding dimensions;
- application of the residual test for the presence of deterministic chaos; and
- calculation of the W statistic.

The Box-Jenkins modelling process included the removal of long-term linear dependencies, which might result from share price appreciation, by employing an extended time series (Mulueri, 1991:31). Using the estimated model and the associated time series, a residual time series was calculated for the share data and its composite. The residuals were then checked for significant autocorrelation coefficients in the lags; however, no significant coefficients existed. As the result of this process, it was determined that each residual series had satisfied the **IID** assumption of the random walk hypothesis. Correlation estimates for each of the resultant residual series were calculated according to the method described by Scheinkman and LeBaron (1989:310-337).

Correlation dimension estimates made from the residuals, θ, are presented in Table 4.18.

Table 4.18 - Correlation dimension estimates for embedding dimensions 1 to 10

Series	1	2	3	4	5	6	7	8	9	10
Short[91]	0.9	1.3	1.6	1.9	2.0	2.2	1.9	2.1	2.2	2.1
Short (Scrambled residual)	0.9	2.0	2.7	4.0	4.4	4.8	4.9	5.1	5.3	5.4
Long[92]	1.0	1.3	1.6	2.1	2.2	2.3	2.4	3.1	3.2	3.3
Long (Scrambled residual)	1.9	2.8	3.2	4.1	4.2	4.5	4.6	5.2	5.3	5.5

Observations which can be made from the results provided in Table 4.18 are that both time series have low correlation dimensions in absolute terms, and both of their correlation dimensions are lower than those of the scrambled data. The general implication of these results indicate that both series exhibit characteristics of nonlinear dynamics in their underlying generating processes. Although no statistic is available to determine whether the correlation estimates are significantly different from each other, apparent indications of nonlinear dynamics in the composite time series are encouraging. However, the findings could be challenged in the sense that the estimation process might not have removed enough linear dependencies in the data, and the process itself could have induced some dependence in the residuals. Furthermore, the evidence of nonlinear dynamic characteristics could be a result of the presence of non-stationarities in the variances of the data, which is not a constant function of time in the residual series.

The level and the stability of the correlation dimension estimates might indicate an effect due to sample size. However, the generated correlations dimensions are low compared with the scrambled residual series, which supports the hypothesis that nonlinear dynamic characteristics exist in both series. Due to the limitations of correlation dimension analysis, (discussed in Chapter

[91] Period 1/2/1991 - 12/31/1992.

[92] Period 1/2/1986 - 12/31/1992.

3, section 3.6.3.2), the BDS W statistic will be employed to resolve the question of significance (refer to Table 4.19).

Table 4.19 - BDS W statistics

Series	1	2	3	4	5	6	7	8	9	10
Short[93]	4.03	4.15	4.17	4.21	5.81	5.96	6.34	6.40	6.63	6.92
Short (Scrambled residual)	1.16	1.18	1.20	1.27	1.55	1.80	2.00	2.18	2.35	3.01
Long[94]	5.68	5.99	6.03	6.34	6.50	6.99	7.76	8.12	8.45	8.70
Long (Scrambled residual)	1.01	1.05	1.10	1.17	1.31	1.43	1.70	2.30	2.48	2.60

It is evident from Table 4.19 that, in each data series, the statistic exceeds the 1.96 value needed (at the 95% confidence level) to reject the null hypothesis of a linear process. Therefore, the null hypothesis that a nonlinear deterministic process does exist on the Johannesburg Stock Exchange is accepted. However, although the W statistic can distinguish between linear and nonlinear processes, it cannot detect whether a process is stochastic or deterministic (Blank, 1991:722). Therefore, additional evidence, such as Lyapunov exponent estimates, is needed to make this distinction.

4.8.4 Lyapunov exponent

Lyapunov estimates for the two data series are presented in Tables 4.20 and 4.21. In the absence of statistics for determining the significance of these estimates, only qualitative observations will be made.

---

93 Period 1/2/1991 - 12/31/1992.

94 Period 1/2/1986 - 12/31/1992.

Table 4.20 - Lyapunov exponents for the period 1/2/1991 - 12/31/1992 for embedding dimensions 2 to 9

Evolution[95]	2	3	4	5	6	7	8	9
5	9.461	7.542	6.777	1.152	0.638	0.357	0.335	0.11
10	-	-	-	-0.114	-0.286	-0.369	-0.323	-0.042
15	-	-	-	0.505	0.618	0.848	1.029	1.099
20	-	-	-	1.303	1.235	1.24	1.279	1.238

Table 4.21 - Lyapunov exponents for the period 1/2/1986 - 12/31/1992 for embedding dimensions 2 to 9

Evolutions	2	3	4	5	6	7	8	9
5	3.536	4.317	4.403	3.643	2.575	1.075	0.769	1.046
10	2.872	2.486	2.634	2.025	1.204	1.316	0.944	0.685
15	3.855	2.076	2.185	1.725	1.276	0.828	0.262	0.879
20	4.85	0.506	0.511	0.355	1.003	0.574	0.009	0.722
25	5.647	0.98	1.034	0.819	0.505	0.663	0.58	0.48
30	4.502	0.843	0.857	0.616	0.608	0.678	0.66	0.386
35	3.568	0.781	0.837	0.647	0.625	0.82	0.926	0.457
40	2.793	0.109	0.514	0.444	0.507	0.883	0.931	0.373
45	2.9	0.602	0.6	0.443	0.27	1.225	1.304	0.216

It is evident from Tables 4.20 and 4.21 that both time series exhibit stable Lyapunov exponents across the embedding dimensions, which implies the presence of chaos. For both series it is also evident that the Lyapunov exponent values decline as evolution lengths increase. According to the literature, this is to be expected.

According to Frank and Stengos (1988:555), "A chaotic system will be quite predictable over very short time horizons. If however, the initial conditions are only known as finite precision, then over long intervals the ability to predict the time path will be lost." This implies that, if chaos cannot be detected at an evolution interval, the deterministic process is not overwhelmed by stochastic noise and the development of forecasting models may be possible. "If the largest Lyapunov exponent is never positive in experiments across evolution lengths, the system is stochastic" (Blank, 1991:724). As shown in Table 4.20, the highest Lyapunov exponent is 9.461.

95 The number of observations over which the two pieces of the trajectory are followed.

However, some existing Lyapunov exponents are positive for short evolutions, turn negative at some longer lengths and then become positive again. This implies that, at some time intervals, stochastic noise becomes dominant, making deterministic forecasting models not empirically viable, even though the underlying system may be completely deterministic in nature. Therefore, it can be suggested that, at times, the market conforms to the efficient market hypothesis. This confirms the findings of Du Toit (1986:9.3) "...the market at times assume[s] the properties of a totally efficient market but at other times prices deviate from the underlying equilibrium values." However, this cannot be claimed for the longer time series, since the largest Lyapunov value was 5.647 (refer to Table 4.21) and there were no negative Lyapunov exponents. This strongly supports the conclusion that both series have a chaotic nonlinear generating process.

4.9 CONCLUSION

This chapter began with the construction of neural networks for the purpose of determining how topologies affected performance. The experiment concluded that a definite correlation exists between the topology of a neural network and the desired outcome. The final neural network model was then compared with a Box-Jenkins model. The comparison clearly showed that neural networks are superior in terms of the accuracy measures employed. Since the correlations of determination of both the neural network model and the Box-Jenkins model were extreme, it was decided to apply additional tools for the purpose of determining if the data series represented a chaotic, deterministic, or nonlinear dynamic process. As a result of the tests performed, the efficient market hypothesis was refuted.

Chapter 5 presents a summary of the research as a whole, offers recommendations, and ends with areas for further research.

CHAPTER 5

SUMMARY, CONCLUSIONS AND RECOMMENDATIONS

It is a test of true theories not only to account for but to predict phenomenon.
-- William Whewell

5.1 INTRODUCTION

This chapter presents a summary of the study as a whole. Conclusions of the most prominent findings are made and some areas for further research are identified. The main thrust of this study has been to investigate whether neural networks can be used to predict future share prices. Furthermore, an overview of the relevant literature regarding neural networks and present share price prediction theories and issues have been provided.

5.2 THE OVERALL PROVING OR DISPROVING OF THE HYPOTHESIS

In Chapter 4, an experimental design was carried out to test the following research hypotheses:

H_1 - Neural networks can forecast share prices seven days ahead.

H_2 - The forecasting accuracy of a neural network model is related to the architecture of the network model.

H_3 - Neural networks represent superior forecasting models relative to Box-Jenkins models.

H_4 - Fluctuations in share prices observed on the Johannesburg Stock Exchange are not the result of purely stochastic processes but, rather, include a nonlinear dynamic process.

Findings for each of these hypotheses will now be discussed.

5.2.1 Neural networks can forecast share prices seven days ahead

The primary purpose of this study was to apply neural networks, as a new and alternative method to standard statistical methods, to the prediction of a group of share prices. Even though statistics and neural networks are closely related, the principal difference between the two fields is that historically, statistics have focused on linear problems, which are relatively traceable, while neural networks have been forced to deal with nonlinearities. To test the above hypothesis, a neural network was constructed with 63 inputs and one output, using 516 data points. The output was composed of the cumulative closing price of a group of shares. The data was split into a training set and a testing set. The results conclusively indicate that the neural network model could predict share prices extremely accurately. Thus, the hypothesis is **accepted** and, accordingly, it can be stated that neural networks can forecast share prices seven days ahead.

5.2.2 The forecasting accuracy of a neural network model is related to the architecture of the network model

It became evident in the literature review that there are design factors, referred to here as the topology, that affect the performance of neural networks. The design factors which influence the performance are:

- The number of hidden layers;
- the number of neurons; and
- the number of inputs.

A genetic algorithm was employed, which begins with an encoded procedure, mutates it, and then uses a specific process to select the mutation with the highest level of fitness according to a pre-defined criterion. Finally, it applies a recombination process to combine characteristics of the selected mutation. The results indicate that the number of neurons and the number of hidden layers do have a considerable effect on the generalization capabilities of a neural network. Furthermore, not discussed in Chapter 4, an analysis-of-variance procedure with the Ducan option was used to ascertain the effect of these two factors on the mean standard error. The results indicate that both the number of neurons and the number of hidden layers are prevalent factors influencing the ability of a neural network to generalize and produce acceptable results. This confirms the findings of Kang (1991:69): "In general, the effect of each of the three factors [number of hidden layers, number of neurons and number of inputs] tends to become more significant as the forecasting horizon increases...particularly, the number of inputs is the most critical factor in the determination of the successful neural forecasting model. Next important comes the number of hidden [neurons]. The effect of the number of hidden layers is less significant than the other factors." It was evident that the number of hidden layers was not a contributing factor since the R^2 decreased slightly when the number of hidden layers was decreased. There was no significant decrease in the training time either.

The last factor which influences the architecture of a neural network is the number of inputs required to achieve the desired output: A criticism against neural networks is that their complexity makes them difficult to understand, which implies that, for one to trust the results of a neural network, the knowledge learned by the networks during the training process should somehow be revealed and confirmed, particularly regarding the correct selection of inputs. However, some inputs have a larger influence on the output than others.

One of the problems with attempting to predict future share prices is that a large number of indicators may be potentially relevant. In order to simultaneously maintain reasonable training times and generate good predictions, it is necessary to develop methodologies for efficiently selecting appropriate inputs. Since a large number of these inputs, as network parameters, may be available, parameter significance analysis can be helpful.

In order to test the impact of the inputs on the neural network model, the variables' impact on the magnitude of the residual for each observation was determined by applying sensitivity analysis. A test of the assumption that a neural network is most sensitive to those variables which are connected with the largest overall interconnection weights was performed. Based on this assumption, specific inputs were removed. However, though training time did decrease, there was no improvement in performance as measured by the coefficient of determination. Overall, however, the hypothesis that the forecasting accuracy of a neural network model is related to the architecture of the network model is **accepted**.

5.2.3 Neural networks represent superior forecasting models relative to Box-Jenkins models

The neural network model was compared with the Box-Jenkins methodology. The purpose of this was to determine the effectiveness of neural network and Box-Jenkins models for both simulated and actual time series predictions. The effectiveness and the accuracy of the two forecasting models were measured by two different error measures:

- Mean squared error (MSE); and
- Mean absolute percentage error (MAPE).

Apart from the two different error measures employed, the coefficient of determination was also calculated for both the neural network and Box-Jenkins models. The research findings clearly indicated that the neural network was superior both in the simulated and actual time-series predictions, measured in terms of MSE, MAPE and R^2. Hence, the hypothesis is **accepted** that neural networks are a superior forecasting model to Box-Jenkins.

5.2.4 Fluctuations in share prices observed on the Johannesburg Stock Exchange are not the result of purely stochastic processes but, rather, include a nonlinear dynamic process

The efficient market hypothesis states that, at any time, the price of a share fully captures all known information about that share and, accordingly, the price behaves like a random walk in time, except when there are changes in information. The research has found the following evidence against the efficient market hypothesis:

- Both the neural network model and the Box-Jenkins model produced extremely significant coefficient of determination figures. With reference to the efficient market hypothesis, by construction, the coefficient of determination must lie between zero and one. The fact that the coefficients of determination were high for the simulated time series (neural networks: $R^2 = 0.98$ and Box-Jenkins: $R^2 = 0.75$) and the actual time (neural networks: $R^2 = 0.92$ and Box-Jenkins: $R^2 = 0.60$) reflects the ability of the neural network and Box-Jenkins, in part, to extract nonlinear regularities from the data sets, suggesting evidence against the efficient market hypothesis.

- Based on the statistical measures mentioned above, it was generally felt necessary to apply tools used in the study of chaos theory on the data sets.

The existence of cases of short-term forecasting success of time series and econometric models implies that financial or economic time series are not always generated by random processes. However, the failure of these models on long-term series indicates that they have not captured the true nature of the underlying generating process. A new methodology, called nonlinear dynamics or "chaos theory" (discussed in Chapter 3), may offer an alternative explanation for the behavior of economic phenomena. Chaos analysis evaluates whether a process is deterministic, based on the assumption that at least part of the underlying process is nonlinear. Inspired by the strong evidence provided by the high coefficients of determination of both the neural network model and the Box-Jenkins model, the efficient market hypothesis may be refuted. The following nonlinear generic-property testing models were employed:

- Rescaled analysis;
- correlation dimension analysis;
- BDS statistic test; and
- Lyapanov exponents.

The generic tools were employed on two sets of data:

- 1/2/1991 - 12/31/1992; and
- 1/2/1986 - 12/31/1992.

The results of the research indicated that the data series had low correlation dimensions of about two to four, which statistically indicates the presence of nonlinearities in both time series, as confirmed by the Hurst coefficients being greater than 0.5 and the BDS W statistic being greater than 1.96. However, although the W statistic can distinguish between a linear and nonlinear generating process, it cannot detect whether a process is stochastic or deterministic. Therefore, additional evidence was required, and Lyapunov exponents were then estimated to assist in making this determination. Both time series exhibit stable Lyapunov exponents across the embedding dimensions, therefore implying the presence of chaos. For both series, it was also evident that the Lyapunov exponent values declined as evolution lengths increased. This strongly supports the conclusion that both the series have a chaotic nonlinear generating process. This supports the use of neural networks as an alternative model for operating on nonlinear data. Hence, the hypothesis that fluctuations in share prices observed on the Johannesburg Stock Exchange are not the result of purely stochastic processes but, rather, include a nonlinear dynamic process is **accepted**.

5.3 LIMITATIONS OF THE STUDY BASED ON THE RESULTS

This study has given rise to two points regarding the suitability of neural networks for short-term predictions of share prices:

- It is rather implausible to expect neural networks to provide acceptable predictions of the actual prices, considering the requirements for precision associated with the problem.

- Neural networks cannot be rejected as candidates for predictors of market direction, given the performance results observed in this study.

5.4 MAJOR CONTRIBUTIONS OF THE STUDY

The major contributions of the study are:

- The first study undertaken in the Republic of South Africa to apply neural networks to the forecasting of share prices.

- The development of a backpropagation neural network for the forecasting of share prices.

- An investigation of the factors affecting the design of a neural network as well as the performance of a neural network, based on statistical analysis.

- A comparison between a neural networks and a Box-Jenkins model using a simulated and an actual time series.

- An introductory overview of chaos theory as well as the tools which can be employed for the purpose of determining if an economic time series is deterministic or stochastic. The findings indicate that the time series includes a nonlinear deterministic process, which could impact debate in the literature concerning the random walk hypothesis and the efficient market hypothesis.

- The provision of a methodological approach in the construction of a neural network model.

5.5 RECOMMENDATIONS

Suggestions for future research on transformations of the input data prior to training a neural network are:

- Preprocess internal data from the target market;
- .reduce noise in data by applying Fast Fourier transformations; and
- transform the factors that classify the state of the market.

Given the promise of neural network technology to financial applications, an extension of this study would be to look at how the technology can be applied to other areas of financial management. The following represent possible areas for further research:

- The construction of a neural network based on specific buy-and-hold strategies which could be employed in the forecasting of the direction of change in share prices and not only of the size of the changes.

- The topology of the neural network structure plays an important role in forecasting. The same neural network topology may not be appropriate for different time series. Therefore, further research into neural network structures, including different numbers of hidden layers and neurons, and types of activation functions are to be explored, contributing to the formulation of a general rule that might be developed for the purpose of determining network structure based on series characteristics.

- The development of a system which incorporates an expert system module for selecting appropriate buy-and-hold strategies and a neural network architecture, for the automatic selection of the most appropriate neural predictors to apply to current market behavior.

- The search space of parameters for training neural networks is very large. A promising approach is to use multiple neural networks, trained using different parameters but the same data, where the output of the neural networks are combined.

- The construction of a genetic algorithm to solve financial portfolio problems related to optimal allocation, portfolio insurance, and performance predictions.

- Endowing neural networks with some initial knowledge involves encoding approximate rules as weights in a neural network and training it using recent data. This may lead to a method of combining rules and data for the purpose of adapting to changes in market environments.

- The construction of a dual adaptive-structure neural network that can predict the short-term trends of price movements and suggest trading strategies.

- The combination of fuzzy logic and mean-variance optimization methods for tactical asset allocation applications, representing an approach which includes interactive problem-solving and supports knowledge refinement.

- The combination of neural networks, genetic algorithms and fuzzy logic for the purpose of designing and implementing trading systems.

- The construction and development of a share-selection neural network represents a final possibility.

5.6 CONCLUSION

The application of neural networks in the disciplines of economics, econometrics and the management sciences is still in its infancy. This study has endeavored to provide insight into the use of neural networks for predicting time series with chaos, random error, and low correlation dimension estimates. Additionally it signifies the potential of neural networks to deal with unstructured problems, inconsistent information and real-time output. The primary value of the study is its extension of previous research, occurring through the implementation of different approaches and methods to problems addressed by previous researchers involved in the construction of models for predicting future share prices.

BIBLIOGRAPHY

ARTICLES

Abdullah, D.A. and Hayworth, S.C. [1993] "Macroeconometrics of stock price fluctuations," *Quarterly Journal of Business and Economics*, vol. 32, no. 1, p. 63.

Affleck-Graves, J.P. and Money, A.H. [1975] "A note on the random walk model and South African share prices," *The South African Journal of Economics*, vol. 43, no. 3, pp. 382-388.

Affleck-Graves, J.F., Money, A.H. and Troskie, C.G. [1980] "An empirical comparison of the performance of different stock market indices," *Investment Analysts Journal*, no. 15, pp. 35-38.

Alexander, M. [1991] "An inside view of neural technology," *Computerworld*, vol. 25, no. 3, p. 17.

Ambrose, B.W., Ancel, E.W. and Griffiths, M.D. [1993], "Fractal structure in the capital markets revisited," *Financial Analysts Journal*, vol. 49, no. 3, pp. 73-77.

Anders, B. [1989] "Chaos theory and market behavior," *Technical Analysis of Stocks & Commodities*, vol. 8, no. 11. p. 31.

Anderson, J.A., Wisniewski, E.J. and Viscuso, S.R. [1988] "Software for neural networks," *Computer Architecture News*, vol. 16, no. 1, p. 28.

Ariovich, G. [1983] "The influence of the gold price on the South African economy," *Chamber of Mines newsletter*, March/June, p. 3.

Asprem, M. [1989] "Stock prices, asset portfolios and macroeconomic variables in ten European countries," *Journal of Banking and Finance*, vol. 13, pp. 596-597.

Barr, G.D.I. [1990] "Macroeconomic identification of the pricing factors on the Johannesburg Stock Exchange," *South African Journal of Business Management*, vol. 21, no. 1, pp. 17-25.

Baumol, W. and Benhabib, J. [1989] "Chaos: Significance, Mechanism, and economic applications," *The Journal of Economic Perspectives*, vol. 3, pp.77-79.

Bethlehem, R.W. [1980] "Interest rates, yield curves and the evaluation of ordinary shares," *Investment Analysts Journal*, no. 15, p. 40.

Bhana, N. [1987] "Take-over announcements and insider trading activity on the Johannesburg Stock Exchange," *South African Journal of Business Management*, vol. 18, no. 1, pp. 198-205.

Bhana, N. [1990] "The performance of secondary share recommendations published in the news media and the effects on the efficiency of the Johannesburg Stock Exchange," *South African Journal of Business Management*, vol. 21, no. 4, pp. 129-135.

Bhana, N. [1991] "Reaction on the Johannesburg Stock Exchange to major shifts in dividend policy," *South African Journal of Business Management*, vol, 22, no. 3, pp. 33-40.

Bhana, N. [1993] "The relationship between growth in money supply and share prices: A test of the efficiency of the Johannesburg Stock Exchange," *Management Dynamics: Contemporary Research*, vol. 2, no. 2, pp. 31-42.

Blank, S.C. [1991] "Chaos in futures markets? A nonlinear dynamical analysis," *The Journal of Futures Markets*, vol. 11, no. 6, pp. 710-728.

Bodie, Z. [1976] "Common stocks as a hedge against inflation," *Journal of Finance*, vol. 31, pp. 259-270.

Brock, W.A. [1986] "Distinguishing random and deterministic systems: Abridged version," *Journal of Economic Theory*, vol. 40, pp. 168-195.

Brümmer, L.M. and Jacobs, P.J. [1981] "Die Johannesburgse effektebeurs as rasionele kapitaalmark," *South African Journal of Business Management*, vol. 12, pp. 53-59.

Chen, N., Roll, R. and Ross, S.A. [1986] "Economic forces and the stock market," *Journal of Business*, vol. 59, no. 3, p. 391.

Cochran, S.J. and Defina, R.H. [1993] "Inflation's negative effects on real stock prices: new evidence and a test of the proxy effect hypothesis," *Applied Economics*, vol. 25, no. 2, p. 263.

Deneckere, R. and Pelikan, S. [1986] "Competitive chaos," *Journal of Economic the Theory*, vol. 40, pp. 13-25.

Eckmann, J.P. and Ruelle, D. [1985] "Ergodic theory of chaos and strange attractors," *Review of Modern Physics*, vol. 57, pp. 617-656.

Fama, E.F. and French, K.R. [1992] "The cross-section of expected stock returns," *Journal of Finance*, vol. 47, iss. 1, pp. 427-465.

Fama, E.F. and Schwert, G.W. [1977] "Asset returns and inflation," *Journal of Financial Economics*, vol. 5, pp. 115-146.

Finkbeiner, A. [1988] "The brain as template," *MOSAIC*, vol. 19, no. 2, pp. 5-10.

Fishman, M.B., Barr, D.S. and Loick, W.J. [1991] "Artificial intelligence and market analysis," *Technical Analysis of Stocks and Commodities*, vol. 9, no 3, p. 18.

Fortune, P. [1991] "Stock market efficiency: An autopsy," *New England Economic Review*, no 3, pp 18-19.

Frank, M. and Stengos, T. [1989] "Measuring the strangeness of gold and silver rates of return," *Review of Economic Studies*, vol. 56, p. 555.

Friedman, M. [1977] "Noble lecture: Inflation and unemployment," *Journal of Political Economy*, no. 85. pp. 451-472.

Geake, E. [1990] "Neural network makes tidy profit," *New Scientist*, no. 1817, p. 18.

Gilbertson, B.P. and Roux, F.J.P. [1977] "The Johannesburg Stock Exchange as an efficient market," *The Investment Analysts Journal*, vol. 9, no 3, p. 21.

Gilbertson, B.P. and Roux, F.J.P. [1978] "Some further comments on the Johannesburg Stock Exchange as an efficient market," *The Investment Analysts Journal*, vol. 10, pp. 223-233.

Glover, F. and Greenberg, H.J. [1989] "New approaches for heuristic search: A bilateral linkage with artificial intelligence," *European Journal of Operational Research (Netherlands)*, vol. 39, no. 2, pp. 121-123.

Goetzmann, W.N. and Jorion, P. [1993] "Testing the predictive power of dividend yields," *The Journal of Finance*, vol. 47, no. 2, pp. 664-665.

Gorman, R.P. and Sejnowski, T.J. [1988] "Analysis of hidden units in a layered network trained to classify sonar targets," *Neural Networks*, vol. 1, no.1, pp. 75-89.

Grassberge, P. and Procaccia, I. [1983] "Measuring the strangeness of strange attractors," *Physica 9D*, pp. 189-208.

Griffith, V. and Southworth, H. [1990] "Chaos theory," *Journal of Banking*, vol. 140, no. 767, pp. 54-55.

Guez, A., Protopopsecu, V. and Barhen, J. [1988] "On the stability, storage capacity, and design of nonlinear continuous neural networks," *IEEE*, vol 28, no 1, p. 80.

Hadassin, I. [1976] "An investigation into the behavior of earnings and share prices of South African listed companies," *The Investment Analysts Journal of South Africa*, vol. 8, pp.13-14.

Hamblin, A.R.P. [1987] "Anatomy of the financial rand," *Investment Analysts Journal*, no. 30, pp. 33-37.

Hawley, D.D., Johnson, J.D. and Raina, D. [1990] "Artificial neural systems: A new tool for financial decision-making," *Financial Analysts Journal*, vol. 46, no. 6, pp. 63-65.

Hecht-Nielsen, R. [1988] "Neurocomputing: Picking the Human Brain," *IEEE Spectrum*, vol. 25, no. 3, p. 131.

Hinton, G.E. [1989] "Connectionist learning procedures," *Artificial Intelligence*, vol. 40, pp. 185-234.

Hinton, G.E. [1992] "Connectionist learning procedures," *Artificial Intelligence*, no. 41, p. 145.

Hong, R. [1988] "Future technology trends and related markets," *Review of Business*, vol. 10, no. 1, pp. 19-21.

Hornik, K., Stinchcombe, M. and White, H. [1989] "Multi-layered feedforward networks are universal approximators," *Neural Networks*, vol. 3, no. 2, pp. 359-366.

Hsieh, D.A. [1991] "Chaos and nonlinear dynamics: Application to financial markets," *The Journal of Finance*, vol. 46, no. 5. pp. 1840-1847.

Hurst, H.E. [1951] "Long-term storage of reservoirs," *Transactions of the American Society of Civil Engineers*, p. 770-779.

James, F.E. [1968] "Monthly moving averages - An effective investment tool ?," *Journal of Financial and Quantitative Analysis*, vol. 12, no. 9, pp. 315-326.

Jones, W.P. and Hoskins, J . [1987] "Back-Propagation," *Byte*, vol. 12, no. 10, pp. 155-162.

Just, R., and Rausser, G. [1981] "Commodity price forecasting with large scale econometric models and the futures market," *American Journal of Agricultural Economics*, vol. 63, pp. 197-208.

Katz, J.O. [1992] "Developing neural network forecasters for trading," *Technical Analysis of Stocks and Commodities*, vol. 10, no 4, p. 59-66.

Knight, R.F. and Affleck-Graves, J.F. [1985] "An empirical evaluation of the effectiveness of South African investment analysts," *South African Journal of Business Management*, vol. 16, pp. 157-160.

Knight, R.F. and Affleck-Graves, J.F. [1987] "An evaluation of dividend signaling on the Johannesburg Stock Exchange," *South African Journal of Business Management*, vol. 18, no. 2, p. 85.

Laing, J.R. [1991] "Efficient chaos: Or, things they never taught in business school," *Barron's*, vol. 71, no. 30, p. 12.

Levy, R.A. [1966] "Conceptual foundations of technical analysis," *Financial Analysts Journal*, vol. 22, no. 4, pp. 83-89.

Lippmann, R.P. [1987] "An introduction to computing with neural networks," *IEEE ASSP Magazine*, vol. 4, no. 2, p. 4.

Lovell-Greene, N.J., Affleck-Graves, J.F. and Money, A.H. [1986] "A survey of investment appraisal methods used by financial analysts in South Africa," *The Investment Analysts Journal*, vol. 10, no. 4, p. 9.

Maddox, J. [1989] "More ways with neural networks," *Nature*, vol. 337, p 403

Malkiel, B. [1979] "The capital formation problem in the United States," *Journal of Finance*, no. 34, pp. 291-306.

Mandelbrot, B.B. [1963] "The variation of certain speculative prices," *The Journal of Business of the University of Chicago*, vol. 36, p. 308.

Mandelbrot, B.B. [1972] "Statistical methodology for nonperiodic cycles: From the Covariances to the R/S analysis," *Analysis of Economic and Social Measurement*, vol. 1. pp. 259-289.

McCulloch, W.W. and Pitts, W. [1943] "A Logical Calculus of Ideas Imminent in Nervous Activity," *Bulletin of Mathematical Biophysics*, vol. 5, pp. 115-133.

Miller, H. M. and Modigliani, F. [1961] "Dividend policy, growth, and the valuation of shares," *Journal of Business*, vol. 34, pp. 411-433.

Mirowski, P. [1992] "From Mandelbrot to Chaos in Economic Theory," *Southern Economics Journal*, October, p. 289.

Mulieri, P.A. [1991] "Stock market price behavior: Random walks and nonlinear dynamics," *Market Technicians Association Journal*, Issue 37, Spring, pp. 28-34.

Naidoo, C. [1990] "Stock broker must be on top of the world," *Sunday Times - Business Times*, 24 June, p. 6.

Neftci, S.N. and Policano, A.J. [1984] "Can chartists outperform the market? Market efficiency tests for technical analysis," *The Journal of Futures Markets*, vol. 4, no. 4, p. 466.

Nelson, C.R. [1976] "Inflation and rates of return on common stocks," *Journal of Finance*, vol. 31, pp. 471-483.

Nichols, N.A. [1993] "Efficient? Chaotic? What's the new finance," *Harvard Business Review*, vol. 71, iss. 2, pp. 50-60.

Niederhoffer, V. and Regan, P.J. [1972] "Earnings changes, analysts forecasts and stock prices," *Financial Analysts Journal*, vol 28, p. 71.

Obermeier, K.K. and Barron, J.J. [1989] "Time to get fired up," *Byte*, vol. 14, no. 8. p. 219.

Ooms, L.L., Archer, A.A. and Van Der M Smit, E. [1987] "The information content of dividends on the Johannesburg Stock Exchange: An empirical analysis," *South African Journal of Business Management*, vol. 18, no. 4, pp.187-197

Page, M.J. and Way, C.V. [1993] "Stock market over-reaction: The South African evidence," *Investment Analysts Journal*, no. 36, pp. 35-47.

Peavy III, J.W. and Goodman, D.A. [1985] "How inflation, risk and corporate profitability affect common stock returns," *Financial Analysts Journal*, no. 5, p. 64.

Pinches, G.E. [1970] "The random walk hypothesis and technical analysis," *Financial Analysts Journal*, vol. 26, no. 2, pp. 104-110.

Ramsey, J.B. and Yaun, H. [1991] "Bias and error bias in dimension calculations and their evaluation in some simple models," *Physical Letters A 134*, pp. 287-297.

Ramsey, J.B., Sayers, C.L. and Rothman, P. [1983] "The statistical properties of dimension calculations using small data sets: some economic applications," *International Economic Review*, vol. 31, no.4, p. 3.

Refenes, A.S., Azema-Barac, M., Chen. L. and Karoussos. P.R. [1993] "Currency exchange rate prediction and neural network design strategies," *Neural Computing and Applications*, vol. 1, no.1, p. 46.

Rockwell, C.S. [1967] "Normal backward, forecasting, and returns to speculators," *Food Research Institute Studies*, vol. 7, no. 6, pp. 107-130.

Rosenblatt, F. [1958] "The perceptron: a probabilistic model for information storage and organization of the brain," *Psychological Review*, no. 65, pp. 386-408.

Roux, F.J.P. and Gilbertson, B.P. [1976] "Trading tests for shares quoted on the Johannesburg Stock Exchange," *Johannesburg Consolidated Investment Company Ltd report, no. F/80*, pp. 1-19.

Sakai, H. and Tokumari, H. [1983] "Autocorrelations of a certain chaos," *IEEE Transactions on Acoustics, Speech and Signal processing*, vol. 28, pp.588-590.

Savit, R. [1988] "When random is not random: An introduction to chaos in market prices," *Journal of Futures Markets*, vol. 8, no. 3, pp. 271-289.

Scheinkman, J.A. and LeBaron, B. [1989] "Nonlinear dynamics and stock returns," *Journal of Business*, vol. 62, pp. 310-337.

Schmitt, L. [1991] "Neural networks solve complex vision problems," *Automation*, vol. 38, no. 8, p. 38.

Shirreff, D. [1993] "Efficient markets and quants' descent into chaos," *Euroeconomy*, July, pp. 60-66.

Sondak, N.E, and Sondak, V.K. [1989] "Neural networks and artificial intelligence," *ACM SIGSE Bulletin*, vol. 21, no. 1, p. 241.

Stein, R.M. [1991] "Real artificial life," *Byte*, vol. 16, p. 289.

Stevens, J.K. [1985] "Reverse engineering the brain," *Byte*, April, pp. 287-297.

Strebel, P.J. [1977] "The limited efficiency of the Johannesburg Stock Exchange," *The Investment Analysts Journal of South Africa*, no. 11, pp 15-21.

Tang, Z., Almeida, C. and Fishwick, P.A. [1991] "Time series forecasting using neural networks vs. Box-Jenkins methodology," *Simulation*, vol. 57, no. 5. pp. 303-305.

Tazelaar, J.M. [1989] "In depth: neural networks," *Byte*, vol. 14, no. 8, p. 214.

The Market Technicians Association board of directors [1991] "Defining technical analysis," *Market Technicians Association Journal*, issue.37, Spring, p. 8.

Tobin, J. [1958] "Liquidity preference as behavior towards risk," *Review of Economic Studies*, no. 25, pp. 65-86.

Touretzky, D.S. and Pomerleau, D.A. [1989] "What's hidden in the hidden layers?," *Byte*, vol. 14, no. 8, pp. 232-234.

Van Coller, J.E.M. [1980] "A system of composite and leading and coinciding indices of the South African business," *Studies in Economics and Econometrics*, pp. 41-73.

Van Den Honert, R.C. and Barr, G.D.I . [1988] "Merger announcements and share price returns - the role of the relationship between acquiring and target firms," *South African Journal of Business Management*, vol. 19, no.1, pp. 1-10.

Van Der Mescht, M.J. and Smit vd M, E. [1993] "Die Suid-Afrikaanse kapitaalmark en aandelebeurs as vooruitskatter van reële ekonomiese aktiwiteit," *Investment Analysts Journal*, Winter, pp. 45-46.

Ver Duin, W. [1990] "Neural Nets: Software that learns by example," *CAE*, vol. 9, no. 1, p. 68.

Van Horne, J.C. and Parker, G.C. [1968] "Technical trading rules: A comment," *Financial Analysts Journal*, vol. 24, no. 4, pp. 128-132.

Webb, A.R., Lowe, D. and Bedworth, M.D. [1988] "A comparison of nonlinear optimization strategies for feedforward adaptive layered networks," *Royal Signals and Radar Establishment Memorandum*, p. 4157.

Wolf, A., Swift, J.B., Swinney, H.L. and Vastano. [1985] "Determining Lyapunov exponents from a time series," *Physica 16D*. July, pp. 285-317.

Xenakis, J.J. [1990] "Brain trust," *Information week*, issue no. 255, p. 41.

Zahedi, F. [1991] "An introduction to neural networks and a comparison with artificial intelligence and expert systems." *Interfaces*, vol. 21, no. 2, pp. 25-38.

Zeidenberg, M. [1987] "Modelling the brain," *Byte*, vol. 12, no. 1, pp. 237-240.

BOOKS

Aleksander, I. and Burnett, P. [1987] *Thinking Machines: The search for artificial intelligence*. London,United Kingdom: Roxby Press Limited.

Aleksander, I. and Morton, H. [1990] *An introduction to neural computing*. London, United Kingdom: Chapman and Hall.

Arbib, M. [1964] *Brains, machines and mathematics*. New York, New York: McGraw-Hill.

Arnold, C.M. [1984] *Timing the market*. Chicago, Illinois: Probus Publishing Company.

Arnold, C.M. [1993] *Your personal computer can make you rich in stocks and commodities*. West Palm Beach, Florida: Weiss Research, Inc.

Bachelier, L. [1964] "Theory of speculation," in *The random character of stock market prices*. (Editor) Cootner, P.H. Cambridge, Massachusetts: MIT Press.

Beale, R. and Jackson, T. [1990] *Neural Computing: An introduction*. New York, New York: Adam Hiller.

Berry, R. and Trigueiros, D. [1993] "Applying neural networks to the extraction of knowledge from accounting reports: A classification study," in *Neural networks in finance and investing*. (Editors) Trippi, R.R. and Turban, E. Chicago, Illinois: Probus publishing company.

Bodie, Z., Kane, A. and Marcus, A.J. [1993] *Investments*. Second edition. Homewood, Illinois: Irwin.

Box, G.P.E., and Jenkins, G.M. [1969] *Time series analysis forecasting and control*. London: Holden-Day.

Brock, W. and Dechert, W. [1991] "Theorems on distinguishing deterministic from random systems," in *Dynamic Econometric Modelling*. (Editors) Barnett, W., Berndt, R.J. and White, P.J. Cambridge: Cambridge University Press.

Caudill, M. and Butler, C. 1990(a). *Naturally Intelligent Systems, vol. 1*. Cambridge, Massachusetts: MIT press.

Caudill, M. and Butler, C. 1990(b). *Naturally Intelligent Systems, vol. 2*. Cambridge, Massachusetts: MIT press.

Churchland, P.S. and Sejnowski, T.J. [1992] *The Computational Brain*. Cambridge, Massachusetts: MIT press.

Cohen, J.B., Zinbarg, E.D. and Zeikel, A. [1987] *Investment Analysis and Portfolio Management*. Fifth edition. Homewood: Illinois, Irwin.

Cootner, P. H. [1964] *The random character of stock market prices*. (Editor) Cootner, P.H. Cambridge, Massachusetts: MIT Press.

Davalo, E. and Naïm, P. [1991] *Des Reseaux de Neurones*. Paris: Eyrolles.

Dayhoff, J.E. [1990] *Neural network architectures: An introduction*. New York, New York: Van Nostrand Reinhold.

De Kock, J. [1989] *The mechanics of the Johannesburg stock exchange*. (Editor) McGregor, R. Johannesburg, Republic of South Africa: Juta and Co Ltd.

Du Plessis, J. [1989] *Charting your way to stock market profits*. Durban, Republic of South Africa: Indexia Research.

Du Plessis, P.G. [1990] "Technical analysis," in *The investment decision*. (Editor) Du Plessis, P.G. Pretoria, Republic of South Africa: Van Schaik (Pty) Ltd.

Du Plessis, P.G. and Mostert, F.J. [1990] "Fundamental analysis of the company," in *The investment decision.* (Editor) Du Plessis, P.G. Pretoria, Republic of South Africa: Van Schaik (Pty) Ltd.

Edwards, R.D. and Magee, J. [1966] *Technical analysis of stock trends.* Fifth edition. Springfield, Massachusetts: John Magee.

Eiteman, W.J., Dice, A.C. and Eiteman D.K. [1966] *The stock market.* Fourth edition. New York, New York: McGraw-Hill Book Company.

Felsen, J. [1975] *Cybernetic approach to stock market analysis versus efficient market theory.* Hickesville, New York: Exposition Press, Inc.

Francis, J.C. [1976] *Investments: Analysis and Management.* Fourth edition. New York, New York: McGraw-Hill Book Company.

Francis, J.C. [1986] *Investments: Analysis and Management.* International edition. New York, New York: McGraw-Hill Book Company.

Gerke, W. and Baun, S. [1993] "Neural networks in financial forecasting - How to develop forecasting models," in the *Proceedings of the first international workshop on neural networks in the capital market.* (Editor) Refenes, A.N. London, United Kingdom: London Business School.

Gitman, L.G. and Joehnk, M.D. [1981] *Fundamentals of Investing.* New York, New York: Harper and Row publishers.

Goodrich, R.L. [1989] *Applied Statistical Forecasting.* New York, New York: Parker Publishing Company, Inc.

Graham, B., Dodd, D.L. and Cottle, S. [1962] *Security Analysis.* New York, New York: McGraw-Hill.

Granville, J.E. [1976] *Granville's new strategy of daily stock market timing for maximum profit*. Engelwood Cliffs, New Jersey: Prentice-Hall Company, Inc.

Grossberg, S. and Gutowski, W. [1987] "Neural dynamics of decisions making under risk: Affective balance and cognitive-emotional interactions," in *Neural Networks and Natural Intelligence*. (Editor) Grossberg, S. Cambridge, Massachusetts: The MIT Press.

Hamburg, M. [1991] *Statistical Analysis for Decision Making*. Fifth edition. Orlando, Florida: Harcourt Brace Jovanovich.

Hanke, J.E. and Reitsch, A.G. [1986] *Business Forecasting*. Newtown, Massachusetts: Allyn and Bacon, Inc.

Hebb, D.O. [1949] *The organization of behavior*. New York, New York: John Wiley and Sons.

Hecht-Nielsen, R. [1990] *Neurocomputing*. Reading, Massachusetts: MIT press.

Hertz, J., Krogh, A. and Palmer, R.G. [1991] *Introduction to theory of neural computations*. Redwood City, California: Addison-Wesley.

Hexton, R. [1990] *Technical analysis in the UK options market*. Barley Mow Passage, London: Heron Publishing Ltd.

Hoff, J.C. [1983] *A practical guide to Box-Jenkins forecasting*. Belmont, California: Lifetime Learning Publication.

Huang, S.S.G. [1973] *A new technical approach to stock market timing*. Second edition. New York, New York: Investors Intelligence.

Joubert, J.J. [1989] *Technical analysis explained*. Weltevredenpark, Republic of South Africa: Investment decision support systems.

Kamijo, K. and Tanigawa, T. [1993] *"Stock price pattern recognition: A recurrent neural network approach,"* in *Neural networks in finance and investing*. (Editors) Trippi, R.R. and Turban, E. Chicago, Illinois: Probus publishing company.

Kimoto, T., Asakawa, K., Yoda, M. and Takeoka, M. [1993] "Stock market prediction system with modular neural networks," in *Neural networks in finance and investing*. (Editors) Trippi, R.R. and Turban, E. Chicago, Illinois: Probus publishing company.

Kohonen, T. [1977] *Associative Memory: A system theoretical approach*. New York, New York: Springer.

Lapedes, A. and Farber, R. [1987] *Nonlinear signal processing using neural networks: Prediction and system modelling*. Los Almos: Los Almos National Laboratory.

Lawrence, J. 1991. *Introduction to neural networks*. (Editor) Luedeking, S. Grass Valley, California: California Scientific Software.

Lawrence, J. 1991. *Introduction to neural networks*. Fourth edition, Luedeking, S. Grass Valley, California: California Scientific Software.

Lukac, L.P., Brorsen, B.W. and Irwin, S.H. [1990] *A comparision of twelve technical trading systems*. Greenville: Traders Press.

Lorie, J.H., Dodd, P. and Kimpton, M.H. [1985] *The stock market :Theories and Evidence*. Homewood, Illinois: Irwin.

Luger, G.F. and Stubblefield, W.A. [1989] *Artificial intelligence and the design of expert systems*. Fort Collins, Colorado: The Benjamin Cummings Publishing company, Inc.

Makridakis, S., Wheelwright, S.C. and McGee. V.E. [1984] *The forecasting accuracy of major time series methods*. New York, New York: John Wiley and Son.

Malkiel, B.G. [1985] *A random walk down wall street*. Fourth edition. New York, New York: Norton and Company.

Maren, A., Harston, C. and Pap, A. [1990] *Handbook of neural computing applications*. New York: Academic Press.

Markstein, D.L. [1966] *How to chart your way to stock market profits*. New York, New York: Parker Publishing Company, Inc.

Minisky, M, and Papert, S. [1969] *Perceptrons*. Cambridge, Massachusetts: MIT Press.

Moody, J.E. and Utans, J. [1992] "Principled architecture selection for neural networks: Applications to corporate bond rating prediction," in *Advances in neural information processing systems 4*. (Editor) Lippmann, R.P. New York, New York: Morgan Kaufmann Publishers.

Moody, J.E. [1992] "The effective number of parameters: An analysis of generalization and regularization in nonlinear systems," in *Advances in neural information processing systems 4*. (Editor) Lippmann, R.P. New York, New York: Morgan Kaufmann Publishers.

Mohr, P.J., Van Der Merwe, C., Botha, Z.C. and Inggs, J. [1991] *A practical guide to South African economic indicators*. Johannesburg, Republic of South Africa: Lexicon.

Muller, B. and Reinhardt, J. [1990] *Neural networks: An introduction*. New York, New York: Springer-Verlag.

Murphy, J.J. [1986] *Technical analysis of the futures markets: A comprehensive guide to trading methods and applications*. New York, New York: Prentice-Hall Company, Inc.

Murphy, J.J. [1991] *Intermarket technical analysis - trading strategies for the global stock, bond, commodity, and currency markets*. New York, New York: John Wiley and Sons, Inc.

Nelson, C.R. [1987] *The investors guide to economic indicators*. New York, New York: John Wiley and Sons.

Nelson, M.M. and Illingworth, W.T. [1992] *A practical guide to neural nets*. Reading, Massachusetts: Addison-Wesley.

Newell, A. and Simon, H. [1981] "Computer science as empirical inquiring: Symbol and search," in *Mind Design*. (Editor) Haugenland. J. Cambridge, Massachusetts: MIT press.

Oldert, N. [1989] *The mechanics of the Johannesburg Stock Exchange*. (Editor) McGregor, R. Johannesburg, Republic of South Africa: Juta and Co Ltd.

Osborne, M.F.M. [1964] "Brownian motion in the stock market," in *The random character of stock market prices*. Cambridge, Massachusetts: MIT Press.

Pack, D.J. and Dowing, D.J. [1983] *Why didn't Box-Jenkins win (again) ?*. Oak Ridge, Tennessee: National laboratory Union Carbide Corporation, Nuclear division.

Pankratz, A. [1983] *Forecasting univariate Box-Jenkins models*. New York: New York: Addison-Wesley.

Peters, E.E. [1991] *Chaos and order in the capital markets: A new view of cycles, prices, and market volatility*. New York: John Wiley and Sons, Inc

Pring, M.J. [1985] *Technical analysis explained.* Second edition. New York, New York: McGraw-Hill Book.

Rahimian, E., Singh, S., Thammachote, T. and Virmani, R. [1993] "Bankruptcy predication by neural networks," in *Neural networks in finance and investing*. (Editors) Trippi, R.R. and Turban, E. Chicago, Illinois: Probus Publishing Company.

Ramsey, J.B. [1990] "Economic and financial data as nonlinear processes," in *The Stock Market: Bubbles, Volatility and Chaos*. (Editors) Dwyer, G.P. and Hafer, P.W: Kluwer.

Refenes, A.N., Zapranis, A.D. and Bentz, Y. [1993] "Modelling stock returns with neural networks," in *Proceedings of the first international workshop on neural networks in the capital market*. (Editor) Refenes, A.N. London, United Kingdom: London Business School.

Rocha, A.F. [1991] *Neural nets: A theory for brains and machines*. New York: Springer-Verlag.

Ryan, C. [1988] *McGregors dictionary of stock market terms*. Johannesburg, Republic of South Africa: Juta and Co Ltd.

Schwager, J.D. [1984] *A complete guide to the futures markets*. New York, New York: John Wiley.

Sharpe, F.W. and Alexander, G.J. [1990] *Investments*. Fourth edition. Engelwood Cliffs, New Jersey: Prentice-Hall International.

Simpson, P.K. [1990] *Artificial neural systems: Foundations, paradigms, applications, and implementations*. Elmsford, New York: Pergamon Press Offices.

Steidlmayer, H.A. [1993] *Profile of chaos*. Portland, Oregon: Icarus Press.

Taveles, R.J., Harlow, C.V. and Stone, H.L. [1974] *The commodities futures game*. New York, New York: McGraw- Hill Book Company.

Teweles, R.J. and Jones F.J. [1987] *The futures game*. Second edition. New York, New York: McGraw-Hill Book Company.

Thompson, R.F. [1985] *The Brain - An introduction to neuroscience*. New York, New York: W.H. Freedman and Company.

Tinic, S.M. and West, P.R. [1977] *Investing in securities: An efficient markets approach*. New York, New York: Addison-Wesley.

Van Wyk, R.J. [1990] *Macroeconomic influence and the investment decision. In the investment decision*. (Editor) Du Plessis, P.G. Pretoria, Republic of South Africa: Van Schaik (Pty) Ltd.

Wassermann, P.D. [1989] *Neural Computing: Theory and Practice*. New York, New York: Van Nostrand Reinhold.

White, H. [1993] }"Economic prediction using neural networks: The case of IBM daily stock returns," in *Neural networks in finance and investing*. (Editors) Trippi, R.R. and Turban, E. Chicago, Illinois: Probus publishing company.

Yoon, Y. and Swales, G .[1993] "Predicting stock price performance: A neural network approach," in *Neural networks in finance and investing*. (Editors) Trippi, R.R. and Turban, E. Chicago, Illinois: Probus publishing company.

CONFERENCE PROCEEDINGS

Arai, M. [1989 "Mapping abilities of three-layer neural networks," *IEEE-INNS International Joint Conference on Neural Networks I*, Washington D.C.

Askew, R.F. [1990] "Perspectives on neural networks," *Proceedings of the first workshop on neural networks: WNN-AIND 90*, Auburn University, Alabama.

Chester, D.L. [1990] "Why two hidden layers are better than one," *IEEE-INNS International Joint Conference on Neural Networks I*, Washington D.C.

Collins, E., Ghosh, S. and Scofield, C. [1988] "An application of a multiple neural network learning system for emulation of mortgage underwriting judgements," *IEEE International Conference on Neural Networks II*, San Diego.

Dutta, S. and Shekhar, S. [1988] "Bond rating: A non-conservative application of neural networks," *IEEE International Conference on Neural Networks II*, San Diego.

Fishwick, P.A. [1989] "Neural network models in simulation: A comparison with traditional modelling approaches," *Proceedings of Winter Simulation Conference*, Washington, D.C.

Hagiwara, M. [1990] "Accelerated backpropagation using unlearning based on Hebb rule," *IEEE-INNS International Joint Conference on Neural Networks*, Washington, D.C.

Hopfield, J.J. [1982] "Neural networks and physical systems with emergent collective computational abilities," *Proceedings of the National Academy of Sciences*.

Irie, B. and Miyake, S. [1988] "Capabilities of three-layered Perceptrons," *IEEE International Conference on Neural Networks II*, San Diego.

Jones, R.D., Lee, L.C., Barnes, C.W., Flake, G.W., Lee, K., Lewis, P.S. and Qian, S. [1989] "Function approximation and time series prediction with neural networks," *IEEE-INNS International Joint Conference on Neural Networks I*, Washington D.C.

Kamijo, K. and Tanigawa, T. [1990] *IEEE INNS International Joint Conference on Neural Networks I*, Washington D.C.

Kimoto, T. and Asakawa, K. [1990] "Stock market prediction systems with modular neural networks," *IEEE-INNS International Joint Conference on Neural Networks I*, Washington D.C.

Pack, D.J. and Downing, D.J. [1983] "Why didn't Box-Jenkins win (again)?," *3rd International Symposium on Forecasting*.

Sharda, R. and Patil, R.B. [1990] "Neural networks as forecasting experts," *Proceedings of the IJCNN Meeting*, Washington D.C.

Stinchcombe, M and White, H. [1989] "Universal approximation using feedforward networks with non-sigmoid hidden layer activation functions," *IEEE-INNS International Joint Conference on Neural Networks I*, Washington D.C.

Veezhinathan, J. and McCormick, B.H. [1988] "Connectionist plan reminding in a hybrid planning model," *IEEE International Conference on Neural Networks I*, Washington D.C.

Weiss, S.M. and Kapouleas, I. [1989] "An empirical comparison of pattern recognition, neural networks, and machine learning classification methods," *Proceedings of the International Joint Conference on Artificial Intelligence II*, Washington D.C.

White, H. [1988] "Economic predictions using neural networks: The case of IBM Daily stock returns," *IEEE International Conference on Neural Networks*, New York.

Wong, F., Tan, P. and Zhang, X. [1992] "Neural networks, genetic algorithms and fuzzy logic for forecasting," *Proceedings of the Third International Conference on Advanced Trading Technologies - AI Applications on Wall Street and Worldwide*, New York.

UNPUBLISHED WORKS

Beechar, N.B. [1986] "Prices benefits of share splits." Johannesburg, Republic of South Africa: Unpublished M.B.A. thesis - University of Witwatersrand.

Bennett, P.G. [1978] "The efficient market hypothesis and the Johannesburg Stock Exchange." Johannesburg, Republic of South Africa: Unpublished M.B.A. thesis - University of Witwatersrand.

Bethlehem, R.W. [1977] "Fundamental analysis: its limitations and use in portfolio selection." Pretoria, Republic of South Africa: Unpublished M.Com thesis - University of South Africa.

Boshoff, J.H. [1983] "A critical appraisal of technical analysis on the Johannesburg Stock Exchange." Pretoria, Republic of South Africa: Unpublished D.Com study - University of South Africa.

Botha, D. [1978] "An investigation of the process underlying share price movements on the Johannesburg Stock Exchange." Pretoria, Republic of South Africa: Unpublished M.Com thesis - University of South Africa.

Brock, W.A., Dechert, W.D., Scheinkman, J.A. and LeBaron, B. [1988] "A test for independence based upon the correlation dimension." Chicago, United States of America: Unpublished working paper - University of Chicago.

Brown, D.J. [1977] "An investigation into the effectiveness of technical share analysis, with particular reference to point and figure charts." Johannesburg, Republic of South Africa: Unpublished M.B.A. thesis - University of Witwatersrand.

Carter, K.J. [1983] "The estimation of security beta coefficients on the Johannesburg Stock Exchange." Cape Town, Republic of South Africa: Unpublished Ph.D - University of Cape Town.

Chang, I-C. [1992] "Neural network applications in time series forecasting." Arlington, United States of America: Unpublished Ph.D study - The University of Texas at Arlington.

Chuah, K. L. [1992] "A nonlinear approach to return predictability in the securities markets using feedforward neural networks." Washington, United States of America: Unpublished Ph.D study - Washington State University.

Chute, R.A. [1983] "A forecasting model for the South African industrial stock market." Pretoria, Republic of South Africa: M.B.L. thesis - University of South Africa

Du Toit, G.S. [1986] "Technical analysis and market efficiency on the Johannesburg Stock Exchange." Pretoria, Republic of South Africa: Unpublished D.Com study - University of South Africa.

Fishman, M.B. [1993] "Various interviews." St. Petersburg, Florida - United States of America.

Greene, M.T. [1975] "Long-term dependence in common stock returns: Evidence and effect of risk return models." Georgia, United States of America: Unpublished Ph.D - George State University.

Haddassin [1976] "An investigation into the behavior of earnings and share prices of South African listed companies." Johannesburg, Republic of South Africa: Unpublished M.B.A thesis - University of Witwatersrand.

Jacobson, M.R. [1989] "Cautionary announcements and the efficient market hypothesis." Johannesburg, Republic of South Africa: Unpublished M.Com thesis - University of Witwatersrand.

Jordan, C.J. [1986] "The Rand/Dollar exchange rate and share returns." Johannesburg, Republic of South Africa: Unpublished M.B.A. thesis - University of Witwatersrand.

Kang, S.Y. [1991] "An investigation of the use of feedforward neural networks for forecasting." United States of America: Unpublished Ph.D - Kent State University.

Klerck, W.G. [1980] "Die ontwikkeling van 'n waardebepalingsmodel vir die evaluering van gewone aandele." Pretoria, Republic of South Africa: Unpublished D.B.L. study - University of South Africa.

Knight, R.F. [1981] "The efficient market hypothesis and a change to L.I.F.O: an empirical study of the Johannesburg Stock Exchange." Cape Town: Republic of South Africa: Unpublished M.Com thesis - University of Cape Town.

McAdam, A. [1991] "Technical analysis in the commodity currency and share markets." Johannesburg, Republic of South Africa: Unpublished M.B.A. thesis - University of Witwatersrand.

McDonald, J.P. [1986] "Die invloed van verdienste, dividende, rentekoerse en inflasie op die markprys van genoteerde aandele." Pretoria, Republic of South Africa: M.Com thesis - University of Pretoria.

Mcquillin, K. [1978] "The construction of a model for stock market trading." Pretoria, Republic of South Africa: Unpublished M.Com thesis - University of South Africa.

Myers, P. [1983] "The gold price and its effect on various sectors on the Johannesburg Stock Exchange." Johannesburg, Republic of South Africa: Unpublished M.B.A. thesis - University of Witwatersrand.

Miller, W.G. [1986] "Die invloed van dividendebeleid op aandelepryse." Pretoria, Republic of South Africa: Unpublished M.B.A. - University of Pretoria.

Paulo, S.B.S. [1984] "The impact of the efficient market hypothesis on the security investment practices of the South African life insurance industry." Port Elizabeth, Republic of South Africa: Unpublished M.Com thesis - University of Port Elizabeth.

Saloner, G. [1977] "The impact of trading volume on share price volatility." Johannesburg, Republic of South Africa: Unpublished M.B.A. thesis - University of Witwatersrand.

Schlosberg, H.H. [1976] "Distribution models for daily log-price relatives." Johannesburg, Republic of South Africa: Unpublished M.B.A. thesis - University of Witwatersrand.

Sen, T., Oliver, R. and Sen, N. [1992] "Predicting corporate mergers using backpropagation neural networks: a comparative study with logistic models." Virginia, United States of America: Unpublished report - Pamblin College of Business, Virginia Tech.

Shave, C. [1976] "Sectoral Stock Exchange indices as leading indicators of sectoral economic activity." Johannesburg, Republic of South Africa: Unpublished M.B.A. thesis - University of Witwatersrand.

Terespolsky, D.J. [1991] "The Hurst phenomenon and share prices." Johannesburg, Republic of South Africa: Unpublished M.B.A. thesis - University of Witwatersrand.

Tsibouris, G. and Zeidenberg, M. [1993] "Interview." Department of Economics and Computer Sciences, University of Wisconsin - Madison.

Umstead, D.A. [1975] "Forecasting stock market prices." Chapel, United States of America: Unpublished Ph.D - University of North Carolina.

Van Eyden, R.J. [1991] "The evaluation of certain technical analysis techniques to determine the future market price of shares on the Johannesburg Stock Exchange." Pretoria, Republic of South Africa: Unpublished M.Com thesis - University of Pretoria.

INDEX